The Hassle-Free Walt Disney World® Vacation

Steven M. Barrett

The Hassle-Free Walt Disney World® Vacation

Published by
The Intrepid Traveler
P.O. Box 531
Branford, CT 06405
http://www.intrepidtraveler.com

Copyright © 2003 by Steven M. Barrett
Second Edition
Printed in Canada
Cover design by Foster & Foster
Maps designed by Evora Taylor
Library of Congress Card Number: 2002101571
ISBN: 1-887140-43-3

Publisher's Cataloging-in-Publication Data. Prepared by Sanford Berman.
Barrett, Steven M.
    The hassle-free Walt Disney world vacation. Branford, CT: The Intrepid Traveler, copyright 2003.
    Includes touring plans for adults and teens, families with children, and seniors; six maps; and material on "attractions that may frighten children."
    PARTIAL CONTENTS: Magic Kingdom. -Epcot. -Disney-MGM Studios. -Disney's Animal Kingdom. -Downtown Disney & the water parks.
    1. Walt Disney World, Florida--Description and travel--Guidebooks. 2. Walt Disney World, Florida--Description and travel--Tours. 3. Theme parks, Orlando region, Florida--Guidebooks. 4. Epcot, Florida--Description and travel--Guidebooks. 5. Disney-MGM Studios Theme Park, Florida--Description and travel--Guidebooks. 6. Travel--Guidebooks (for seniors). 7. Travel--Guidebooks (for parents and children). I. Title. II. Title: Walt Disney World vacation. III. Title: Disney World vacation. IV. The Intrepid Traveler.
    917.5924

Trademarks, Etc.

About the Author

Photo by Jon Thomas

Author Steven M. Barrett, paid his first visit to Walt Disney World in the late 1980s, after attending a medical conference in Orlando. He immediately fell under its spell, visiting it twice yearly with family and friends for the next several years, offering touring advice to the less initiated, and reading almost everything written about the WDW theme parks. When a job in his field of emergency medicine opened up not far from WDW in 1998, Barrett, a Texas native, Air Force veteran, and former Oklahoma City medical professor, relocated to the Orlando area from Houston, Texas. He began visiting the WDW parks every chance he got to enjoy the attractions, sample the restaurants, and escort visiting friends and relatives. Eventually, their feedback made him realize he had better advice on touring the parks than they could get anywhere else; so he decided to write this book. He continues to visit the parks almost every week, finding them every bit as magical as they appeared to him on that first visit over a decade ago.

Dedication

I dedicate this book to my wife Vickie and son Steven, who willingly accompanied me on countless research visits to Walt Disney World and added invaluable insight to the advice in this book.

Table of Contents

Maps

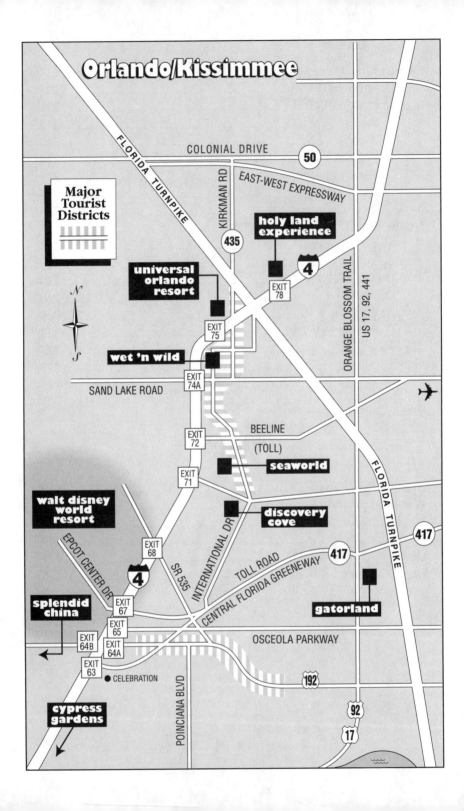

Introduction

No doubt about it, Walt Disney World is one of the most entertaining places anywhere. Yes, I admit it, I'm a rabid WDW aficionado. I have yet to find a ride or attraction at WDW that I didn't enjoy, and I've experienced all of them many times. I began trekking to this mecca of tourism years ago on vacations once or twice yearly. Now I live nearby and can explore the wonders of Walt Disney World Resort whenever I have the time (that is, as often as I can manage it).

Early on, I noticed an anomaly as I wandered the parks. Despite the worldwide appeal of WDW, some visitors weren't enjoying themselves! Many of these folks had planned their monster vacation months ahead of time and weathered their kids' salivating impatience for weeks, only to arrive at WDW and quickly wither in the crowds, the heat, and the ubiquitous long lines. Recently, I was on a boat ride from the Magic Kingdom to Fort Wilderness, and a man uttered a complaint that I've often heard at WDW: "This is supposed to be a vacation? I've been here five days, and I'm more tired than when I left home. I don't feel like I've had a vacation at all!"

I began to wonder: What could people do to enhance their WDW experience? Some of the answers are obvious and have been mentioned in other guidebooks. Some of the advice is not so obvious and is mentioned only in this book. What I've tried to accomplish in these pages is to give both first-time visitors and seasoned WDW pros the nuts and bolts tips and information for a hassle-free WDW vacation.

This new 2003 edition contains updated touring plans, descriptions and ratings of new attractions, a new section on photo tips, and a general update on Walt Disney World Resort that is current as we go to press. If you follow my recommendations and touring plans, you will be as prepared as possible for a successful voyage to WDW. Enjoy!

Steven M. Barrett

CHAPTER ONE:

Planning Your WDW Vacation

A few miles southwest of Orlando, Florida, lies one of the most popular spots on earth, Walt Disney World Resort (WDW). This huge complex contains four separate theme parks, more than two dozen hotels, scores of restaurants, a campground, water parks, golf courses, miniature golf courses, two evening entertainment complexes, a shopping and daytime entertainment district, an adult educational venue for business groups, and a sports complex. Whew! WDW is magical but it's also complicated and often crowded. The unprepared visitor can easily be overwhelmed and left with less than magical memories: long lines, heat and sunburn, exhaustion, expensive food, crying kids.

Don't let that happen to you. WDW is a wonderful place to visit. With proper planning, any WDW visit can be fun from beginning to end. This book is dedicated to giving you the insider tips, practical advice, and customized touring plans you need to have one of the best vacations of your life.

When to Go

You can have fun any time of the year at WDW. In terms of crowds, however, the best time to go is the period from after the Thanksgiving weekend until the week before Christmas (the last days of November and the first two and one-half weeks of December), when the parks are

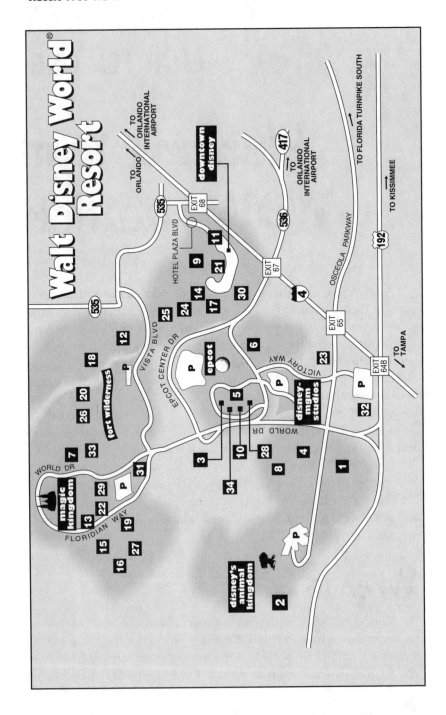

1 All-Star Resorts
2 Animal Kingdom Lodge
3 Beach Club
4 Blizzard Beach
5 BoardWalk
6 Caribbean Beach
7 Contemporary
8 Coronado Springs
9 Disney Institute
10 Dolphin
11 Downtown Disney
12 Eagle Pines Golf Course
13 Grand Floridian
14 Lake Buena Vista Golf Course
15 Magnolia Golf Course
16 Oak Trails Golf Course
17 Old Key West
18 Osprey Ridge Golf Course

19 Palm Golf Course
20 Pioneer Hall
21 Pleasure Island, in Downtown Disney
22 Polynesian
23 Pop Century Resort (opening Spring 2003)
24 Port Orleans French Quarter
25 Port Orleans Riverside
26 River Country (closed at press time)
27 Shades of Green
28 Swan
29 Transportation and Ticket Center
30 Typhoon Lagoon
31 WDW Speedway
32 Wide World of Sports
33 Wilderness Lodge
34 Yacht Club
P Parking

least crowded. The next best times to visit are the first part of November through the weekend preceding Thanksgiving, January 4 through February 7, and the week after Easter through early June.

The most crowded times to come are Christmas Day through New Year's Day, Thanksgiving weekend, the week of Presidents' Day, spring break for colleges, the two weeks around Easter, and mid June through late August. If you visit during the these ultra-busy times of the year, you can expect to pay more for your hotel room and you won't be able to experience as many attractions because long lines build early in the day. However, theme park hours are longer during the busiest seasons and there is more live entertainment on offer.

At slower times of the year, some attractions will probably be closed for maintenance or refurbishment, park hours will be shorter, and you'll have less live entertainment to choose from. These drawbacks are outweighed, however, by the pleasant ambiance created by lighter crowds and generally shorter lines. Furthermore, cooler weather tends to prevail during slower times of the year.

The slower late November and early December time period offers an additional benefit: Walt Disney World is perhaps at its most beautiful during the slowest time of the year! Christmas decorations abound in the parks and hotels. For example, the five million (and still counting) lights in the "Osborne Family Spectacle of Lights" are draped over the streets of the *Backlot Tour* area of Disney-MGM Studios. In addition, special Christmas events, shows, and parades are scheduled in the parks for your enjoyment. At Epcot, you can make reservations for the "Candlelight Processional," a program

At Christmas time, the main lobby of the Grand Floridian is graced by a towering Christmas tree. It's worth a special trip just to marvel at it.

that includes a choir, orchestra, and a guest celebrity who reads the Christmas story in America Gardens Theater at U.S.A. The American Adventure Pavilion. At Magic Kingdom, tickets go fast for "Mickey's Very Merry Christmas Party," scheduled for ten or so December nights, usually from 7:00 p.m. to 12:00 a.m. This party includes special holiday shows, a Christmas parade, caroling, complimentary family photographs (recently, the photo area near *Pirates of the Caribbean* was one of the least crowded), and free hot chocolate and cookies. Since many attractions remain open for party guests, it's a great excuse for Disney to keep the Magic Kingdom open late.

You've probably noticed that the best times of year to visit WDW are during the school year. A message for parents with kids: it's worthwhile to take your kids out of school to visit WDW if they can afford the short absence from the classroom. Otherwise, try for late May or early June, before the summer crowds hit their peaks.

Gay visitors take note: the unofficial "Gay Pride" day(s) are generally celebrated around the first weekend in June and many celebrants visit the Magic Kingdom on Saturday of that weekend.

Where to Stay

One of the most important decisions you'll make once you've picked dates for your visit is whether to stay "on property" or "off." Staying "on property," that is, at a Walt Disney World Resort hotel or campground, confers several important advantages.

Special privileges for on-property guests

On-property guests get free parking and free, generally efficient transportation to and from the theme parks and around WDW. They get free delivery of their theme park purchases to their rooms, and can charge most of those purchases to their hotel bill. WDW Resort hotel guests can purchase a flexible admission ticket, called the Ultimate Park Hopper Pass, that gives them the privilege of being able to enter any part of WDW any time they want during opening hours. Those who hold multi-day admission passes are eligible to purchase special "E-Ride" tickets that let them stay late at the Magic Kingdom at various times during the year. They can also can reserve golf tee times up to 90 days in advance — 60 days earlier than off-property guests.

Staying on property can be especially beneficial during very busy periods such as major holidays. During these periods, the crowds at one or more of the theme parks sometimes reach capacity. When that happens, the park's parking lot is closed and only Disney property guests arriving via Disney transportation are allowed to enter. The same thing can happen at the minor parks (especially Blizzard Beach and Typhoon Lagoon water parks) during the summer.

The most important reason for staying on property, however, is the property itself. When you stay on-property you are immersed in that magical Disney ambiance. Walt Disney World Resort hotels are themed, uniquely and beautifully. You'll feel transported far away from your everyday environment.

The downside is expense. Staying off property can be more economical, with lower hotel and food costs. Room rates on WDW property range from $77 a night for a double at Disney's All-Star Resorts (Fort Wilderness campsites can go for as little as $34 a night!) to more than $500 a night. In contrast, you can find off-property lodging within a reasonable driving distance from WDW for $50 a night and sometimes less. (Rates will vary seasonally wherever you stay.)

Tip: Wherever you book, be sure to note the hotel check-in time on your reservation confirmation form and plan your arrival accordingly.

The E-Ride privilege

The E-Ride name goes back to the days when Disney sold tickets to individual rides and designated them alphabetically. The "E" ticket was the most popular and most expensive. Sporadically throughout the year (and not every day of the week), Disney property guests with multi-day admission tickets (or annual or seasonal passes) can purchase an E-Ride ticket for $12 or so. These tickets allow guests to come back into the Magic Kingdom for three hours after the official closing time and enjoy certain of its more popular attractions. WDW limits the number of E-Ride tickets it sells for any one night to keep the park relatively uncrowded. If you're eligible and you'd like to play late in the Magic Kingdom (and the program is available when you're there), go ahead and have fun. The lines will probably be manageable. Ask about availability at Magic Kingdom's Guest Relations window.

Early Entry

In the past, on-property guests have been entitled to Early Entry to the Magic Kingdom, Epcot, and Disney-MGM Studios on certain days of the week, usually an hour to an hour and a half before the general public. WDW suspended the Early Entry program in fall 2001. It may be reinstated at some point, but Disney has made no announcements one way or the other as we go to press. If it is reinstated, Guest Services at your Disney hotel will be able to tell you which parks are scheduled for Early Entry days during your stay.

WDW Lodgings

The highest quality (and most expensive) hotel at Walt Disney World

Resort is Disney's Grand Floridian Resort & Spa on the monorail to the Magic Kingdom. On the second tier, but not far behind in terms of quality, are Disney's BoardWalk Inn and Villas, Disney's Beach Club Resort, and Disney's Yacht Club Resort (all three are Epcot resort hotels), Disney's Animal Kingdom Lodge, and Shades of Green, open exclusively to people connected with the U.S. military. In the

Ask at Guest Services to schedule a Garden Stroll through the grounds of the picturesque Beach or Yacht Club Resorts.

same quality category, Disney's Old Key West Resort has nice studio rooms but is more isolated from the theme parks than the others.

The third tier of hotels, in terms of quality, includes Disney's Polynesian Resort and Disney's Contemporary Resort (both on the Magic Kingdom monorail), Disney's Wilderness Lodge and Villas, the Villas at the Disney Institute, and the WDW Swan and WDW Dolphin hotels (Epcot resort hotels popular with convention and meeting planners).

Moderate quality (and less expensive) hotels include Disney's Port Orleans French Quarter Resort, Disney's Port Orleans Riverside Resort, Disney's Coronado Springs Resort, and Disney's Caribbean Beach Resort. The budget hotels at WDW are Disney's All-Star Resorts and Disney's Pop Century Resort (opening in 2003). These less expensive hotels have smaller rooms with only one bathroom sink.

A brief rundown on the ambiance of each of the Disney resort hotels follows. See "Good Things to Know About," below, for reservations web sites and phone numbers.

Deluxe

(generally start at more than $200 per night):

- Grand Floridian Resort & Spa (over $329 per night). Serviced by the Magic Kingdom monorail, this hotel complex looks like a Victorian oceanside resort, complete with white wood buildings and red shingle roofs. In the center of the main building is a spacious lobby surrounded by several floors of elegant concierge rooms.
- Beach and Yacht Club Resorts (over $289 per night). Two of the five Epcot resort hotels, the Beach and Yacht Club Resorts are situated at the "back door" of Epcot. These wood-trimmed hotels are reminiscent of Atlantic coast resorts of the past.
- BoardWalk Inn and Villas (over $289 per night). BoardWalk shops and restaurants front this sprawling red, yellow, and pastel

wood-trimmed hotel complex, located in the Epcot resort area across a lake from the Beach and Yacht Club Resorts.

- Shades of Green. If you're active duty or retired military, the Shades of Green Hotel is an exceptionally good deal. Located near the Grand Floridian, but not connected to the Magic Kingdom monorail, this secluded, recently renovated countryside hotel is surrounded by golf courses. The Shades of Green hotel is operated by the U.S. Military and is available only to military personnel. Room rates are based on military or civilian grade; call 407-824-3600 for information or 407-934-7639 for current prices and reservations.

At one end of the Polynesian Resort is a short walkway to the Transportation and Ticket Center.

- Old Key West Resort (over $249 per night). Not far from the Disney Institute, these pastel villas are spread about in clusters and decorated with Key West designs and landscaping.
- Polynesian Resort (over $299 per night). Connected to the Magic Kingdom monorail and next to the Transportation and Ticket Center, this complex of Pacific island themed buildings rests in a lush tropical landscape.
- Contemporary Resort (over $234 per night). Connected to the Magic Kingdom by monorail and a walking path, this A-frame futuristic hotel and its adjacent garden buildings has a 15th-floor observation deck overlooking the Magic Kingdom.
- Animal Kingdom Lodge (over $204 per night). New in spring 2001 and modeled on an African game lodge, this resort is not far from Disney's Animal Kingdom theme park. Most of the rooms overlook an expansive, savanna-like preserve, which is home to birds, zebras, antelopes, giraffes, and other exotic creatures.
- Wilderness Lodge and Villas (over $194 per night). Located on Bay Lake near Fort Wilderness, the Wilderness Lodge is a convincing rendition of national park lodges from the early 1900s, complete with a geyser and "mountain spring" swimming pool.
- WDW Swan and Dolphin Resorts (over $325 per night). WDW handles their reservations, but the WDW Swan is owned by Westin and the WDW Dolphin by Sheraton. These sister Epcot resort structures are designed and decorated in a unique art deco style.
- The Villas at the Disney Institute. These secluded villas in diverse styles offer deluxe one-, two-, and three-bedroom accommodations (some in "Treehouse Villas" on stilts). Closed for refurbish-

ment as we go to press, they are scheduled to reopen in 2004.

Moderate

(approximately $133 to $205 per night):

- Port Orleans Resort—French Quarter. Located next to Port Orleans Resort—Riverside and a slow boat ride away from Downtown Disney, this resort is reminiscent of the French Quarter of New Orleans. In the center of the swimming pool is a water slide down a sea serpent's tongue.

- Port Orleans Resort—Riverside. A boat trip away from Downtown Disney, Port Orleans Riverside looks like a sprawling plantation mansion in the rural South. Ol' Man Island is a recreational area with a playground, pool, and fishing hole. The food court sports a waterwheel that powers a working cotton press.

Legend has it that Walt Disney himself helped design the Treehouse Villas near the Disney Institute.

- Coronado Springs Resort. A short bus ride from Disney's Animal Kingdom and Blizzard Beach, this resort brings to mind Mexico and the American Southwest. The guest buildings are spread around a lake. Water flows down a Mayan pyramid into the main swimming pool.

- Caribbean Beach Resort. Five brightly colored guest villages named after Caribbean islands surround a large lake. The main swimming pool is themed after an old island fort. The resort is a short bus ride away from both Epcot and Disney-MGM Studios.

Value

(approximately $77 to $119 per night):

- All-Star Movies, All-Star Music, and All-Star Sports Resort. This budget resort is amusingly themed with bright colors and oversized embellishments, such as huge Dalmatians, hockey masks, football helmets, baseball bats, soda cups, cowboy boots, guitars, a walk-through jukebox, and many other amazing sights. Although the ambiance is fun, each room is quite small with only one sink. The resort is a short bus ride away from both Disney's Animal Kingdom and Blizzard Beach.

- Pop Century Resort (opening in 2003). Located near Disney's Wide World of Sports, this budget resort celebrates twentieth-century American Pop Culture with such oversized icons as Play-Doh, hula hoops, and Rubik's Cubes. Classic phrases ("Boogie down," "You dig?") adorn the buildings. Guest rooms are small with only one bathroom sink.

- Fort Wilderness. One of the nicest campgrounds in the U.S., Fort Wilderness offers cabins for rent (they cost more than $224 per night), as well as sites for camping vehicles and tents (about $34 to $72 per night). The campground has biking and hiking trails, boating, fishing, swimming, horseback riding, hayrides, a petting farm, an evening campfire program, and courts for tennis, basketball, volleyball, and tetherball. The popular *Hoop-Dee-Doo Musical Revue* (separate admission) is here (see "Good Things to Know About," below). The Magic Kingdom is a rather slow boat ride away.

Tip: If you stay on property, sample the TV channels that describe WDW attractions the first night of your stay, if you have enough energy.

Downtown Disney Hotel Plaza Lodgings

Downtown Disney Hotel Plaza lodgings have the advantage of being on Disney property close to the Disney theme parks, but they do not confer all the advantages of staying "on property." They have their own bus service to the theme parks, which is not as timely as the Disney bus service available elsewhere in WDW. And while themed, they aren't themed as extensively as the main WDW property resorts.

There are seven hotels at the Downtown Disney Hotel Plaza:
- Best Western Lake Buena Vista Hotel 407-828-2424
- Courtyard by Marriott 407-828-8888
- DoubleTree Guest Suites Resort 407-934-1000
- Grosvenor Resort 407-828-4444
- Hilton Resort 407-827-4000
- Hotel Royal Plaza 407-828-2828
- Wyndham Palace Resort 407-827-2727

These hotels are value-priced to very expensive ($89 to $500 a night and up for a double). The lowest room rates are usually advertised by Best Western.

Nearby Off-Property Lodgings

The highest quality hotels off WDW property but still nearby are the Hyatt Regency Grand Cypress (407-239-1234), the Marriott Orlando World Center (407-239-4200), the Peabody Orlando (407-352-4000), the Renaissance Orlando Resort (407-351-5555), and the Gaylord Palms Resort (407-586-0000). These hotels are comparable in quality to the best WDW resorts but tend to be less pricey ($180 to $250 or more per night for all but the Peabody, which starts at over $350). Celebration Hotel, located in the quaint and scenic Disney-associated town of Celebration, Florida, is a fine lodging with an early 1900's design and rooms priced at over $150 per night.

Some good quality and moderately priced hotels ($80 to $170 per night) off WDW property are Holiday Inn Family Suites (407-387-5437), Hawthorne Suites Hotel (407-351-6600), Radisson Resort Parkway (407-396-7000), Radisson Barcelo Hotel (407-345-0505), Crowne Plaza Resort (407-239-1222), Embassy Vacation Resort (407-238-2500), Embassy Suites Hotel (407-345-8250), and Sierra Suites Lake Buena Vista (407-239-4300).

You can order a free "Orlando Accommodations Guide and Vacation Package" from the Orlando/Orange County Convention and Visitors Bureau. Call 800-255-5786 or 407-363-5871 and allow two to three weeks to receive it.

Getting There

Orlando is one of the country's top tourist destinations. You can drive there, bus there, train there, or fly there. Once there, you'll find it easiest to navigate the area and the many pleasures of Walt Disney World by car. If you plan to spend all your time at Disney, however, you can get by using WDW buses, monorails, and boats. You'll just find it a lot less convenient. Many visitors either drive their own cars or fly and then rent a car.

By air

WDW is just a 30- to 40-minute drive from the Orlando airport. If you don't want to rent a car, you can taxi to your hotel ($34 to $50 plus tip for up to nine people to lodgings in and near WDW). Less efficient than a taxi are the shuttle bus services operated by Mears and Transtar (about $16 per person, children under 4 ride free). Or take a limo ($50 to $70 for up to five riders).

Airlines to Orlando from the U.S.:

Air Tran	800-247-8726
America West	800-235-9292
American	800-433-7300
ATA (American Trans Air)	800-435-9282
Continental	800-525-0280
Delta	800-221-1212
Frontier	800-432-1359
Jet Blue	800-538-2583
Midwest Express	800-452-2022
Northwest	800-225-2525
Pan American (to Sanford airport)	800-359-7262
Southwest	800-435-9792
Spirit	800-772-7117
United Airlines	800-241-6522
US Airways	800-428-4322
Vintage	800-852-0275

Airlines to Orlando from Canada:

Air Canada	888-247-2262
Air Transat	877-872-6728
America West	800-235-9292
American Airlines	800-433-7300
Continental	800-231-0856
Delta	800-221-1212
Northwest	800-225-2525
United	800-241-6522
US Airways	800-428-4322

Airlines to Orlando from the U.K.:

American	08457-789-789
British Airways	08457-733-377
Continental	0800-776-464
Delta	0800-414-767
United	08458-444-777
US Airways	08456-003-300
Virgin Atlantic	01293-450-150

Charter Airlines to Sanford from the U.K.:

Air 2000 (www.air2000.com)

Britannia Airways (www.britanniaairways.com)
JMC Airlines (www.jmcholidays.com)
Monarch Airlines (www.monarch-airlines.com)
My Travel (www.mytravelgroup.com)
Note: Sanford, Florida is located about a 50-minute to an hour's drive north of WDW.

By car

WDW is located close to Kissimmee, Florida, in Osceola county, just south of Orlando, which is in Orange county. The area's major highway, Interstate 4 (I-4) runs east-west across Florida, but roughly northeast to southwest through the Orlando metro area. WDW is located west of I-4 and north of US 192 (also called Highway 192 and Irlo Bronson Highway), which runs east to west through Kissimmee, crossing I-4 at Exit 64.

Four exits from I-4 lead into WDW. Your choice will depend on your ultimate destination. The most northerly exit, 68, takes you onto Highway 535. Take a left to Hotel Plaza Boulevard and the Downtown Disney area. Exit 67 is your best route to Epcot. Exit 65 directs you to Disney's Wide World of Sports Complex and Disney's Animal Kingdom. The southernmost exits, 64 and 62, lead to Highway 192 and Disney's Wide World of Sports Complex, Disney's Animal Kingdom, Disney-MGM Studios, and further north to Magic Kingdom.

From the airport: If you're driving a rental car from Orlando International Airport, take either the Bee Line Toll Expressway (north airport exit) to I-4 or the longer and slightly more expensive Central Florida Greeneway (south airport exit) straight to Epcot Center Drive in the center of WDW. Bring several dollars in cash or quarters for either tollway and more cash for your return trip. The Bee Line Expressway has colorful billboards advertising some of the exciting attractions of WDW and Universal Orlando. The Central Florida Greeneway is less congested and passes through uncluttered countryside.

Getting Around WDW

In most cases, the easiest method for navigating WDW is by private car. A car also gives you the freedom, time permitting, to visit some of Orlando's other stellar attractions, such as Universal Orlando,

SeaWorld, and Discovery Cove. If you drive to WDW, no problem. If you fly into Orlando, plan to rent a car for the duration of your stay. To avoid disappointment, reserve your rental car prior to your arrival — well prior if you will be coming at a busy time of year (see "When to Go," above). Budget at least $45 a day or $220 weekly for a midsize car.

Getting around WDW can be complicated. So ask your hotel Guest Services for a WDW map or get one before you arrive. If you are staying on property, ask for the combination **WDW map and transportation guide**. The latter lists WDW buses, monorails, and boats. You'll find it especially useful if you don't have a car.

Note: Disney transportation begins about an hour and a half to two hours before park opening times and continues to function two hours (and sometimes more) after the parks close. (See the following chapters for more about getting to each of the theme parks.)

Two exceptions to the navigate-WDW-by-car rule: You won't need a car if you are staying at the Polynesian, Grand Floridian, or Contemporary Resort and plan to spend most of your time at the Magic Kingdom (MK). You can ride the monorail to the MK directly from these hotels; you can also walk to the MK in about ten minutes from the Contemporary. You also won't need a car (though you will find it an advantage to have one) if your primary destination is Epcot and you stay in one of the Epcot resort hotels. These hotels are just a five- to ten-minute walk from the rear Epcot entrance.

Admission Tickets

Your choice of admission ticket will depend on how long you want to stay and how much freedom you want to move around within WDW. Note that child passes are available to children 3 through 9 years of age, while children under 3 are admitted free. Special tickets (such as the "After 2 p.m. One Park Pass") are available for convention attendants. Prices listed are for 2002 and are rounded up to the nearest dollar amount, but prices may increase at any time and are likely to be higher in 2003. Likewise, pass names and options may change at any time. To verify prices and options for the dates of your visit, check online at www.disneyworld.com or call 407-824-4321 or 407-827-4166.

Discounts of 3% to 5% are available to AAA members, Disney timeshare owners, and Disney Club members. A one-year club membership costs about $40; call 800-654-6347 to join.

Note: All admission passes except the One-Day ticket include free use of WDW transportation.

One-Day ticket

Adults	–	$48
Children (3 to 9)	–	$38

Good for one day only and for one park only (Magic Kingdom, Epcot, Disney-MGM Studios, or Disney's Animal Kingdom).

Multi-Day tickets

4-Day or 5-Day Park Hopper Passes:

4-Day:	Adults – $192	Children (3 to 9) – $152
5-Day:	Adults – $217	Children (3 to 9) – $172

Allow you to switch from one major theme park to another (if you desire) without limitation for four or five days. You don't have to use the days consecutively, and unused days never expire. These tickets do not admit you to the minor parks and entertainment areas. Passes with unused days bought before the opening of Disney's Animal Kingdom can be upgraded (for more money) to include admission to the new park.

5-Day, 6-Day, or 7-Day Park Hopper Plus Passes:

5-Day:	Adults – $247	Children (3 to 9) – $197
6-Day:	Adults – $277	Children (3 to 9) – $222
7-Day:	Adults – $307	Children (3 to 9) – $247

Admit you to the four major theme parks as well as these minor parks and entertainment areas: Pleasure Island, the water parks, and Disney's Wide World of Sports. You choose two, three, or four options among the minor areas depending on the number of days (five, six, or seven) on your pass, and you can switch from one park to another (if you desire) without limitation for the length of your pass. You don't have to use the days consecutively and unused days never expire. You can visit more than one park or entertainment area in one day, but any use of the pass on a given day counts as a day used. So if you should spend the day outside of WDW and then use your pass in the evening to go to Pleasure Island, say, you've used up a full day on your pass. Furthermore, the options expire as you use them. So, for example, if you visit two water parks in one day, you use up two options. Passes with unused days bought before the opening of Disney's Animal Kingdom can be upgraded (for more money) to include admission to that park.

Disney's Ultimate Park Hopper Pass:

Available only to WDW hotel and campground guests. The cost varies by length of stay. For example:

2-Day: Adults – $116   Children (3 to 9) – $93
10-Day: Adults – $402   Children (3 to 9) – $315

Call 407-824-4321 or 407-827-4166 for current information.

Admits the guest to the four major theme parks and all minor parks and entertainment areas (including *DisneyQuest* in Downtown Disney). It can be purchased for any length of stay of two days or longer, but you can't use this pass on future visits. Some vacation packages include Disney's Ultimate Park Hopper Pass. If you want to save money, ask to drop the first and/or last day(s) of your stay from your pass because you'll probably be too busy to take full advantage of them.

Annual Passes

Theme Park Annual Pass:

Adults   – $349
Children (3 to 9)   – $297

Allows unlimited entry to the major theme parks for one year. The pass can be used in more than one park on the same day and includes use of the WDW transportation system. Renewals are cheaper. Call 407-824-4321 or 407-827-4166 for current information.

Premium Annual Pass:

Adults   – $469
Children (3 to 9)   – $399

Allows unlimited entry to the major and minor parks plus the entertainment areas (including DisneyQuest). Otherwise, it is just like the Theme Park Annual Pass (see above).

Annual Passes confer a number of benefits in addition to the flexibility of unlimited entry to the parks. Passholders park free on WDW property. They receive seasonal discounts at selected resort hotels on property, as well as discounts (usually 10%) on food at certain restaurants, select merchandise at numerous (but not all) shops in Downtown Disney, certain Disney backstage tours (you have to call and ask which ones), a Family Portrait sitting fee, a "Leave a Legacy" tile purchase, and certain recreation (parasailing, waterskiing, wakeboarding, some boats, and the *Richard Petty Driving Experience* packages). Passholders also get 10% off one Grand Floridian spa treatment, 30% off golf fees at certain times, 50% off miniature golf, and a free subscription to the quarterly *Mickey Monitor* newsletter. Passholders also receive a 10%

discount on National Car rentals. Occasionally they are invited to priority reviews of new attractions.

Note: The specific benefits change from time to time.

Special passes for Florida residents

WDW offers a number of incentives to Florida residents, including a Seasonal Pass (good for entry to the major theme parks during slower times of the year); a Disney Dining Experience membership (which offers benefits such as a 20% discount at many WDW restaurants); separate Annual Passes to Pleasure Island, DisneyQuest, and the water parks; and an annual golf pass for discounted greens fees. Floridians can also purchase Annual Passes at a discount (about 17% off the regular Annual Pass price). During slower times of the year, Florida residents can get seasonal discounts on One-Day tickets. Call 407-939-6244 for current prices and information and be prepared to provide proof that you are a state resident.

Choosing your tickets

With so many options to choose from, selecting the pass that's best for you can be tricky. Here are some things to think about:

• How many days do you have to devote to WDW?

• Are you interested in visiting every major and minor park plus the entertainment areas, or are only some of them of interest to you?

• Do you plan to return to the area within the next year? Ever?

If you want to see a lot of WDW and won't be back within a year, the Hopper passes are the best buys because they give you the most flexibility and unused days never expire. For example, say the park you are visiting today gets too crowded for your comfort; you can use a Hopper pass to switch to another park.

Here are some guidelines for getting the best value for your time and money based on the number of days you have to spend.

Note: If the Early Entry program is in effect when you visit, take advantage of it if you are staying on Disney property (see "Early Entry," above). If you're not, plan your park visits carefully. You want to avoid any park that is open for Early Entry on its Early Entry day(s). On those days, the parks are already crowded by the time they open to other guests. Call 407-824-4321 for an Early Entry update.

If you have one day. Choose a park to visit. Buy a One-Day ticket and use the appropriate one-day touring plan (see *Chapters Two* through *Five*). Visit Pleasure Island (extra cost) and the rest of Downtown Disney (no admission cost) after the park closes if you still have energy.

If you have two days. Choose two parks to visit and buy two One-Day tickets (ask for a discount on the second ticket). Or purchase Disney's Ultimate Park Hopper Pass if you're staying on property and want to see more of WDW. Visit the parks of your choice and follow the appropriate one-day touring plans. If you have Disney's Ultimate Park Hopper Pass, you can switch parks whenever you want and pick up the touring plan of your choice at the appropriate place. Consider visiting Pleasure Island (no extra cost with Disney's Ultimate Park Hopper Pass) and the rest of Downtown Disney the second night.

If you have three days. Choose three parks to visit and buy three One-Day tickets (ask for discounts on the second and third tickets). Or buy Disney's Ultimate Park Hopper Pass if you're staying on property and want to see more of WDW. Tour the three parks (or more if you switch parks with Disney's Ultimate Park Hopper Pass) following the appropriate touring plans. Consider visiting Pleasure Island (no extra cost with Disney's Ultimate Park Hopper Pass) and the rest of Downtown Disney the last night.

If you have four days. Buy a 4-Day Park Hopper Pass or Disney's Ultimate Park Hopper Pass (if you're staying on property and want to see more of WDW). Visit all four major theme parks and follow the appropriate touring plans. You can switch parks as desired with the Park Hopper passes. Consider visiting Pleasure Island (no extra cost with Disney's Ultimate Park Hopper Pass) and the rest of Downtown Disney your last night.

If you have five days. Buy the 5-Day Park Hopper Pass, 5-Day Park Hopper Plus Pass, or Disney's Ultimate Park Hopper Pass (if you're staying on property and want to see more of WDW). Follow a two-day touring plan for either the Magic Kingdom or Epcot, depending on your interests, and one-day touring plans for the other three parks. Switch parks as you see fit.

Alternatively, if you'd like to see more of the Orlando area, buy 4-Day WDW tickets and use a one-day touring plan for each. Then buy separate admission(s) to other area attractions that interest you, such as Kennedy Space Center (about an hour's drive to the east), one of the Universal Orlando theme parks, SeaWorld, or Discovery Cove. Consider visiting Pleasure Island on a Disney day (no extra cost with a Hopper Plus Pass or Disney's Ultimate Park Hopper Pass) and the rest of Downtown Disney the last night of your visit.

If you have six days. Buy the 6-Day Park Hopper Plus Pass or Disney's Ultimate Park Hopper Pass (if eligible). Visit the four major theme parks and switch parks as you please. Follow the two-day touring plans for the Magic Kingdom and Epcot and the one-day touring plans for the other two parks. Alternatively, buy a 4- or 5-Day Pass and work in visits to other area attractions during the remaining day or days. Consider visiting Pleasure Island and the rest of Downtown Disney the last night of your stay. (If you have a Hopper Plus Pass, visit Pleasure Island on a Disney day so that the admission charge is covered by your pass.)

If you have seven days. Buy a 7-Day Park Hopper Plus Pass or Disney's Ultimate Park Hopper Pass (if eligible) and switch parks at your pleasure. Follow the two-day touring plans for the Magic Kingdom and Epcot and the one-day plans for the other two parks. For the seventh day, use the second day touring plan for Disney-MGM Studios, visit a Disney water park, or revisit attractions at any of the other major Disney parks. Alternatively, buy a 4-, 5- or 6-Day Pass or Disney's Ultimate Park Hopper Pass and visit other area attractions in your remaining time. Consider visiting Pleasure Island and the rest of Downtown Disney your last night. (If you have a Hopper Plus Pass, visit Pleasure Island on a Disney day so that the admission charge is covered by your pass.)

If you have eight or more days. Buy a 7-Day Park Hopper Plus Pass or, if eligible, Disney's Ultimate Park Hopper Pass for your length of stay. Work in the two-day touring plans for the Magic Kingdom, Epcot, and Disney-MGM Studios and the one-day touring plan for Disney's Animal Kingdom. Swim in a Disney water park, revisit your favorite attractions, and review *Chapter Seven* for insider information about other fun things to do at WDW. See Pleasure Island and the rest of Downtown Disney one evening on a Disney ticket day (if you have a Hopper Plus Pass). Alternatively, buy shorter passes and spend the rest of your time exploring other area attractions. Isn't it great to have so many choices?

Note: For more information about other area attractions, see my publisher's books, *Universal Orlando* and *The Other Orlando: What To Do When You've Done Disney and Universal.* Or check out the publisher's web site: www.TheOtherOrlando.com.

When an Annual Pass makes sense

The Annual Pass makes sense financially if you visit more than seven days per year (7 times the single day rate of about $48 is about the price of a regular Annual Pass) or if you live in Florida, visit frequently, and want to take advantage of the discounts. If you spend one long visit per year and want to check out the minor parks and attractions, then the Park Hopper Plus Pass or Ultimate Park Hopper Pass are the best options. The Premium Annual Pass (which admits you to both the major and minor parks) makes sense if you visit 10 or more days per year and want the minor park option.

Buying your tickets

You can purchase multi-day passes before you go by phone (407-824-4321), over the Web (www.disneyworld.com), or by mail (Walt Disney World, Box 10140, Lake Buena Vista, FL 32830-0030 Attn: Ticket Mail Order). You'll pay a $3 handling fee on the above orders. Make checks payable to Walt Disney World Company and allow three to four weeks for delivery. You can also purchase select passes from your travel agent or at your local Disney Store.

In Florida, passes can be bought at a number of sites. They include the Orlando International Airport Disney Store, the Ocala Disney Information Center on I-75 in Ocala, Florida, the WDW hotels, the Transportation and Ticket Center near the Magic Kingdom, Downtown Disney Guest Relations, and the park and entertainment area entrances. You'll save time by buying your tickets before you get to the parks, where ticket lines are often long.

Note: Not all types of passes are available at every location, so you may want to call 407-824-4321 to confirm availability of the ticket or pass you want.

Some passes are also available from ticket brokers at a slight or no discount. Look for the broker's license to be sure you are dealing with a legitimate agent. And be sure you know what you'd pay in the park or at a Disney store before you plunk down your money.

Package deals

Vacation packages appeal to many visitors. They're simple and you can save money if you take advantage of all the elements. But that's a big "if." Often, you won't have the slightest interest in some of the elements, or if interested, won't have the time for all of them. When that's the case, the package is likely to cost you more than buying separately the elements you really want. So if you're interested in a package vacation to WDW, be prepared to do some studying. Many different packages are available. Sit down with several that look appealing, do the budget arith-metic, factor in the convenience of-fered by the pack-age, and make cer-tain that you're willing and able to

The Annual Pass makes sense over any park hopper pass if you stay more than seven days (and visit only the major theme parks) or if you plan one or more return visits within a year.

take advantage of all the features you're paying for. Furthermore, read the fine print to make sure you aren't paying too much. Some packages are loaded with features that few families or individuals could reasonably use during their vacation because of time and energy limitations. At a minimum, check the cost of any package you're seriously considering against the cost of purchasing separately the elements you're really after. Also keep in mind that you can buy WDW's Hopper Passes and save any unused days for future use if you plan to return to WDW someday.

WDW vacation packages. If you're interested in a WDW package, get a free "Walt Disney World Resort Vacation Brochure" from your travel agent. Or order it (two or more months in advance of your visit) from the Walt Disney Travel Company by calling 800-828-0228 or 407-934-7639.

Good Things to Know About

You will have the best time — and fewest hassles — if you know a bit more about your options ahead of time.

Budgeting

What does it cost to visit WDW? It depends on the choices you make. A family of four (two adults, one teenager, one child) will spend about $400 per day at WDW **excluding** lodging and transportation. This cost includes tickets, a light breakfast and lunch, a $100 dinner, a few light snacks in the parks, and a few souvenirs. A couple could get by on $150 a day per person (**including** admission tickets and lodging) with some careful budgeting. You'll minimize your expenditures by staying in a hotel off property and eating light food from hotel snack areas and from vendors and fast food eateries in the theme parks.

However, part of the unique magic of Walt Disney World Resort exists in the on-site hotels and restaurants (character meals, for example). You'll pay more for these experiences, but you'll take home many more special memories.

Car rentals

Call the agency of your choice and reserve a car well ahead of your trip—three to six months ahead if you are coming at Christmas time. A good rule of thumb is to book your car when you book your hotel. Budget at least $45 a day or $220 weekly for a midsize car.

Child care

As you'd expect, child care is readily available to Orlando area visitors from a number of reputable agencies. You can drop your children off or arrange for in-room care. Most agencies that offer in-room services charge a four-hour minimum plus a travel fee for the babysitter, with the hourly rate determined by the number of children. Expect to pay $11 to $14 per hour for one child plus $1 to $2 per hour more for each additional child. Travel fees range from $8 to $12. Some agencies charge extra for care that begins after 9:00 p.m. Check with your hotel concierge for a list of reputable services. Here are phone numbers for a few:

- All About Kids (407-812-9300)
- Fairy Godmothers (407-277-3724)
- Kid's Nite Out (407-827-5444)

The last will also accompany solo kids age 3 to 12 to the theme parks and can be hired to accompany families who feel the need of an extra adult to help manage the little ones.

WDW provides nighttime fun for guests ages 4 to 12 through several children's clubs: The Harbor Club at the BoardWalk Resort (407-939-3463); The Never Land Club at the Polynesian Resort (very popular, 407-939-3463); The Cub's Den at Wilderness Lodge (407-939-3463); Simba's Cubhouse at the Animal Kingdom Lodge (407-938-3000); The Mouseketeer Clubhouse at the Contemporary Resort (407-824-1000, ext. 3038); The Sandcastle Club at the Yacht and Beach Club Resorts (407-939-3463), and The Mouseketeer Club at the Grand Floridian Resort (407-824-2985). Call the listed numbers for information and reservations; rates run about $8 per hour.

During the day, WDW offers various educational and fun youth programs; call 407-939-8687 for information and reservations (for example, for Magic Kingdom children's tours) or 407-939-3463 for the Pirates Cruise or the Wonderland Tea Party (both at the Grand Floridian).

FASTPASS and Singles lines

Consider using these time savers whenever theme-park lines start to lengthen. **FASTPASS** is available for a number of popular attractions in each of the four major theme parks (check the park Guidemaps). This option saves you time in line by giving you a ticket now for later admission to the attraction with a shorter wait. To get one, place your admission ticket through the slot in the FASTPASS turnstile near the entrance to the attraction you've chosen. You will receive a slip of paper with a time period for you to return (e.g., 1:20 p.m. to 2:20 p.m.). You simply return to the separate FASTPASS

You can get a FASTPASS for another attraction: after you use your current FASTPASS; one minute or more after your current FASTPASS time window begins (for example, at 1:21 p.m. if your current time window is 1:20 p.m. to 2:20 p.m.); or two hours or more after your current FASTPASS was issued regardless of its return-time window.

entry line at any time during that period and your wait will be shorter than the general admission queue. You won't be admitted earlier than your allotted time range but sometimes the attendant will admit you later.

Tip: FASTPASS tickets are often unavailable during the late afternoon or evening hours.

Note: Eligibility rules governing when you can get a FASTPASS for another attraction change from time to time and may be different when you visit. Most likely to change: the two-hour wait requirement. It may be cut to as little as 45 minutes. Check your FASTPASS ticket.

Single-rider lines (aka, singles lines) are sometimes available for popular attractions, such as *Test Track* at Epcot and the *ChairLift* at Blizzard Beach; just ask a Disney attendant at the park Tip Board. These lines are used to fill the empty seats in ride vehicles. Singles lines have shorter waits, but your party will usually be split up to fill the seats as they become available.

Guests with disabilities

WDW is fully accessible to persons with disabilities. For a free copy of Disney's "Walt Disney World Guidebook for Guests with Disabilities," call 407-939-6244 two or more months in advance of your visit.

Important web site addresses

You can gather information, investigate vacation packages, buy theme park admission tickets, and make hotel and restaurant reservations with your computer if you use the Internet. The following web sites are especially helpful:

- www.disneyworld.com — A comprehensive Disney web site with many useful links.
- www.wdwinfo.com — A more personal site for WDW updates that is maintained by Disney aficionados; includes bulletin boards full of advice.
- www.hiddenmickeys.org — Hidden Mickey freaks, here's the place for you (and me).
- www.wdwig.com — An unofficial but comprehensive source of Disney advice and information.
- www.TheOtherOrlando.com — Objective, updated information about virtually all of Orlando's non-Disney attractions.
- www.floridakiss.com — Site of the Kissimmee-St. Cloud Convention and Visitors Bureau (Kissimmee is the town closest to WDW) with many links.
- www.orlandoinfo.com — Site of the Orlando/Orange County Convention and Visitors Bureau with many links.

Mouse talk

Disney calls its theme park employees "cast members." "Walt Disney Imagineers" are the folks who dream up and build WDW's wonderful environments and attractions. Guests staying at WDW's resort hotels and campground are "on-property" guests.

Park hours

Theme park hours are subject to change. Call 407-824-4321 a few days before you arrive for park hours during your visit and find out if the Early Entry program will be in effect during your visit. Then reconfirm the hours with hotel Guest Services after you arrive. Note that these are the "official" hours. The theme parks actually admit guests earlier. For example, if the official opening time for the Magic Kingdom (on a non Early Entry day) is listed as 9:00 a.m., you will be admitted to Main Street, U.S.A. at 8:30 a.m. and the remainder of the park will open at 9:00 a.m. Occasionally when the official opening time is 9:00 a.m., you'll be admitted to Main Street as early as 8:00 a.m. and to the rest of the park at 8:30 a.m. If you don't know this nuance of Disney magic and arrive "on-time" at 9:00 a.m., you'll find Main Street already buzzing with guests.

Parking

Parking at the four major theme parks is free for WDW property guests and Annual Passholders, $6 per day for others. Once you've paid for the day at one park, you can leave and reenter the same lot or switch to the lot at another major WDW park without paying again (simply show your parking receipt). Parking is free for everyone at Downtown Disney, the water parks, Disney's Wide World of Sports Complex, its five golf courses, and its two miniature golf courses.

Pets

Can't bear to leave your pet at home? Call 407-824-6568 for WDW boarding information and vaccination requirements. Overnight pet stays cost $11 (WDW Resort hotel guests pay $9), and day stays cost $6. Pets can stay with you for an additional fee of $3 per night if you camp at certain sites in the Fort Wilderness Campground.

Resting places

Busy as they are, each of the major theme parks offers some inviting places to sit and relax awhile. I list them for you in the appropriate chapters. Enjoy.

Switching off

Disney provides this option for parties with two or more adults and one or more children who are too young or frightened to experience a particular attraction. Initially you wait in line together. When the group reaches the loading area, one adult rides while the other adult and the kid(s) are directed to a specific area to wait. When the first adult disembarks and takes the kid(s), the second adult gets on the ride without a wait. A third adult in the group can ride twice, once with each of the other adults.

Switching off is available at some attractions in all the parks; they are listed in the "Attractions That May Frighten Children" sections of *Chapters Two, Three, Four,* and *Five*. If you want to take advantage of it, tell all Disney attendants you encounter as you move through the queue that you want to switch off.

Visiting other area attractions

If you plan to check out Universal Studios Florida or Islands of Adventure during your stay, call ahead (407-363-8000) for park hours and to find out if any movie or TV production is scheduled during your stay. You may also want to pick up a copy of my publisher's book *Universal Orlando* for a complete guide to Universal's attractions (see www.TheOtherOrlando.com).

WDW (and related) phone numbers

Use these numbers to get the information you need before you head out and while you're there:

General Information	407-824-4321
Hotel Reservations	407-934-7639 / 407-824-8000
or for the Swan & Dolphin	
(not operated by Disney)	800-227-1500
Dining Reservations	407-939-3463
All-Star Resorts:	
Sports	407-939-5000
Music	407-939-6000
Movies	407-939-7000
Animal Kingdom Lodge	407-938-3000
Beach Club Resort	407-934-8000
Blizzard Beach	407-560-3400
BoardWalk Resort	407-939-5100
Caribbean Beach Resort	407-934-3400
Centra Care (walk-in medical clinic	
and 24-hour hotel in-room services)	407-239-7777 / 407-238-2000
Contemporary Resort	407-824-1000
Coronado Springs Resort	407-939-1000
Disabled Guests Special Requests	407-939-7807
Disney Institute Resort	407-827-1100
Dolphin Resort	407-934-4000
Fantasia Gardens Miniature Golf	407-560-8760
Fort Wilderness Campground	407-824-2900
Golf Reservations and Information	407-939-4653
Grand Floridian Beach Resort	407-824-3000
Guided Tour Information	407-939-8687
Guided VIP Tours	407-560-4033
House of Blues Information	407-934-2583
Lost and Found	

lost yesterday and before	407-824-4245
lost today at Magic Kingdom	407-824-4521
lost today at Epcot	407-560-7500
lost today at Disney-MGM	407-560-3764
lost today at Animal Kingdom	407-938-2265
lost today at Fort Wilderness	407-824-2726
lost today at Downtown Disney	407-828-3058
Mail Order and Merchandise Return	407-363-6200
Old Key West Resort	407-827-7700
Outdoor Recreation Reservations	407-939-7529
Pleasure Island Information	407-934-6300
Polynesian Resort	407-824-2000
Port Orleans Resort—French Quarter	407-934-5000
Port Orleans Resort—Riverside	407-934-6000
River Country Information	407-824-2760
Shades of Green (U.S. Military) Hotel	407-824-3400
Swan Resort	407-934-3000
Tennis Reservations and Lessons	407-939-7529
Typhoon Lagoon Information	407-560-4141
Weather Information	407-827-4545
Wide World of Sports	407-363-6600
Wilderness Lodge Resort	407-824-3200
Winter Summerland Miniature Golf	407-560-3000
Yacht Club Resort	407-934-7000

What to do on arrival day

If you have an Annual Passport or an Ultimate Park Hopper Pass, you can go to a major park (follow the afternoon and evening parts of the appropriate touring plan; see *Chapters Two, Three, Four,* and *Five*). Otherwise don't burn a day of your other passes. Instead, try one or more of the following options: swim — don't sunburn!; spa; play miniature golf; visit DisneyQuest, a water park, Fort Wilderness (petting farm, hayride, campfire show), Cirque du Soleil, a dinner show, Downtown Disney, or Pleasure Island; explore your hotel or other hotels; ride the monorail; rent a boat or a BoardWalk surrey bike; enjoy a hotel or character dinner; watch the Electrical Water Pageant; look for Hidden Mickeys in the hotels or other WDW areas; get married at the Wedding Pavilion!

See *Chapters Six* and *Seven* for more on most of these options.

What to do on departure day

Schedule a character breakfast; revisit favorite attractions (if your ticket allows); consider arrival day options you haven't yet tried.

What to Bring

1. An over-the-counter analgesic, such as Aspirin, Tylenol, Advil, or Aleve, plus an over-the-counter motion-sickness remedy if you are prone to motion sickness (you may need it for simulator rides).

2. Sunburn protection (SPF 15 or higher).

3. Lip balm.

4. Bandage strips and first-aid cream.

5. Two pairs of thin socks for each foot if you tend to blister.

6. Moleskin (buy at a pharmacy) to place over "hot spots" on feet before they blister. If the tender spot is already blistered, cut a hole in a square of moleskin and place the hole over the blister; if the tender area is just a red spot, cover the entire spot with moleskin.

7. Small scissors to cut moleskin. (Just be sure to pack them in your checked luggage if you fly; no sharp objects are allowed in carry-on bags.)

8. Hats or caps (the Florida sun is very strong).

9. Swimsuits if your family likes to swim, and also to wear under your clothes for wet rides (like those at Disney's Animal Kingdom) and the interactive fountains you'll find at most of the theme parks. Remove your (or their) regular clothes before the drenching experiences and you'll have dry clothes to wear for the rest of the day.

10. Small towels to dry wet skin and a cloth for cleaning spectacles (you will get wet on certain rides and in the interactive fountains).

11. Broken-in walking shoes (you'll walk several miles or more daily in the parks). Bring two pairs of shoes if you can so you'll have a dry pair available if your shoes get drenched on a wet ride or in a sudden summer downpour.

12. Compact ponchos for rain protection. Also consider small umbrellas for rain and sun protection, especially if you're visiting in the summer.

13. Lightweight jackets or sweaters for cooler months (November through March, especially in the evenings) and air-conditioning.

14. Brightly colored, loud shirts and blouses if you want to volunteer for shows.
15. Nice clothes (jackets for men) if you plan to eat at Victoria & Albert's at the Grand Floridian or at Arthur's 27 at the Wyndham Palace. (Tie optional for both.)
16. A fat pen for autographs. (Fat pens are easier for the Disney characters to handle.)
17. Autograph book (or buy one at the airport Disney Store, your hotel, or in the parks).
18. A pen and note paper for writing down your parking locations (if you plan to have a car at WDW).
19. Camera with plenty of film. (Film and disposable cameras are available in the parks, but you'll generally pay more there than you would at home.)
20. Clear plastic water bottles.
21. A Walt Disney World Resort map if you're driving. (Check with your local book store or download a map from one of the WDW-related web sites.)
22. Several dollars (preferably in quarters) for the tollway if you plan to fly in and rent a car at the airport.
23. A few more dollars for tipping the hotel baggage handlers.
24. Your pet's vaccination record if you bring a pet.
25. Your admission tickets! (if purchased ahead of time).

Where to Eat

WDW offers plenty of choice when it comes to food and eateries. Priority seating reservations are recommended for most full-service restaurants in WDW, so plan ahead if you can. With "priority seating" you don't actually have a reservation, but you'll be seated as close as possible to the assigned time and ahead of walk-ins. During busy periods, priority seating works best near popular restaurants' opening times (that's why the touring plans for each park emphasize eating early lunches and dinners if possible). Furthermore, prime tables are more often available to early diners. Some of the prime locations you may want to try for are window seats at the California Grill in the Contemporary Resort, seats close to the aquarium glass wall (in the first three rows of tables) at the Coral Reef Restaurant in Epcot's Living Seas Pavilion, and seats overlooking El Rio del Tiempo (The River of Time) at the San Angel Inn Restaurant in Epcot's Mexico Pavilion.

Restaurant recommendations and ratings

To give you an overview of the wide range of choices and prices available to you at WDW's full-service restaurants, and make it as easy as possible for you to compare them, I decided to group my ratings together alphabetically instead of separating them by theme park or other venue. You'll find restaurant recommendations for the theme parks below, followed by recommendations for restaurants outside the parks, and then by my ratings of all the WDW eateries. The touring plans for each park include additional recommendations.

Note: All parks have fresh fruit stands and fast food is available in abundance. Restaurant hours and menus change periodically.

Magic Kingdom

The Plaza Restaurant at the end of Main Street has decent food, and you can get seated quickly if you're at the door when it opens for lunch at 11:00 a.m. even if you don't have priority seating reservations. Tony's Town Square Restaurant near the Main Street Train Station also has decent food; try the *Lady and the Tramp* character waffles for breakfast (8:30 a.m. to 10:45 a.m.). Priority seating reservations are recommended at the generally good character meals at The Crystal Palace buffet (breakfast, lunch, dinner), Cinderella's Royal Table (breakfast), and Liberty Tree Tavern (dinner).

Fast food abounds in the Magic Kingdom. You might try the apple pie in the restful surroundings of Aunt Polly's Dockside Inn or the fruit cobbler and cappuccino at Sleepy Hollow (eat at the quiet park behind Ye Olde Christmas Shoppe).

Note: If you're already at Magic Kingdom and want priority seating reservations, walk to the restaurant of your choice when the park opens and see what's available.

Epcot

Epcot serves some of WDW's best park food. All eleven World Showcase countries (see *Chapter Three*) have restaurants, ten are full-service eateries, while the one at U.S.A. The American Adventure offers counter-service. The full-service restaurants are picturesque and worthwhile. Restaurant Marrakesh in Morocco offers entertainment (music and belly dancing) with lunch and dinner. The Biergarten in

Germany has musicians performing afternoons and evenings. In the Coral Reef Restaurant (expensive) in The Living Seas Pavilion, you sit and eat near floor-to-ceiling windows that allow you to see marine life in the huge aquarium. Character meals (breakfast, lunch, dinner) are available in The Garden Grill Restaurant in The Land Pavilion.

Note: If you're at Epcot and want priority seating reservations, talk with the personnel at Guest Relations (to the left of *Spaceship Earth*) when the park opens and see what's available.

Disney-MGM Studios

The Hollywood Brown Derby, named for the original Brown Derby in Hollywood, California, cooks up this park's tastiest food. The Sci-Fi Dine-In Theater Restaurant and the 50s Prime Time Cafe offer only fair food but unique and memorable ambiance. At Sci-Fi, you sit in small convertible cars at a "drive-in" movie theater and watch trailers from old science fiction films while you eat. At Prime Time, a motherly server brings your food ("Better clean your plate!") while you watch fifties' sitcom segments on small TVs. Mama Melrose's Ristorante Italiano offers decent Italian fare. Entertaining character meals (breakfast, lunch) are available at the Hollywood & Vine buffet. For fast food, try the Backlot Express for burgers and sandwiches or the Toy Story Pizza Planet for pizza and cappuccino.

Note: If you're at Disney-MGM Studios and want priority seating reservations, walk to the priority seating window near the corner of Hollywood and Sunset Boulevards when the park opens and see what's available.

Disney's Animal Kingdom

The only full-service restaurant here is the Rainforest Cafe, which serves good food in a jungle atmosphere. It's a fun place to eat. You can enter the restaurant from inside or outside the park, so you don't have to buy park admission to eat here. A character breakfast with Donald Duck and friends is available at Restaurantosaurus, a counter-service restaurant. Fast food eateries are scattered around the park, and the food and ambiance are generally good.

Elsewhere in WDW

You'll find plenty of worthwhile WDW restaurants outside of the theme parks. The two best restaurants in WDW are Victoria & Albert's (expensive) at the Grand Floridian Resort & Spa and the California

Grill (expensive) at the Contemporary Resort. The Marketplace at Downtown Disney has a second Rainforest Cafe (moderate) equal in quality to the one in Disney's Animal Kingdom. The Portobello Yacht Club restaurant (expensive) at Pleasure Island and Palio restaurant (expensive) at the Swan hotel offer good Italian food. Other very good eateries include: Kimonos (Japanese) at the Swan hotel; the Flying Fish Cafe (seafood) and Spoodles (Mediterranean tapas) at the BoardWalk Resort; Citricos (Mediterranean fare) and Narcoossee's (seafood) at the Grand Floridian Resort; Artist Point (seafood) at Wilderness Lodge; Shula's Steak House at the Dolphin hotel; Yachtsman Steakhouse at the Yacht Club Resort; Fulton's Crab House at Pleasure Island; Olivia's Cafe (American) at Old Key West Resort; Jiko (African) at the Animal Kingdom Lodge.

Dinner shows

The best dinner show at WDW is *Hoop-Dee-Doo Musical Revue*, an energetic song and dance show with tongue-in-cheek humor at Fort Wilderness Pioneer Hall. You can reserve one of three nightly performances (5:00 p.m., 7:15 p.m., or 9:30 p.m.). The show is popular, so make your reservations months in advance. You can book up to two years ahead, which gives you some idea of the revue's popularity. Your other dinner-show option is *The Polynesian Luau Dinner Show* at the Polynesian Resort. It's entertaining and has decent food. The price is the same for either show: Adults $47.80, children $24.81. Book either one by calling 407-WDW-DINE.

Character meals outside the parks

You'll find decent character breakfasts in the hotels at such restaurants as the Cape May Cafe in the Beach Club Resort (Goofy and friends), 'Ohana in the Polynesian Resort (Mickey and friends), Chef Mickey's in the Contemporary Resort, and 1900 Park Fare in the Grand Floridian Resort (Mary Poppins and friends). Hotel restaurants offering good character dinners include 1900 Park Fare in the Grand Floridian Resort (Winnie the Pooh and friends) and Chef Mickey's in the Contemporary Resort. The specific characters at these meals change from time to time. So call ahead if you want to be sure you'll be dining with your favorites.

Money-saving tip: Eat light food for breakfast (most hotels have a snack area with cereals, fruit, milk, etc.). Then buy from vendors and counter-service eateries in the theme parks.

A final note: The tastiest (and safest) seafood is served in restaurants that specialize in seafood.

WDW Full-Service Restaurants Rated

- Rating: * to * * * * *
- Approximate Cost (for soup or salad and main course, without drinks, dessert or tip):
  - Expensive (over $25 per person)
  - Moderate ($15 to $25 per person)
  - Inexpensive (less than $15 per person)
- Meals Offered: Breakfast (B), Lunch (L), Dinner (D)
- † Next to the meal designation, for example (B†), means the restaurant offers an "all you can eat" buffet at that meal

Note: Restaurant opening hours, menus, and prices change periodically, and eateries may be refurbished or replaced.

Restaurant	Location	Cuisine	Rating	Price
Akershus (L†,D†)	Norway, Epcot	Norwegian	* * *	Moderate
Alfredo di Roma (L,D)	Italy, Epcot	Italian	* * *	Expensive
Arthur's 27 (D)	Wyndham Palace	Gourmet	* * * *	Expensive
Artist Point (D)	Wilderness Lodge	Seafood	* * *	Moderate
Baskervilles (B†,D†)	Grosvenor Resort	American	* *	Moderate
Benihana (D)	Hilton Resort	Japanese	* * *	Moderate
Biergarten (L†,D†)	Germany, Epcot	German	* *	Moderate
Big River Grille (L,D)	BoardWalk	American	* *	Moderate
Bistro de Paris (D)	France, Epcot	French	* * * *	Expensive
Boatwright's (B,D)	Port Orleans/Rvsd	Cajun	* *	Moderate
Boma (B†,D†)	Animal King. Ldg	African	* * *	Moderate
Bongo's (L,D)	Disney West Side	Cuban	* *	Moderate
California Grill (D)	Contemporary Res	American	* * * * *	Expensive
Cape May Cafe (B†,D†)	Beach Club Resort	Buffet	* * *	Moderate
Cap'n Jack's (L,D)	Disney Marketplace	Seafood	* * *	Moderate
Captain's Tavern (D)	Caribbean Beach	Seafood	* *	Moderate
Le Cellier Steakhouse (L,D)	Canada, Epcot	Steak	* * * *	Moderate
Chef Mickey's (B†,D†)	Contemporary Res	Buffet	* * *	Moderate
Chefs de France (L,D)	France, Epcot	French	* * * *	Moderate

Cinderella's Royal Table (B,L,D)	Magic Kingdom	American	* *	Moderat
Citricos (D)	Grand Floridian	Mediterran.	* * * *	Expensive
Concourse Steakhouse (B,L,D)	Contemporary	Steak	* * *	Moderate
Coral Cafe (B†,L,D†)	Dolphin Resort	American	* *	Moderate
Coral Reef (L,D)	Living Seas, Epcot	Seafood	* * * *	Expensive
Courtyard Cafe (B†,L,D)	Courtyard Marriott	American	* *	Moderate
Crystal Palace (B†,L†,D†)	Magic Kingdom	Buffet	* * *	Moderate
ESPN Club (L,D)	BoardWalk	American	* *	Moderate
50s Prime Time Cafe (L,D)	Disney-MGM	American	* * *	Moderate
Finn's Grill (D)	Hilton Resort	Seafood	* *	Moderate
Flying Fish Cafe (D)	BoardWalk	Seafood	* * * *	Expensive
Fulton's Crab House (B,L,D)	Pleasure Island	Seafood	* * * *	Expensive
Garden Grill (B,L,D)	The Land, Epcot	American	* * *	Moderate
Garden Grove (B,L,D)	Swan Resort	American	* *	Expensive
Giraffe Grill (B†,L,D)	Royal Plaza Resort	American	* *	Moderate
Grand Floridian Cafe (B,L,D)	Grand Floridian	American	* *	Moderate
Hollywood & Vine (B†,L†,D†)	Disney-MGM	American	* * *	Moderate
Hollywood Brown Derby (L,D)	Disney-MGM	American	* * * *	Expensive
House of Blues (L,D)	Disney West Side	American	* * *	Moderate
Jazz Company (D)	Pleasure Island	American	* *	Moderate
Jiko (D)	Animal King. Ldg	African	* * * *	Expensive
Kimonos (D)	Swan Resort	Japanese	* * * *	Moderate
Kona Cafe (B,L,D)	Polynesian Resort	Asian	* * *	Moderate
Liberty Tree Tavern (L,D)	Magic Kingdom	American	* * *	Moderate
Mama Melrose's (L,D)	Disney-MGM	Italian	* * *	Moderate
Marrakesh (L,D)	Morocco, Epcot	Moroccan	* * *	Moderate
Maya Grill (B†,D)	Coronado Springs	Mexican	* * *	Expensive
Narcoossee's (D)	Grand Floridian	Seafood	* * * *	Expensive
Nine Dragons (L,D)	China, Epcot	Chinese	* * *	Expensive
1900 Park Fare (B†,D†)	Grand Floridian	Buffet	* * *	Expensive

Official All-Star Cafe (L,D)	Wide Wld of Sports	American	* *	Moderate
'Ohana (B,D)	Polynesian Resort	Polynesian	* * *	Expensive
Olivia's Cafe (B,L,D)	Old Key West	American	* * *	Moderate
The Outback (D)	Wyndham Palace	Steak	* * *	Expensive
(Note: not part of the Outback Steakhouse restaurant chain)				
Palio (D)	Swan Resort	Italian	* * *	Expensive
Planet Hollywood (L,D)	Disney West Side	American	* * *	Moderate
Plaza (L,D)	Magic Kingdom	American	* * *	Moderate
Portobello Yacht Club (L,D)	Pleasure Island	Italian	* * *	Expensive
Rainforest Cafe (B,L,D)	Animal Kingdom	American	* * *	Moderate
Rainforest Cafe (B,L,D)	Disney Marketplace	American	* * *	Moderate
Rose & Crown (L,D)	UK, Epcot	English	* * *	Moderate
San Angel Inn (L,D)	Mexico, Epcot	Mexican	* * *	Expensive
Sci-Fi Dine-In (L,D)	Disney-MGM	American	* *	Moderate
Shula's (D)	Dolphin Resort	Steak	* * * *	Expensive
Spoodles (B†,D)	BoardWalk	Mediterran.	* * *	Moderate
Streamers (B†,L,D)	DoubleTree Suites	American	* *	Moderate
Tempura Kiku (L,D)	Japan, Epcot	Japanese	* * *	Moderate
Teppanyaki (L,D)	Japan, Epcot	Japanese	* * *	Expensive
Tony's Town Square (B,L,D,)	Magic Kingdom	Italian	* * *	Moderate
Traders (B,D)	Best Western	American	* *	Moderate
Trail's End (B†,L†,D†)	Fort Wilderness	Buffet	* * *	Moderate
Victoria & Albert's (D)	Grand Floridian	Gourmet	* * * * *	Expensive
Watercress Cafe (B†,L,D†)	Wyndham Palace	American	* *	Moderate
Whispering Canyon (B,L,D)	Wilderness Lodge	American	* * *	Moderate
Wolfgang Puck (L,D)	Disney West Side	Californian	* * *	Expensive
Yacht Club Galley (B,L,D)	Yacht Club Resort	American	* * *	Moderate
Yachtsman Steakhouse (D)	Yacht Club Resort	Steak	* * * *	Expensive

Basic Rules for Touring

1. Don't try to do everything. Each theme park, with the possible exception of Disney's Animal Kingdom, is too large to experience fully in one day. If you come to WDW intending to experience every attraction, you'll probably be disappointed. Furthermore, you'll quickly reach sensory overload, that point during the day when the kids are crying and you're no longer having fun.

2. Wake up early, arrive at the park early, and take a break in the afternoon either back at your hotel or in the park itself (see touring plans). This approach will provide the most time-efficient method for visiting the more popular attractions and let you recharge your engines during the afternoon break. Furthermore, you'll prevent sensory overload and avoid the worst of the afternoon heat. If you decide to sleep in, just pick up the appropriate touring plan later in the morning (a few steps before lunchtime) and try to catch the more popular attractions with FASTPASS (see "Good Things to Know About," above), during afternoon and evening parades, or in the hour before closing.

3. If you're visiting WDW to play golf or attend a conference, go to the parks after your morning recreation and follow the afternoon and evening portions of the appropriate touring plan(s). To avoid the longest lines, try to experience the more popular attractions during parades or in the hour before the park closes. In addition, use the FASTPASS or singles line options when available (see above) to minimize your waits for some popular attractions.

4. Don't stand in too many long lines. A long wait is more than 15 to 20 minutes. Current attraction wait times are posted on park Tip Boards (sometimes inaccurate) and in front of most attractions (usually accurate), or you can ask the Disney attendant. Waiting in queues can be exhausting, especially for children. As you follow the touring plans, the lines may become unbearably long later in the morning or early afternoon. At this point, you have several alternatives: You can use the FASTPASS and singles line options; you can skip down the touring plan to less congested attractions, or you can leave the park you're in and switch to another (if your ticket allows) — in essence combining touring plans for different parks on the same day. Just pick up the next park's touring plan at an appropriate point. The act of switching

parks will also provide a break of sorts, offering you a change of scenery.

5. Relax! You'll encounter many hyperkinetic vacationers in the theme parks, running to and fro, dragging crying kids behind them, jostling for position before parades and character greetings. Some of these folks don't get to WDW very often and are trying to pack too much into too short a time. Are these people really having fun? Avoid them if you can and seek quieter surroundings.

6. Avoid sunburn, dehydration, and exhaustion. If you start losing steam at any point, seek a rest area (consult the list of rest areas for each park in the appropriate chapters), take some refreshment in a cool place, or leave the park for your hotel. Drink frequently, even if you or your kids don't feel thirsty. Bring or rent a stroller for kids six and under.

   Note: The larger double strollers are more difficult to maneuver around the parks (especially when the parks are crowded).

7. Bring small snacks, such as gum or mints, into the parks in your shoulder bag or fanny pack. They come in handy between meals.

8. Convince your family, *before* you enter the parks, of the benefits of following the touring plans you'll find in the upcoming chapters. They will minimize waiting in lines while offering maximum opportunities for experiencing the best of WDW. They should also prevent time-consuming and sometimes emotional arguments and discussions about what everyone wants to do next. Convince your kids that they will meet plenty of characters during their visit, so hopefully they won't stop in their tracks every time they spot a Disney character off to the side. On the other hand, if your child seems desperate at times and the line for the character isn't too long, go ahead and queue up.

   The touring plans take busy periods into account and suggest strategies for dealing with them whether you are staying on property or off. One strategy is to arrive early, visit until the park becomes too crowded for comfort, and then switch to another less crowded park if your ticket allows. Another is to give yourself a "time out" by taking a rest break in the park itself. Either way, later in the day your time is best spent enjoying the least crowded attractions (these are listed for each park) and stage shows.

   Tip: On really crowded days, visit Epcot. It is large enough and offers enough shows to accommodate crowds enjoyably even when WDW is packed.

Note: Some children do better if they visit Magic Kingdom last. If they see it first, they may not enjoy the other parks quite as much because they may expect all of WDW to be just like Magic Kingdom.

9. Keep your camera readily available. Consult the park Guidemaps for "picture spot" locations that you may come upon as you follow the touring plans. Be alert for the many special picture moments that will inevitably happen.

   Note: See "Bringing the Magic Home," below, for photo tips.

10. If you get around WDW by car (recommended), write down your parking location on a piece of paper that you keep with you. Do this *every* time you park your car, even at the hotels.

11. Be ready for surprises. Attractions are periodically updated, changed completely, or closed for refurbishment. Times, schedules, shows, and parades vary continually. Furthermore, attractions occasionally break down, and inclement weather may cause cancellation of parades or temporary closing of certain rides.

    This book is current as of the date of publication, but don't be dismayed if you encounter a few surprises during your vacation. Even the Guidemap you pick up at the park entrance occasionally has erroneous information. Ask one or more cast members (Disney employees) if you have questions.

Hidden Mickeys

A long tradition with the "Imagineers" (see "Mouse Talk," above) is to build or paint the silhouette of Mickey Mouse into rides and attractions. Most of these silhouettes are not obvious, thus the "hidden Mickey" term. Some Disney fans become experts at hidden Mickey lore, and web sites exist that cover this arcane area.

Ask at Hotel Guest Services for guides to hidden Mickeys and other difficult-to-spot animal figures located throughout the Wilderness Lodge and the Animal Kingdom Lodge Resorts.

When Disney cast members are hired, certain of them are given review sheets that list the location of some hidden Mickeys. A few such locations are listed in each of the next four chapters. If you're interested, try to find them when you're in the parks. Most Disney cast members will happily point out nearby hidden Mickeys if you ask.

Attraction Ratings Explained

In the following four chapters, you'll find ratings of each park's attractions, along with descriptions of each ride or exhibit. Here is what the stars mean:

* * * * *	The Very Best
* * * *	Outstanding
* * *	Very Good
* *	Good
*	Average but still fun

Using the Touring Plans

The touring plans are the heart of this book. They are customized to the preferences of adults and teens, families with younger children, and seniors, and they work — better than you could ever imagine. I've tested and perfected them over a number of years with the help of numerous friends, friends of friends, and other visitors who turned to me (the WDW fanatic) for help in making their WDW theme park visits as magical as possible. BUT the plans aren't intended for armchair reading. If you've never visited the WDW theme parks and simply read the touring plans, you're likely to find them a little confusing.

Trust me. Once you are in the parks, you'll find these touring plans a breeze to follow. Visitors who've used them tell me they are like having your own personal tour guide. Follow them and you'll avoid the long lines and the exhaustion and frustration that can set in when you don't know what to do first or how to pace yourself.

If you're visiting WDW for the first time, using these plans will help to ensure a truly magical experience. And if you are a repeat visitor, the plans will help you savor the magic as you never have before.

A Special Note on Early Entry

There is no telling whether Disney will reinstate its Early Entry program for WDW Resort guests (see page 18). You can check the current status before your visit by calling 407-824-4321. Operators there will have all the details on which parks are offering Early Entry and on which days of the week — if and when the program is restored. Meanwhile, in hopes that it will return, I have included special touring plans for Early Entry days in this edition. By all means, take advantage of them if you are eligible. Plan to arrive at least 90 minutes before the official opening time on Early Entry days, and then follow the appropriate Early Entry touring plan in *Chapters Two, Three*, or *Four*.

Note: If the Early Entry program is reinstated and you are not staying on Disney property — thus are not eligible for Early Entry — I strongly advise visiting any park scheduled for Early Entry on another day of the week. On Early Entry days, the park will be crowded by the time it opens to the general public.

Accuracy and Other Impossible Dreams

I have tried to be as accurate and up-to-date as possible. But complete accuracy is an unattainable goal. As noted in #11, above, Walt Disney World is always changing — tweaking attractions, adding new lodging, restaurants, and entertainment venues, and adjusting prices and ticket options. Most likely to change are the prices and ticket options. Like any business, WDW reserves the right to change these at any time without notice. So it is possible, even probable, that there will be changes after the deadline for this book. Just to be on the safe side, when you are planning your trip, visit Disney's web site to check the latest price information: www.disneyworld.com

A special word about closings

WDW closes attractions periodically for maintenance, refurbishing, or replacement. So it is likely that one or more of the attractions in this book will be closed when you visit. If it has been replaced, you'll probably find the new attraction as good or even better than its predecessor. Simply note the name and include it in your touring plan in place of the old attraction.

Bringing the Magic Home

Nearly every visitor to Walt Disney World tries to capture the magic in photos, but all too often the results fall short of the goal. Here are some tips to help you get shots you'll enjoy viewing for years to come. Special thanks to my colleague Mark Ahrens, ER Nurse and photography enthusiast, for his help with this section.

1. The most efficient and least cumbersome camera for taking pictures in the parks is a simple disposable. The fixed focus lens is usually set to photograph subjects four to six feet away from the camera. So long as you keep that in mind when you take your pictures, you're likely to find the image quality acceptable. If you decide to go this route, buy several disposables at a discount store before your trip (they're more expensive at WDW).

2. If you desire higher quality photos or more flexibility, a range finder 35 mm auto-focus camera provides the best image quality for the cost. These cameras are available for $100 to $200 and offer such features as a zoom lens, self-loading, self-winding, and a built-in flash. Choose a camera you find comfortable to hold, with buttons that are easy to operate. The zoom feature will help you capture images in the distance — exotic animals at Disney's Animal Kingdom, for example.

3. Test your camera before taking it with you on vacation (unless, of course, it is a disposable). Read the owner's manual. If you're buying an upscale camera, shoot a roll of film in the store and test all the features (flash, zoom lens, and so on). Ask for instruction if you need help. Then leave the store and have the film developed at a one-hour processing center. If the pictures don't turn out well, return to the store and find out why. Or exchange your purchase for a different camera.

4. Come prepared. Use fresh film. (Check each roll to make sure that the expiration date hasn't passed.) Bring extra camera batteries with you. Store extra disposable cameras and film cartridges in a locker at the parks to lighten your load while touring. You may want to stash exposed film there, too.

5. Put your name and address on your camera(s) and film canisters with adhesive mailing labels or the like. That way if you drop one, you're likely to get it back. (Theme park guests tend to turn in found objects.)

6. Take a number of pictures of the subject if you can. Professional photographers take numerous photos to get the few that stand out. If you feel a photo op coming on, start clicking away! Try different angles and perspectives, sometimes tilting the camera to a 45-degree angle, for example, for variety. Always include close-ups, and be sure your subject isn't wearing a hat or sunglasses in

every shot; both can obscure the face.

7. Take some pictures when your subject isn't posing. One trick is to stand behind a character to capture the spontaneous facial expressions of your child approaching and greeting the character. If you're alert — and lucky — you may get a photo of a first-time visitor's glimpse of Main Street and Cinderella Castle as he or she comes out from under the Train Station arches.

8. Include yourself! Ask strangers or cast members to take photos of you with your group, especially at one of the "Kodak picture spots" listed in the park Guidemaps. You can take self portraits, too. Use the delayed-action shutter button on fancy cameras or hold the camera at arm's length if you're using a simple disposable unit.

9. Come up with a theme. For example, your kids trying on different hats or posing with their favorite characters or character merchandise. My teenage son once took pictures of his friends coming out of each restroom in the countries of World Showcase at Epcot!

10. Keep your cool. If your kids, pals, or significant other get tired of posing or waiting while you do elaborate set-ups, be content with snapping them in action for a while. Remember, candid shots are often the most magical.

CHAPTER TWO:

The Magic Kingdom

One of the most visited theme parks on earth, the Magic Kingdom (MK) is the original place of magic and fantasy at Walt Disney World Resort, and it never disappoints its visitors. There's something here for everyone, although the parent will likely leave the MK with a list of favorite attractions different from the list of his or her teenager or child.

Attractions Described & Rated

Main Street, U.S.A.

Guests pass through the MK entrance turnstiles, under the arches of the overhead WDW Railroad tracks, and into Town Square, which funnels folks onto Main Street. The Main Street shops open a half-hour before the rest of the MK and close up to an hour after the official closing time.

Main Street is a re-creation of a small town American street of the early 1900s. As you enter Town Square, City Hall will be to your left, with a fire station and shop next door. At City Hall, you can pick up Guidemaps (in seven languages) and get information about dining, character greeting, lost and found, and other topics of interest from helpful Disney cast members. Inside the Camera Center, next to Tony's Town Square Restaurant, are interesting interactive photography exhibits.

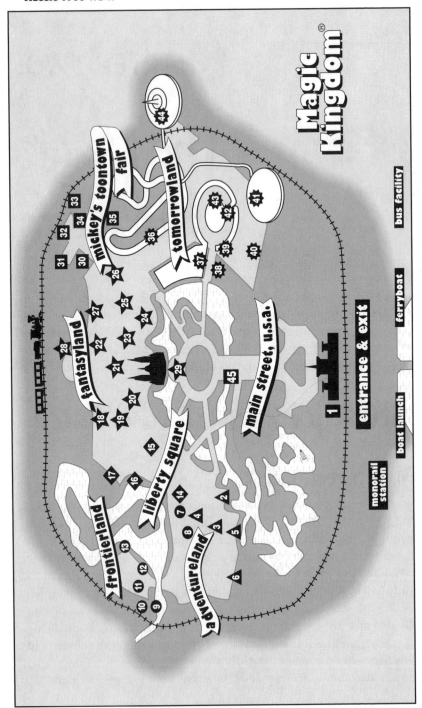

1 WDW Railroad, Entrance

adventureland

2 Swiss Family Treehouse

3 The Enchanted Tiki Room Under New Management

4 The Magic Carpets of Aladdin

5 Jungle Cruise

6 Pirates of the Caribbean

frontierland

7 Frontierland Shootin' Arcade

8 Country Bear Jamboree

9 Splash Mountain

10 WDW Railroad

11 Big Thunder Mountain Railroad

12 Raft to Tom Sawyer Island

13 Mike Fink Keelboats (currently closed)

liberty square

14 "The Diamond Horseshoe Saloon Revue"

15 The Hall of Presidents

16 Liberty Square Riverboat

17 The Haunted Mansion

fantasyland

18 "it's a small world"

19 Peter Pan's Flight

20 Mickey's PhilharMagic

21 Cinderella's Golden Carrousel

22 Dumbo the Flying Elephant

23 Snow White's Scary Adventures

24 Fairytale Garden

25 The Many Adventures of Winnie the Pooh

26 Mad Tea Party

27 Fantasyland Character Festival

28 Ariel's Grotto

29 Castle Forecourt Stage

mickey's toontown fair

30 Minnie's Country House

31 Toontown Hall Of Fame

32 Mickey's Country House

33 WDW Railroad

34 Donald's Boat

35 The Barnstormer at Goofy's Wiseacre Farm

tomorrowland

36 Tomorrowland Indy Speedway

37 The ExtraTERRORestrial Alien Encounter

38 The Timekeeper

39 Buzz Lightyear's Space Ranger Spin

40 Galaxy Palace Theater

41 Walt Disney's Carousel of Progress

42 Tomorrowland Transit Authority

43 Astro Orbiter

44 Space Mountain

main street, u.s.a.

45 Guest Information Board

Along Main Street are places to eat, shops, and an old-time barber shop. You can ride a fire engine or a horse-drawn trolley from Town Square down Main Street to the central hub in front of Cinderella Castle (and back to Town Square if you get off and queue up again).

You can send mail from the mailbox on Main Street (check your Guidemap for location), or any other mailboxes you see in the theme parks. The postmark will read "Lake Buena Vista, FL"

Look up at the store windows above the street. The "proprietors" are people who were actually involved in the early Disney company or people Walt Disney used as "front names" so he could secretly buy at market value the property on which he built WDW. Look back at the window above the Plaza Ice Cream Parlor and find the name of the man himself, Walter E. Disney. Walt wanted guests to see his name as they were leaving the main part of the Magic Kingdom.

Walt Disney World Railroad

> *Rating:* * *
> *Type:* Gentle train ride with audio tour guide
> *Time:* About 20 minutes to circle the park
> *Steve says:* A great way to relax and rest your legs

Take a pleasant, scenic journey around the MK on the WDW train. Keep your eyes and ears open for the Audio-Animatronics frontier and American Indian scenes along the way. The three stops are Main Street, Frontierland, and Mickey's Toontown Fair. You can ride for as long as you want. Only the Main Street Station has no wheelchair access.

Note: Folks in the first car are occasionally subjected to engine exhaust fumes.

Adventureland

The flower-covered bridge to Adventureland suggests you're entering an exotic paradise. The environment here evokes the Pacific and Caribbean Islands with a sprinkling of Africa and Asia. Adventureland has shops, eating places, and attractions.

Swiss Family Treehouse

> *Rating:* * * *
> *Type:* Outdoor walk-through exhibit

Time: 10 - 15 minutes, but dally longer if you wish

Steve says: Kids of all ages should have a treehouse like this!

You pass through the entry turnstile into an imaginative trail that winds up and through a replica of the treehouse built by the ship-wrecked Robinson family. It's fun to visually explore the fascinating details of the various "rooms" of the house. Try to follow the intricate water delivery system throughout the huge tree.

Note: If you want to linger at sights in the Swiss Family Treehouse, move to the side of the walkway and let those behind you pass by.

The Magic Carpets of Aladdin

Rating: * *

Type: Flying, steerable carpets

Time: Less than 2 minutes

Steve says: Eye-pleasing circle ride

Colorful, four-seater carpets whiz around in lofty circles. However, these magical carpets have a bit more zing than other circle rides: the two riders in the front control vertical movement, while the two rear riders can tilt the carpet nose up or nose down. It's rather like sitting on a real flying carpet! Fly high to avoid the water-squirting camel.

The Enchanted Tiki Room — Under New Management

Rating: * *

Type: Musical show with singing robotic birds

Time: 16 minutes

Steve says: Especially fun for younger kids

The first Disney Audio-Animatronics attraction, this amusing show takes place above your head as you sit in a dark, cool room. The attraction was updated to add Iago (from *Aladdin*) and Zazu (from *The Lion King*) to the veteran choir of brightly colored birds. Even the flowers and tiki statues sing!

Jungle Cruise

Rating: * * * *

Type: Outdoor boat tour

Time: 9 - 10 minutes

Steve says: Fun for everyone; the boat skipper has everyone smiling

A classic Disney attraction, *Jungle Cruise* takes you gently down the great jungle rivers of the earth. Along the way, you pass Audio-Anima-

tronics elephants, hippos, and other animals. The boat skipper's jokes
are corny yet still amusing and seem perfectly in tune with the ride. Be
sure to look at the "back side of water."

Tip: After the early morning, the lines are usually long here for the
rest of the day, especially during busy seasons.

At the exit is **Shrunken Ned's Junior Jungle Boats**, which are miniature boats navigated by your remote control around a pond studded
with various jungle obstacles. They're not free; you have to buy a one-
dollar token to make the boats operate for about two minutes.

Tip: Save *Shrunken Ned's* for downtime. It's fun but if you've only
one day in the MK, you'll want to spend it experiencing the more exciting attractions.

Pirates of the Caribbean

> Rating: * * * *
> Type: Indoor boat ride past pirate scenes
> Time: About 8 minutes
> Steve says: A classic attraction; not scary except for one small
>   boat drop

The queue area and the boat ride take you back in time to pirates
searching for island treasures. Your boat initially passes pirate skeletons, then swooshes down a mild water drop back to the time when
those pirates were alive and pillaging. You float by incredibly detailed
sets and Audio-Animatronics figures as the pirates invade and conquer
an island town. Look for the hairy pirate leg dangling from a bridge
above you and the jail door lock shaped like Mickey Mouse's head. The
waiting lines generally move quickly, but even this ride can be a long
wait during afternoons in busy seasons.

Frontierland

The main thoroughfare through Frontierland takes you back in
time to the days of the Old West. The frontier ambiance is so realistic, a
Western movie could be filmed here! Frontierland has its own unique
shops and eating places. The *Walt Disney World Railroad* makes one of
its three stops right by *Splash Mountain*.

Country Bear Jamboree

> Rating: * * *
> Type: Indoor theater show with singing bears

Time: 15 minutes

Steve says: Toe-tapping country-hillbilly style music

These Audio-Animatronics bears bring smiles to just about everyone as they sing a series of humorous country and hillbilly songs from a stage facing the theater. Many in the audience will clap and sing along. A special holiday show runs for several weeks during the Christmas season.

Frontierland Shootin' Arcade

Rating: * *

Type: Shooting gallery

Time: A few minutes per session

Steve says: A fun diversion

This shooting arcade will entertain children and teenagers until they run short of coins (There is a 50-cent charge for each 1- to 2-minute session). The guns shoot infrared beams at targets scattered around a town in the Old West. Expect humorous and unique visual and sometimes auditory effects (tombstones that rise up or spin, a howling coyote, a galloping ghost rider in the sky) as your rifle scores direct hits on the hapless bull's-eyes.

Splash Mountain

Rating: * * * * *

Type: Log flume ride through a mountain

Time: 10 - 11 minutes

Steve says: A fun feast for the eyes and ears and a gut check for the stomach

This attraction is the favorite of some folks. Hollowed-out log boats take you on a more than half-mile journey inside the mountain and past riverside scenes that showcase singing and talking Audio-Animatronics characters from the Disney movie *Song of the South*. Brer Fox chases Brer Rabbit to the "Laughing Place," while other Brer characters regale you with song as you float by. Several small water drops prepare you for the big 52-foot drop into a "briar patch" (the "Laughing Place") near the end of the ride.

On the way down the big drop, you'll be photographed, and you can check out the picture at the end of the ride. You may want to buy your picture at least once, since these *Splash Mountain* photos are some of the best mementos of WDW vacations.

Tip: To enhance the thrill of the drop, some riders raise their arms straight up. Unfortunately, these high hands can block the faces of riders in the seats behind them. If you sense a hand raised in front of you, tilt left in your seat before the flash to preserve your frightened mug for posterity.

The big drop often gets riders wet, especially those in the front seat. Riders on the right side of the boat will also frequently get wet during the journey. Since the boat seats are usually moist, you'll notice that just about everyone exiting in front of you will have a damp derriere!

Note: See "The Dash to Splash," page 83, for insider directions on the fastest way to get to *Splash Mountain* at opening time.

Height restriction: Kids must be 40" or taller to ride.

Big Thunder Mountain Railroad

Rating: ★★★★
Type: Outdoor roller coaster
Time: 3 - 4 minutes
Steve says: Moderately fast coaster with dips and turns, no loops

BTMR is a roller coaster that winds and dips around and through a big mountain past various mining and desert scenes, including mountain animals, falling rocks, and geysers. The sights from the train are humorous and entertaining. The roller coaster ride itself is tame for teenagers, but many older folks will find it jarring enough. The experience is more thrilling if you hold your arms straight up during drops and turns. You can study the flooded mining town scene at a more leisurely pace from the *WDW Railroad* train as it passes by Big Thunder Mountain.

Height restriction: Kids must be 40" or taller to ride.

Mike Fink Keelboats

Rating: ★★
Type: Outdoor gentle boat ride
Time: About 10 minutes
Steve says: Scenic and relaxing, but skippable

These small boats putter down the Rivers of America around *Tom Sawyer Island* along the same route and scenery as the *Liberty Square Riverboat*. Each keelboat is guided not by an underwater rail but by a skipper who controls the rudder of the free-floating vessel and recounts an entertaining spiel along the way. Guests sit inside the boat or on top on benches which are exposed to the elements. By the way, Mike

Fink was a Mississippi River keelboat captain and a contemporary of Mark Twain. This attraction closes at dusk.

Note: Disney has closed Mike *Fink Keelboats* till further notice. It has not announced a replacement, and as it sometimes reopens attractions, I've kept it in this edition.

Tom Sawyer Island

Rating: * * *
Type: Elaborate outdoor playground
Time: As long as you want, minimum 20 minutes
Steve says: A place where kids and adults become excited explorers

Take a raft over to *Tom Sawyer Island* and enter the world of Mark Twain's famous character. This forested island has caves, bridges, a frontier fort, winding trails, and other interesting discoveries. Don't miss the escape tunnel from the back of the fort. If you're flagging a bit in the early afternoon, head over to Aunt Polly's Dockside Inn for rest and refreshment while the younger folks explore the island. *Tom Sawyer Island* closes in the early evening.

Liberty Square

This small but beautiful section of the Magic Kingdom re-creates America during the Revolutionary War. In the middle of Liberty Square is the Liberty Tree, a large spreading live oak with 13 lanterns hanging from its branches (representing the 13 original colonies), and a replica of the cracked Liberty Bell. Liberty Square has its own shops and eateries.

"The Diamond Horseshoe Saloon Revue"

Rating: * * *
Type: Indoor live musical western show
Time: About 30 minutes
Steve says: An enjoyable lunch option, but arrive early for a decent seat

This fast-moving live song and dance show is humorous and entertaining. The jokes and one-liners are reminiscent of the *Hoop-Dee-Doo Musical Revue* show in Fort Wilderness (see "Good Things to Know About" in *Chapter One*), and the performers move around and through the audience. Show times are listed in the Magic Kingdom Times Guide.

Reservations are not required, and you can walk in at any time before or during the performance. The dance hall also has a fast-food counter inside.

Note: Disney periodically experiments with the length of the show; so it may be a bit longer or shorter when you see it.

The Hall of Presidents

Rating: * * *
Type: Indoor historical theater show
Time: 23 minutes
Steve says: Moving and patriotic, a fitting attraction for Liberty Square

The first part of the show is a patriotic movie-screen review of important moments in American history. The show ends with an impressive on-stage presentation of all the U.S. presidents (thanks to Audio-Animatronics). Each president responds with a nod as his name is called and, during the roll call, the presidents act almost like real people: they fidget and even whisper to each other! Their clothes and furniture are historically accurate, so the history buffs in the audience can get deeply absorbed in the details. Your kids might even learn something. But don't use the word "educational" in front of them beforehand or they might want to skip this attraction. The show starts every 30 minutes.

Liberty Square Riverboat

Rating: * * *
Type: Outdoor gentle boat ride
Time: 16 - 18 minutes
Steve says: A relaxing tour around *Tom Sawyer Island*

This paddle-wheel steamboat, called the Liberty Belle, tracks through the half-mile long Rivers of America on an underwater rail. The journey is laid-back and pleasant, and the boat passes a variety of frontier and Old West scenes on the riverbanks. Stand at the front or rear of the boat toward the center on either level for the best view of both riverbanks. Listen to the recorded spiel and learn some river lore of the American past, like the meaning of "mark twain": two fathoms or twelve feet deep (mark one is one fathom). "Mark twain" is deep enough for safe passage for these riverboats. You'll also hear some humorous aphorisms from famed writer Mark Twain himself.

Note: You won't hear the spiel as well if you stand at the rear of the boat on the lower level near the paddle wheel; the noise muffles the speaker. This attraction sometimes closes at dusk. The Liberty Belle leaves the dock on the hour and the half-hour.

The Haunted Mansion

Rating: ****
Type: "Dark ride" through haunted house
Time: About 9 minutes
Steve says: Not scary, except for small children

Inside this imposing old house, Disney visits Halloween in a tongue-in-cheek style. The lighthearted journey begins in a dark room where the walls and pictures stretch. Then you step onto a "doom buggy" which takes you past all manner of ghosts and spooky (but humorous) special effects, such as a banquet hall with dancing ghosts and a cemetery where the dead come alive and drink tea. In fact, there's so much to see, it's difficult to take it all in on just one ride through. Look for the "hidden Mickey" in the arrangement of dishes in one of the individual place settings on the large dinner table, and read a few of the humorous tombstone epitaphs on the left side of the walkway on your way in or out.

Fantasyland

An imaginative and dreamy place, Fantasyland is what some people conjure up when they think of the Magic Kingdom. This land sits just behind Cinderella Castle, so it's easy to see why some folks are drawn to Fantasyland as one of their first stops. Fantasyland has its own unique shops and places to grab a bite.

Cinderella Castle

There's no ride in the Castle, but Cinderella's Royal Table (a restaurant) is here. While walking through the Castle, note the beautiful mural along the walls that tells the Cinderella story. Before the evening fireworks, an acrobatic woman performs Tinker Bell's Flight as she "floats" down a wire stretching from a high point on Cinderella Castle to a rooftop in Tomorrowland.

"it's a small world"

Rating: ***
Type: Indoor boat ride
Time: 11 - 12 minutes

Steve says: A family favorite; try to guess the different cultures

Inside a cool and restful building, a boat floats you gently past singing and dancing dolls representing the dress and culture of many nations of the Earth. You'll sing along with German oompah bands, scarlet-garbed Tower of London guards, Japanese kite fliers, Don Quixote tilting at windmills, and much more. The melodic theme song is soothing and easily learned, and repetitive enough that it will probably remain locked in your subconscious for the rest of your life. This ride is a good choice if you're feeling hot and need a rest because the lines are rarely long and the boats load quickly.

Peter Pan's Flight

Rating: * * * *
Type: "Dark ride" in suspended boats
Time: 3 - 4 minutes
Steve says: A classic theme ride

This short indoor flight in soaring ships is a perennial favorite of many guests. A sprinkling of pixie dust allows you to fly from Wendy's house out over London (the cars on the streets far below really move), past the Big Ben clock, and then to Never Land. The atmosphere is absorbing and delightful as Peter Pan and his friends eventually vanquish Captain Hook and his pirates.

Mickey's PhilharMagic

Rating: Not open at press time
Type: 3-D theater show
Steve says: Sounds like a winner

Scheduled to open sometime in 2003, Mickey's PhilharMagic will star the main mouse himself and other Disney characters. Disney is billing this as a "3-D film spectacular" complete with in-theatre effects, a 150-foot wide screen, and plenty of Disney music.

Cinderella's Golden Carrousel

Rating: *
Type: Carousel ride
Time: 2 - 3 minutes
Steve says: Slow loader; not worth a long wait

Every horse is different on this colorful and intricate merry-go-round. Notice the Cinderella story pictures above the horses. The ride is fun, but the real beauty is in the details of the *Carrousel*.

Dumbo the Flying Elephant

Rating: * * for most visitors; ***** for young children
Type: Flying, steerable elephants
Time: About 2 minutes
Steve says: A must for young children

Most folks have been on rides of this type at local carnivals and fairs. However, this circular ride in Disney elephant vehicles is frequently represented in pictures of the Magic Kingdom, and it's the favorite ride of many young children who visit WDW. Your joystick controls the height of the elephant vehicle.

Note: The lines are long all day, except early in the morning just after the park opens. Even if the queue is long, however, you will be giving your child a long-lasting and cherished memory by waiting patiently for your turn to fly with Dumbo.

Ariel's Grotto

Rating: *
Type: Elaborate character greeting area and water playground
Time: About 1 minute, once you get to her
Steve says: Fun for small children; memorable photo for the family album

This small area tucked away at the back of Fantasyland is a combination spurting water playground and greeting area for an autograph and picture with Ariel, the mermaid. WDW has placed several of these interactive fountains around the theme parks. Each one consists of a soft matted area with holes from which water spurts randomly to various heights and shapes. The first one at Epcot near the central walkway to World Showcase was an instant hit, and it's delightful to observe children completely lose themselves in innocent play here as they dart in and out among the water spurts. In fact, these playgrounds are magnets for young children. If you turn your head for only a second as you and your child approach the area, your young one will be dripping wet before you can even utter a sound. Get in line whenever you want to meet Ariel.

Another character area near *Ariel's Grotto* is the **Fantasyland Character Festival,** which is located where the queue for the now-defunct *20,000 Leagues Under The Sea* ride used to be. Various characters are available here for pictures and autographs.

Note: The lines are often long.

Snow White's Scary Adventures

Rating: * * *
Type: "Dark ride"
Time: 2 - 3 minutes
Steve says: Revisit some classic characters

The Dwarves' diamond mine car takes you winding along a track past indoor scenes of Snow White in peril. The Dwarves try to help as Snow White runs from the evil Queen. The wicked Witch pops out several times and frightens some young children, but the story ends happily as you wave goodbye to Snow White and the Prince. Nevertheless, some youngsters remember only the scary Witch.

Caution: If you're concerned about your child's reaction, please prepare him or her before this ride if possible or skip it altogether; it may not be worth the risk of spoiling the rest of the day at the Magic Kingdom.

The Many Adventures of Winnie the Pooh

Rating: * * * *
Type: "Dark ride"
Time: 4 - 5 minutes
Steve says: A must ride for children; fun for adults, too

Your "Hunny Pot" vehicle moves indoors through scenes from *Winnie the Pooh* stories. You meet Pooh, Kanga, Roo, and Owl coping with the wind on a "Blustery Day," then your car bounces along with Tigger deeper into the Hundred Acre Wood. The next scene is the inside of Pooh's house, where you enter Pooh's dream about Heffalumps and Woozles. Your "Hunny Pot" bobs through the "Floody Place," where Piglet is saved from going over a waterfall. Final scenes are the "Hero Party" with Pooh's friends, then Christopher Robin and Pooh skipping into the horizon. The attraction is happy and uplifting and is accompanied by classic *Winnie the Pooh* music.

Mad Tea Party

Rating: * *
Type: Outdoor spinning ride
Time: About 2 minutes
Steve says: A favorite for teenagers (and for adults who like to whirl)

These teacups spin you as the entire floor rotates. You can spin even faster by turning the wheel at the center of the teacup. When the ride stops, you may feel like the dizzy mouse that periodically pops out of the teacup at the center of the ride.

Mickey's Toontown Fair

This small, colorful land is truly a haven for kids. They can meet Mickey here (as well as a slew of other characters), tour Mickey's and Minnie's houses, ride a cool kiddies' roller coaster, and get wet in *Donald Duck's Boat*. You can shop at the Judge's Tent and quell the munchies with a stop at the snack area. To get to Mickey's Toontown Fair, ride the *Walt Disney World Railroad* or walk the short path from Fantasyland or the little-used path from the side of the Tomorrowland Arcade.

Minnie's Country House

Rating: ★ ★ ★
Type: Walk-through house exhibit
Time: 5 - 10 minutes, sometimes longer for young children
Steve says: Worth a visit no matter what your age

Walk at your own pace through this wonderfully detailed house, filled with interesting pictures and knickknacks. Push the big button on Minnie's telephone and listen to some of her answering machine messages. Her kitchen is really cool, especially after you open the refrigerator door and feel the frosty air.

Toontown Hall of Fame

Rating: ★ ★
Type: Indoor area for meeting characters
Time: Up to 10 minutes for each group greeting (not counting the time waiting in line)
Steve says: A great place for adding to the autograph books, but it can be time consuming

Located between Mickey's and Minnie's houses, this big tent is where you and your kids can meet a bunch of characters who cluster at the end of three different queues. For example, one recent grouping had classic Disney characters in one room (Chip 'n' Dale, Daisy Duck, Donald Duck, Uncle Scrooge or Roger Rabbit), Winnie the Pooh and pals in a second room (Tigger, Piglet, and Winnie), and Minnie Mouse and her friends (Goofy, Pluto) in the third room.

Note: Only three characters may be present at any given time, and one or more characters change(s) every half-hour. Toward the front of the line, you will be ushered into the room with 10 to 15 other guests for about a 10-minute visit with the characters. You have to queue up all over again for each of the other rooms.

Mickey's Country House

Rating: * * *
Type: Walk-through house exhibit
Time: About 10 minutes. Add 10 - 30 minutes (depending on the crowd) if you want to meet Mickey Mouse in the Judge's Tent out back
Steve says: Mickey's home is fun for all ages, but unless the waiting line at the Judge's Tent is short, it's easier to meet Mickey at one of his character meals.

Walk through Mickey's house and revel in the detail. The Imagineers must've had great fun designing these rooms, the backyard, and garage. Mickey's friends are still working at remodeling the kitchen, which is quite a mess. Don't miss Pluto's doghouse in the back, and note that the vegetables in the garden magically grow Mickey ears! The sidewalk behind the house leads to Mickey's Judge's Tent, where you and your children can line up and meet the Main Mouse in person. If you don't want to enter the Judge's Tent, exit through Mickey's garage.

Donald's Boat

Rating: * *
Type: Spurting water playground
Time: As long as you want; your children may not want to leave
Steve says: Your kids will get wet

Like *Ariel's Grotto*, this spurting fountain playground provides a wet antidote to hot afternoons. Kids love to explore the boat while trying in vain to dodge the random water spurts from the sides of the leaky vessel.

The Barnstormer at Goofy's Wiseacre Farm

Rating: * * *
Type: Short, outdoor roller coaster for kids
Time: Less than one minute
Steve says: Adults enjoy this one, too

This roller coaster zips you up and around and then through the walls of Goofy's barn. Although the ride is short, it's fun, especially for kids.

Age/height restrictions: Children under 3 years of age or less than 35" tall cannot ride.

Tomorrowland

This glistening, futuristic land should rightfully be entered from above, preferably along a beam of light from a hovering spaceship. If you don't command such a vehicle, stand in the middle of Tomorrowland, near the *Astro Orbiter* ride, and turn slowly around. You'll feel as if you are on a sci-fi movie set of the past. Tomorrowland, colorful during the day, is especially striking after dark with its bright neon lights. Like the MK's other lands, it has its own themed shops and eating places.

Tomorrowland Indy Speedway

Rating: * *

Type: Outdoor miniature raceway

Time: 4 - 5 minutes

Steve says: Great fun for children, but be wary; you can get rammed from behind

Slow-moving gasoline powered miniature cars putter over guide rails along a winding track. The cars are painted and decorated to resemble racing cars. Preschool and elementary school children enjoy this ride, and the fun is enhanced by the loud car engine noises. Teens and adults find it less exciting.

Height restriction: You have to be 52" or taller to drive by yourself.

The ExtraTERRORestrial Alien Encounter

Rating: * * * *

Type: Indoor special effects scare-fest

Time: 12 minutes (not counting a 5 - 6 minute pre-show)

Steve says: Horror in the dark; you'll hear screams aplenty (maybe your own!)

This attraction is a departure from the typical WDW entertainment. The purpose of *Alien Encounter* is to frighten you. The somewhat morbid pre-show sets you up for the scary experience inside the main arena. An alien monster is mistakenly transported from a faraway planet to a holding chamber in the center of your theater. The lights go out and mayhem follows as the alien escapes to flap around above and behind you. The area around you is equipped with various special effects that suggest the monster is moving (and eating) all around you in the dark. You'll feel his breath on the back of your neck and fluid (blood?) dripping on your legs from above. All in all, it's pretty scary, and you won't leave the exit doors with the usual warm and fuzzy Disney glow.

Height restriction: Kids have to be 44" or taller to get in.

Caution: The experience is too frightening for small children. Even 9- and 10-year-olds will often say they didn't enjoy it (without admitting to having been scared).

The Timekeeper

Rating: * * *
Type: Indoor time-travel movie in Circle-Vision
Time: 20 minutes
Steve says: Imaginative, humorous movie

You stand alongside a rail to watch an entertaining Circle-Vision movie (the scenes unfold on screens encircling the viewers). A robot equipped with cameras for eyes is sent in a time machine on a journey across recent centuries. The robot transmits "live" camera shots to your movie screen, including artists at work such as young Mozart and Leonardo da Vinci, then Jules Verne and H.G. Wells. Jules Verne hitches a ride to the present and beyond, and he joyfully witnesses some of his visions come to fruition. The acting is convincing and the dialogue witty and rapid-fire (one of the narrators is Robin Williams).

Note: The Timekeeper is open seasonally, typically during busy periods, and it may close before the park closes (consult your Times Guide).

Buzz Lightyear's Space Ranger Spin

Rating: * * * *
Type: Indoor, interactive track ride
Time: About 5 minutes
Steve says: Great fun for all ages

This indoor ride is more interactive than most: you can turn and even spin your car and shoot simulated laser guns at multiple targets. Your mission is to help Buzz Lightyear save the universe from the villainous Emperor Zurg and his warriors. At the end of the ride, your total shooting score is displayed in front of you on the dashboard. The cars seat two, and your fellow soldier's shooting score is tallied separately. To maximize your score, hold down the firing button while you turn the laser gun and car for the best target angles.

Walt Disney's Carousel of Progress

Rating: * * *
Type: Indoor theater show with changing tableaus
Time: About 18 minutes
Steve says: Especially interesting for adults

This attraction has endured well. You sit in a comfortable indoor theater which revolves around stage sets of an Audio-Animatronics family as they grow older gracefully. The theme of the show is progress, especially the evolution of the American home with its ever more complicated appliances and entertainment gadgets. The scenes take you from the early part of the 20th century all the way forward to the computer age. The 1950s' kitchen is reminiscent of the 50s Prime Time Cafe at Disney-MGM Studios. As at *The Hall of Presidents*, your kids might actually learn something here while having fun at the same time!

Note: *Carousel of Progress*, like *The Timekeeper*, is open seasonally, typically during busy periods, and it may close early (consult your Times Guide).

Tomorrowland Transit Authority

Rating: * *
Type: Gentle tram ride
Time: 10 - 12 minutes
Steve says: A unique view of Tomorrowland from above

A slow-moving tram takes you on a restful and scenic journey around Tomorrowland, both outdoors and inside the various attraction buildings. The overhead spiel during the ride is entertaining. There's rarely a long wait, so this ride is a good bet during hot or crowded times of the day.

Astro Orbiter

Rating: * * *
Type: Flying, steerable rockets
Time: Less than 2 minutes
Steve says: Grand panoramic view over the Magic Kingdom

You ride an elevator up to the loading platform then climb into a small rocket that flies you in circles high in the air. It's a futuristic *Dumbo* ride, as a control stick allows you to select and adjust the height of your rocket. The view from the ride is a large part of the fun. Be prepared to get dizzy, unless you're accustomed to rides that move in rapid circles.

Space Mountain

Rating: *****
Type: Indoor roller coaster
Time: About 3 minutes
Steve says: Exhilarating, worth riding again and again

This roller coaster ride in the dark is the favorite attraction of many visitors to the Magic Kingdom. The long entrance path inside the futuristic cone-shaped building winds past visual effects about astronomy that set the mood for your blastoff into space. The coaster ride is filled with dips and spiraling turns (no loops), as asteroids whiz by overhead. If you can hold your gaze upwards long enough, you'll spot galaxies and other space matter moving through the blackness. *Space Mountain* is not as terrifying as well-known roller coasters at other theme parks, but the ride is great fun if your neck, back, and inner ear are up to it.

Height restriction: Kids have to be 44" or taller to ride.

Note: See "The Race to Space," page 82, for insider tips on the fastest way to get to *Space Mountain* first thing in the morning.

Special Attractions

Parades. The Magic Kingdom offers two parades, one daily in the afternoon and another in the evening on most days of the year. In busy seasons, it adds a second evening parade. Different characters appear in the afternoon and evening, so parade fans will want to catch them both.

Fireworks. Weather permitting, most evenings end with *Fantasy in the Sky*, a fireworks display that offers a magical end to your day in the Magic Kingdom.

Attractions with Minimal Waits (Usually)

- *Swiss Family Treehouse.* On crowded days, this attraction may have a wait.
- *The Enchanted Tiki Room.* The wait is usually the time until the

next show, except on really crowded days.

- *Shrunken Ned's Junior Jungle Boats.* You may have to wait for the next available remote control stand. It costs money to play — one dollar per short session.
- *Frontierland Shootin' Arcade.* You may have to wait a short time for the next available gun. It costs money to play — 50 cents per short round.
- *"The Diamond Horseshoe Saloon Revue."* Wander inside 15 minutes before the next show — check your Times Guide for the performance schedule. Sit downstairs or in the balcony.
- *The Hall of Presidents.* The wait is usually the time until the next show, except on very crowded days.
- *Liberty Square Riverboat.* The wait is usually the time until the next ride.
- *"it's a small world."* On really crowded days, this attraction may have a wait.
- *Donald's Boat.* This interactive fountain usually has room for a few more guests.
- *Walt Disney's Carousel of Progress.* The wait is usually the time until the next show.
- *Tomorrowland Transit Authority.* If this ride has a wait, chances are the entire park is very crowded.
- *The Timekeeper.* The wait is usually the time until the next show.

Attractions That May Frighten Children

(Remember that "switching off' is available at some of these attractions; see *Chapter One,* "Good Things to Know About," and below.)

- *Pirates of the Caribbean.* May frighten toddlers.
- *Splash Mountain.* The drop at the end of this ride can frighten anyone. Switching off is available.
- *Big Thunder Mountain Railroad.* This roller coaster is fast enough to frighten children and seniors. Switching off is available.
- *The Haunted Mansion.* The mansion's dark ambiance may frighten young children.
- *Snow White's Scary Adventures.* This ride has a tradition of frightening preschoolers.
- *Mad Tea Party.* Can cause motion sickness in anyone.
- *The Barnstormer at Goofy's Wiseacre Farm.* This zippy roller coaster can frighten young children.

- *Alien Encounter.* Scary experience for anyone. Not recommended for children 10 and under. Switching off is available.
- *Space Mountain.* Intense roller coaster in the dark can frighten anyone. Switching off is available.

Least Crowded Restrooms

- The restrooms to the left off Main Street in a small alcove between Casey's Corner and The Crystal Palace restaurant.
- The restrooms on the right side of *Pirates of the Caribbean*.

Especially Attractive at Night

- *Big Thunder Mountain Railroad*
- *Cinderella's Golden Carrousel*
- *Astro Orbiter*

Resting Places

- The quiet park in Liberty Square behind Ye Olde Christmas Shoppe.
- The benches in the small alcove to the right of the entrance to *Pirates of the Caribbean*.
- The benches under the shed at the edge of the rose garden between the two entrance bridges to Tomorrowland.
- The sitting area by the Sunshine Tree Terrace in Adventureland.
- The chairs at the end of the cul-de-sac to the right, halfway down Main Street as you're entering the park.

Hidden Mickeys

Here are just a few of the hidden Mickeys you may want to look for in the Magic Kingdom:

- *"it's a small world"* — As you are floating through the tropical segment, look up and find the hanging vines that curve down from the ceiling. One of the vines has leaves shaped like Mickey's frontal silhouette, with the round head and two round ears.
- *The Haunted Mansion* — As you are passing by the ghostly dining room, observe the left end of the large banquet table below. One of the place settings (a plate and two small dishes) is usually arranged like Mickey's frontal silhouette.

- *Frontierland Shootin' Arcade* — In one target area toward the front is a three-lobed cactus shaped like Mickey's head and ears.
- *Splash Mountain* — Toward the end of the ride after the big drop, look to your right as you're floating toward the riverboat with singing fowl. A white cloud on the wall is shaped like Mickey reclining on his back with his head on the right. You can also see this Hidden Mickey from the *Walt Disney World Railroad* train as it passes by.
- *Pirates of the Caribbean* — Near the end of the boat ride, on the right side, is a jail with prisoners who are trying to coax a dog to bring them the jail keys. The lock on the jail door is shaped like Mickey's head.
- *Walt Disney's Carousel of Progress* — In the last scene, a pepper grinder on the kitchen counter has Mickey ears.
- *Tomorrowland Transit Authority* — Toward the end of the ride, your car passes a woman getting her hair done. Her belt buckle sports a Mickey head.
- *The ExtraTERRORestrial Alien Encounter* — In the waiting area, certain poles with electrical conduits are decorated with hieroglyphics. Mickey appears as one of the icons in the symbols.

Touring The Magic Kingdom

Getting to the Magic Kingdom can be a less than magical experience, especially if you are staying off property and want to arrive early, as I recommend. The following tips will help you arrive with minimal frustration. Once you're there, follow the appropriate touring plan for a hassle-free visit.

Getting to the entrance turnstiles if you are staying on property

Guests staying on Disney property have a major advantage over those staying elsewhere because they can take Disney transport directly from their hotels to the MK turnstiles. Grand Floridian and Polynesian Resort guests can hop a resort monorail or a boat (the boats are usually slower), while guests of the Contemporary Resort can take a resort monorail or a special walkway to the Magic Kingdom; the walk takes about 10 minutes. The other Disney properties (except Fort Wilderness and the Wilderness Lodge) provide bus service directly to the entrance turnstiles (See "Caution," below). Fort Wilderness and the Wilderness Lodge provide boat service to the entrance turnstiles but bus service only to the Transportation and Ticket Center (TTC) across the Seven Seas Lagoon from the MK. Ask at your hotel Guest Services how long it will take you to get to the Magic Kingdom entrance.

Caution: Buses that arrive prior to one hour before the park's official 9:00 a.m. opening time will drop you at the Transportation and Ticket Center (TTC), where you will be stuck waiting with all the off-property guests for the monorail and ferry to begin running. Ask the bus driver where you will be dropped before you board to avoid any unpleasant surprises.

Getting to the entrance turnstiles if you are staying off property

You cannot go directly to the turnstiles, but will enter the MK by way of the Transportation and Ticket Center (TTC), where the parking lot is located. Once you've parked, you will hop a shuttle to the boarding area for transport to the MK. Your choices are the express monorail or the ferryboat. (Note that the ferries don't always operate in the afternoons during slower times of the year.) The monorail is a few minutes faster (the trip takes four to five minutes), but it often has a longer wait than the ferry (which takes six to seven minutes). If the monorail entry ramp is packed with people, take the ferry if it is in or approaching the dock. Also take the ferry if a magical approach is more important to you than a speedy one. Budget a total of 15 to 25 minutes for your entire trip from parking lot to entrance turnstiles.

In the early morning hours when you're striving to arrive early, the ferries and express monorail from the TTC often do not even begin to operate until 30 minutes before the official opening time. That happens to be about when the Magic Kingdom begins to admit guests at the entry turnstiles! Message: WDW clearly favors its resort guests at times like these.

Insider tip #1: During slow seasons, guests staying off property can sometimes gain the Disney resort-guest advantage. Drive early to the Contemporary or another monorail resort and tell the parking lot guard that you're having breakfast at the hotel. Then eat an early breakfast (especially if you haven't eaten already), leave your car in the lot, and walk (about 10 minutes from the Contemporary) or ride the hotel monorail (budget 20 to 25 minutes) to the MK entrance. If you decide to try this strategy, be sure to make dining reservations before your arrival. WDW hotel parking areas are gated to keep out non-guests. The guard may check your name against the restaurant's reservations list before letting you in. Don't be too disappointed if you can't get in. WDW employees (cast members), who are off duty and visiting the Magic Kingdom, often park their cars in a lot at the Contemporary Resort to the left of the guard gate and close to the walkway to the Magic Kingdom. During busy periods, the guard turns them away from this lot, presumably to keep it clear for Contemporary Resort guest use.

Another option for off-property guests is the bus. Some public and hotel shuttle buses make regular runs to the TTC during MK operating hours.

Insider tip #2: If your admission ticket allows you to switch from one WDW theme park to another without penalty and you'd like to combine a morning visit to the Magic Kingdom with an afternoon visit to Epcot, you have another transportation option. Park your car in the morning at Epcot. Then take the Epcot monorail to and from the MK via the TTC. Allow about 25 to 35 minutes one way. You'll save yourself the considerable hassle of having to retrieve your car from the MK parking lot and re-park it at Epcot. And when you leave for the evening, your car will probably be more conveniently located than it would have been had you parked it in mid afternoon.

How early should you arrive?

Whatever your mode of transport, plan to arrive early in the day, preferably before opening time, so that you can experience the major rides and attractions with minimal waits. If you are a Disney property guest, plan to arrive at the entrance turnstiles about 35-40 minutes before the official opening time. If you're not staying on Disney property, plan to arrive at the Transportation and Ticket Center 50 to 60 minutes before the official opening time if you already have your admission tickets, and an hour or more before the official opening time if you have to purchase your tickets. If you follow this advice, you will be able to ride at least two and possibly four or more popular attractions before the lines become long. But don't despair if you aren't an early riser; the touring plans below can be picked up any time of the day. Just be aware that you will have to make some hard choices about what to skip.

Note: If you are visiting on or near a major holiday, add 30 minutes to each of the above times.

Entering the Magic Kingdom

At the MK entrance, monorail passengers usually head for the closest turnstiles on the left side of the entrance plaza, while ferryboat and bus riders head for the closest turnstiles on the right side.

Tip: If you're in the middle or back of a mass of disembarking monorail riders, check out the entrance turnstiles on the right side of the entrance plaza. These gates may be relatively uncrowded if the ferry or a bus hasn't unloaded for a while. If you're disembarking with a mass of ferryboat or bus passengers, check out the turnstiles on the left side. If a monorail hasn't unloaded for a while, these gates on the left side may be uncrowded. Furthermore, if the morning lines are long at all entrance turnstiles, line up in an outside queue. Sometimes an attendant will open up a nearby turnstile at the last minute, and you may be positioned to move with other excited guests to the new and shorter queue.

Have your admission ticket ready (plus your hotel room key for Early Entry privileges). If you don't have a park Guidemap and Times Guide yet (they are available at the WDW hotels), pick them up as soon as you can. Sometimes they are piled on the entry turnstiles for entering guests. Frequently, a small Guidemap stand is located inside the entrance turnstiles before or beneath the arched walkways under the Main Street train station. Otherwise, you can pick them up at City Hall to the left of Town Square or at the counters of the stores and outside merchandise stands along Main Street.

What you ride first will depend on your interests. I recommend *Dumbo the Flying Elephant* for parties with preschoolers (although older children may also place this ride high on their lists). For others, I recommend *Space Mountain* or *Splash Mountain*. If it's a tie between *Mountains*, go to *Space Mountain* first.

Getting to the 'Mountains'

Two fascinating rituals occur each morning at the Magic Kingdom as visitors to the MK attempt to be first in line at two of the park's most popular rides, *Space Mountain* and *Splash Mountain*. When the park opens on non Early Entry days (usually 30 minutes before the official opening time), or if you arrive near the official opening time on any day, you're admitted through the entrance turnstiles and onto Main Street. The rest of the park is roped off and will not admit guests until the official opening time. Some otherwise sane folks gather at the rope at the end of Main Street with impatient anticipation of that exhilarating first-of-the-morning ride on *Space Mountain*. Others line up at the ropes to Adventureland giddy with anticipation of the *Splash Mountain* experience. By the time the overhead welcoming announcements are over and the hapless Disney cast members begin to pull the ropes back, the nervous excitement of the early morning crowd has reached a fever pitch.

Now there's no holding back. The stampede that ensues can be unstoppable, despite Disney's best intentions. Make no mistake about it, these are no walks in the park. In fact, if you are walking to either *Mountain*, prepare to get bumped and jostled. Parents with strollers, beware! Wild-eyed and breathless *Mountain* junkies of most ages (anyone who can jog or run) will be hurtling by you. For the safety of everyone, parents with strollers or those in wheelchairs should stay at the fringes of the frantic rush. On a crowded day, inadvertent jostles and sometimes collisions between people are not unusual. Folks may drop sunglasses or caps, stop to retrieve them, and risk a rugby-style encounter from behind.

These morning races are unique and memorable, and you can enjoy them firsthand even if you just walk fast. However, don't overexert yourself in the excitement. You have a long fun day ahead; don't spoil it with an untimely injury or exhaustion. Even if you are not among the first in line, you won't have a very long wait if you head to the *Mountain* of your choice first thing.

Note: On Early Entry days, *Splash Mountain* will be closed till the park's official opening time and *Space Mountain* may or may not be open.

Tip: WDW periodically attempts to control these morning dashes. You may be instructed to walk briskly behind a Disney cast member to the *Mountain* entrances. If you encounter this method of crowd control, follow instructions but be prepared to dash with other excited guests when the entrance is in sight. Even Disney can't always prevent these last-second dashes.

Here are my tips for putting yourself near the front of the crowd to the *Mountain* of your choice:

The Race to Space

The closest rope to *Space Mountain* is *either* the one at the end of Main Street to the right past the Plaza Ice Cream Parlor and near the Plaza Pavilion *or* the rope at the first bridge to Tomorrowland. The exact position of these ropes varies from time to time. Ask the Disney attendant if the bridge rope will be moved forward (a few minutes before the official opening time) to the edge of Tomorrowland at the far end of the bridge. If the answer is yes, or if the rope has already been moved, line up at this rope. *Space Mountain* is slightly to the left past *Alien Encounter* and then straight ahead. Disney began this rope-moving maneuver to counteract the advantage that the rope near the Plaza Pavilion offered joggers to *Space Mountain*.

If the answer is no, the rope near the Plaza Pavilion is the closest rope for the race to *Space*. You will power walk, jog, or run toward and through the left side of the Plaza Pavilion restaurant and into Tomorrowland. Pass *The Timekeeper* (or its replacement) on your right, then pass *Alien Encounter* on your left. Be careful not to get entangled in the waiting area chains at *Alien Encounter*; take a wide berth around the last posts of this waiting area. Now you can see the *Space Mountain* building. Head straight for it and you'll spot the entrance. Unless you're a fast sprinter with some endurance and get to *Space Mountain* ahead of them, you can easily follow the speedy teenagers to the entrance.

If you're pushing a stroller, you can still move briskly, but please don't move along beside other strollers. This will inadvertently create an obstacle for the out-of-control sprinters who may be coming up behind you — a potentially dangerous situation. For safety's sake, strollers and wheelchairs should move along the sides of the paths to *Space Mountain* and not in the midst of the mayhem.

Once you arrive, slow down a bit and try to sense where people are. The inside queue area is long and dark, so it's easy to collide with someone in front of you. If you have time, note the interesting astronomical exhibits and photographs along the walls of the entrance queue area.

Tip: Space Mountain has two coaster tracks. Generally only one will be operating at opening. If you have a choice between the right or left tracks, choose the side that seems less crowded or the side that you haven't been on before. The two tracks differ slightly, though the general effect is the same. At the end of the ride, feel free to ride the moving sidewalk (instead of walking or jogging) and view the interesting and humorous science fiction exhibits along the side.

Note: If you're staying on Disney property and Early Entry is in effect (see page 51), most attractions in Fantasyland and Tomorrowland will be operating when you enter early. The rest of the park will be closed until the official opening time. *Space Mountain* may or may not be operating initially. Check with Guest Services in your hotel or look for an explanatory placard inside the entrance turnstiles to find out which attractions (specifically *Space Mountain*) are open. Or ask the turnstile attendant at the entrance.

If *Space Mountain* is open, you have to hustle down Main Street with the rest of the early entrants. For the shortest route, remember to turn right off Main Street at the Plaza Ice Cream Parlor so you can head through the Plaza Pavilion as described above. However, in the early morning this route is sometimes blocked by a rope and a Disney attendant! If so, continue on to the first open route to Tomorrowland on your right, jog past *Alien Encounter*, and angle slightly left to *Space Mountain*.

If *Space Mountain* is not open initially, ask the entrance turnstile attendant (he or she may not know) or any attendant near Tomorrowland when it will open. Take in other attractions in Fantasyland or Tomorrowland while you wait (consult the appropriate Early Entry tour plan below), then line up as close as you can to *Space Mountain* 15 minutes before opening. (You'll usually be able to line up past the *Tomorrowland Indy Speedway* entrance within sight of the *Space Mountain* entrance.) When the attendant says "go," you can dash the short distance to the entrance.

The Dash to Splash

When the Magic Kingdom turnstiles open (usually 30 minutes before the official opening time), line up at the ropes to Adventureland. For the shortest route, stand close to the rope in front of the Crystal Palace Restaurant. In front of this restaurant is a bridge to Adventureland. When the rope drops after the welcome spiel at the official opening time, walk fast, jog or sprint across this bridge and turn left into Adventureland. When you spot the *Swiss Family Treehouse* on your left, slow down, and look right to find a passageway to Frontierland. Go through this passageway, veer left, and look for *Splash Mountain*; it's left of *Big Thunder Mountain Railroad*. Go straight to the end of the wide path through Frontierland; the entrance to *Splash Mountain* is sometimes at the top of this path. I recommend that you get a FASTPASS for *Splash*

Mountain and ride *Big Thunder Mountain Railroad* first.

Note: If Early Entry is in effect, *Splash Mountain* will not be operating at first. Follow the Early Entry tour plan (if you are eligible for it) until 15 minutes before the park's official opening time, then buy some coffee or other refreshments in Fantasyland and line up at the rope between Fantasyland and Liberty Square. When the rope drops, hightail it through Liberty Square to the Frontierland path to *Splash Mountain*.

Caution: Occasionally, the speaker near the Liberty Square rope doesn't work, so the Disney attendant there can't hear the park opening spiel and therefore doesn't drop the rope when the park officially opens. When this happens, you may not have a chance of being at the front of the *Splash* line! By the time you get to it, the Frontierland path may already be clogged with folks who waited at the Main Street ropes (where the attendant could hear the spiel and dropped the ropes on time). So be sure to ask the attendant if the speaker has been functioning lately. If there is any doubt, leave Liberty Square and line up at the rope near Cinderella Castle. You'll find it at the entrance to the small walkway to Liberty Square (just past the Cinderella fountain). Even if the speaker isn't working at this location, you'll have a better vantage point to sense when the Main Street ropes drop. When your rope drops, hustle down this path, turn right into Liberty Square, then veer sharply left just before the Liberty Tree. Follow the path around the left side of the big tree and into Frontierland.

Note: The dash to *Splash* is longer than the race to *Space*. Unless you're in excellent aerobic shape, you need to pace yourself. Don't worry about the competition; although many folks start out sprinting, you'll pass by tiring joggers whose legs and lungs gave out toward the end of the Frontierland path. Some folks take the first train to Frontierland at opening time. The joggers (but not the casual walkers) will beat the train riders to *Splash Mountain*.

Lines to *Splash Mountain* remain long all day, and big rushes occur after parades as people in Frontierland make a beeline to the entrance.

One-Day Touring Plans for Adults and Teens

(See "A Special Note on Early Entry," page 51.)

You won't be able to experience every attraction in the Magic Kingdom in a single day, but following this plan will ensure that you'll experience the best the MK has to offer adults and teens.

This plan assumes you will arrive at opening time. If you want to sleep in, just pick up the non Early Entry plan around step five. If the park is crowded and you arrive late, consider skipping the afternoon break and use the time to visit attractions that usually have minimal waits; or consult your Times Guide for stage shows. Use FASTPASS or the singles line option (when available) for crowded attractions.

Note: I consider a wait of more than 15 to 20 minutes "too long."

Adults and Teens One-Day Plan for Early Entry Days

(WDW property guests only)

1. Ride *Space Mountain*. (See "The Race to Space," page 82, for the best way to get to it.) If the Main Street ropes are up, line up at the one by the Plaza Ice Cream Parlor or at the first bridge to Tomorrowland. (Remember: this rope may be moved up to the far end of the bridge.) Resist the urge to ride it again; there's a lot more fun stuff ahead.

    If *Space Mountain* is not open initially, ask a Tomorrowland attendant when it will open. Then continue with the touring plan and line up near *Space Mountain* about 15 minutes before it opens.

2. Exit straight ahead. Pass *Astro Orbiter* on your left, and ride *Alien Encounter*.

3. Exit *Alien Encounter*. Turn left and take the route to Fantasyland past *Tomorrowland Indy Speedway*. Walk into Fantasyland past *Mad Tea Party* and ride *The Many Adventures of Winnie the Pooh*.

4. If you have more than 25 minutes before the official opening time, turn left, head past *Cinderella's Golden Carrousel* on your left, and ride either *Peter Pan's Flight* or *Snow White's Scary Adventures* if the wait is five minutes or less.

5. 15 minutes before the official opening time, line up at the rope between Fantasyland and Liberty Square. Ask the Disney rope attendant if the speaker is working so you can hear the park opening spiel. If there's any doubt, walk back through Fantasyland, turn right just before Cinderella Castle, pass by the Cinderella fountain, and line up at the rope on the small walkway to Liberty Square. If you have a few minutes, buy some coffee or refreshments to enjoy while you wait at the rope.

6. When the rope drops, hurry through Liberty Square to Frontierland. Or, if you're at the second rope by Cinderella Castle, go down the Liberty Square path and turn right at the Sleepy Hollow eatery and then left before the Liberty Tree to enter Frontierland. Hustle to the end of the Frontierland path, then get a FASTPASS for *Splash Mountain* to ride later. Turn left to the nearby entrance to *Big Thunder Mountain Railroad* and ride.

7. Exit *Big Thunder Mountain Railroad*. Return to ride *Splash Mountain* at your allotted time. The entry queue may split into two sides. *Tip:* If both lines seem about equally long, choose the left side; it's shorter at the loading dock.

8. Pick up the following plan at step 4. Skip any steps you've already done today.

Adults and Teens
One-Day Plan for Non Early Entry Days

1. Ride *Space Mountain*. (See "The Race to Space," page 82, for the best way to get to it.) Resist the urge to ride it again; there's a lot more fun stuff ahead.

2. Walk back through Tomorrowland past *Alien Encounter* on your right. Walk to the left side of the central hub and onto the path to Adventureland. Turn right just past *Swiss Family Treehouse* and pass through a tunnel to Frontierland. Turn left and walk to the end of the Frontierland path, then get a FASTPASS for *Splash Mountain* to ride later. Turn left to the nearby entrance to *Big Thunder Mountain Railroad* and ride.

3. Return to *Splash Mountain* at your allotted time. The entry queue may split into two sides.
Tip: If both lines seem about equally long, choose the left side; it's shorter at the loading dock. Ride *Splash Mountain*.

4. Exit *Splash Mountain*, turn left onto the first bridge to the Frontierland walkway. Turn left, walk through Frontierland, and grab some refreshment in Frontierland or Liberty Square. Take a short break. Liberty Square has a good fruit stand.
5. Walk through Liberty Square, keep to the left and ride *The Haunted Mansion*. Get a FASTPASS if the wait is too long.
6. Exit *The Haunted Mansion* and return to Frontierland. Walk to the *Country Bear Jamboree* on your left and enjoy the show.
7. Consider an early lunch. The Plaza Restaurant at the end of Main Street opens at 11:00 a.m. and is a good place for lunch. Fast food eateries like Pecos Bill Cafe in Frontierland are a good bet. Another option is to check your Times Guide for the next *"Diamond Horseshoe Saloon Revue"* show, where you can enjoy a sandwich along with high-spirited entertainment. You can wander into the theater anytime and eat before or during the show.
8. Go to Adventureland by way of one of the passageways from Frontierland (by either *"The Diamond Horseshoe Saloon Revue"* or *Country Bear Jamboree*). Ride *Pirates of the Caribbean*.
   Tip: Choose the left queue if it's open; it's often shorter.
9. Exit *Pirates of the Caribbean* and turn left. Pass by *Splash Mountain* and turn left to *Walt Disney World Railroad*. Ride the train around the entire park and exit at Mickey's Toontown Fair on your second pass.
10. Visit *Mickey's Country House* and *Minnie's Country House* and enjoy the colorful details of Mickey's neighborhood.
11. If you're staying on Disney property and feel tired, consider leaving the park at this point (via the train to Main Street) to refresh yourself at your hotel for a few hours. Have your hand stamped at the exit for re-entry and keep any parking receipts. Return to the park when you feel re-energized and pick up the touring plan where you left off. If the timing is right, eat an early dinner in your hotel or at the park on your return and then resume the touring plan after dinner if the park is open late.
    Alternative: If you need a rest but are staying off property, leaving may be more trouble than it is worth. Simply rest in a shady spot for a while in mid-afternoon. The quiet park across from the Sleepy Hollow eatery behind Ye Olde Christmas Shoppe in Liberty Square is a good place.
    Note: If the Magic Kingdom is too crowded for your comfort and your ticket allows, switch to a non Early Entry Disney park at this

point and start with the afternoon or evening section of the appropriate touring plan.

12. Walk through Mickey's Toontown Fair toward *Mad Tea Party* and turn left into Tomorrowland. Get a FASTPASS for *Buzz Lightyear's Space Ranger Spin*, then see *The Timekeeper* (or its replacement), which is across from *Alien Encounter*.

13. Exit *The Timekeeper* (or its replacement). Ride *Buzz Lightyear's Space Ranger Spin* at your allotted time.

14. Cross Tomorrowland to *Walt Disney's Carousel of Progress*. Enjoy the show.

15. Exit the show. Cross Tomorrowland past *The Timekeeper* (or its replacement) on your left, and walk through or around the central hub on the right. Enter Liberty Square and walk to *The Hall of Presidents* on your right. Enjoy the show.

16. Exit the show. Turn right to the *Liberty Square Riverboat* (it sometimes closes at dusk). If the wait is 10 minutes or more, grab a snack from a vendor in Liberty Square or Frontierland and refresh yourself as you wait. On the *Riverboat*, listen to the overhead spiel for some humorous Mark Twain aphorisms.

17. Disembark. Turn left and walk past Columbia Harbour House eatery to Fantasyland. Walk to *Mickey's PhilharMagic* on your right side. Enjoy the show if it has opened and the line is not too long.

18. Most Fantasyland attractions are crowded in the afternoon and early evening. If the wait for *Peter Pan's Flight*, *Snow White's Scary Adventures*, or *The Many Adventures of Winnie the Pooh* is 15 minutes or less, go ahead and ride one or all of them now. Use FASTPASS for one of the rides if it is available (consult your Guidemap).

19. Ride *"it's a small world"* across from *Peter Pan's Flight*. The wait for *"it's a small world"* is usually not too long.

20. Leave Fantasyland through Cinderella Castle and enjoy the elaborate mosaic mural inside on the Castle wall. Turn left and walk to the second entrance to Tomorrowland. Walk past *The Timekeeper* (or its replacement) and *Astro Orbiter* on your left to *Tomorrowland Transit Authority*. While you're enjoying the *Tomorrowland Transit Authority*, consider your dinner options if you don't already have priority seating reservations. The Crystal Palace Buffet is a good bet (Disney characters visit your table) if you can get there early.

21. Eat dinner.

22. How you spend your remaining time will depend on when the park closes. At a minimum, plan to see one of the evening parades and the fireworks show. If there is time before the parade, consider visiting one or more of the following attractions: *The ExtraTERRORestrial Alien Encounter* (scary, not upbeat), *Swiss Family Treehouse* (requires climbing stairs), *The Enchanted Tiki Room* (lighthearted musical fare, but skippable for many folks) or *The Magic Carpets of Aladdin*.

    20 to 30 minutes before parade time, find a viewing spot in Frontierland. Ask a Disney cast member where the parade is starting from. If it begins at Main Street, you have 15 or more minutes after starting time before the parade hits Frontierland. Send someone for refreshments if you wish.

    Later, watch the fireworks from the main bridge to Tomorrowland. Before the fireworks, Tinker Bell floats down from near the top of Cinderella Castle to a rooftop in Tomorrowland.

    After dark and during one of the evening parades (preferably the early one if there are two), check out *Jungle Cruise* (use FASTPASS if it's available; consult your Guidemap). Check the Tip Board across from Casey's Corner for approximate attraction wait times (but be aware that it's not always accurate).

23. Close down the park with any last-minute attractions you want to see and shop on Main Street on your way out. Enjoy the Disney window scenes at the Emporium shop.

One-Day Touring Plans for Families with Children

(See "A Special Note on Early Entry," page 51.)

You won't be able to experience every attraction in the Magic Kingdom in a single day, but following this plan will ensure that you'll experience the best the MK has to offer you and your children.

This plan assumes you will arrive at opening time. If you want to sleep in, just pick up the non Early Entry plan around step five. If the park is crowded and you arrive late, consider skipping the afternoon break and use the time to visit attractions that usually have minimal waits; or consult your Times Guide for stage shows. For crowded attractions, use FASTPASS or the singles line option (if you and your children are comfortable with it) when available.

Be aware that only collapsible strollers are allowed on the *Walt Disney World Railroad*. Leave any noncollapsible stroller at the station and retrieve it later. Or get a replacement stroller with your rental receipt at your destination.

Note: I consider a wait of more than 15 to 20 minutes "too long."

Families with Children
One-Day Plan for Early Entry Days

(WDW property guests only)

1. Rent strollers, if needed, past the entrance turnstiles to the right at the archway under the *Walt Disney World Railroad*.
2. Line up at the rope nearest Cinderella Castle. When the rope drops, or if the rope is not up, head up either walkway and through Cinderella Castle to Fantasyland and ride *Dumbo the Flying Elephant*. If your kids enjoyed the ride, get back in line and soar on *Dumbo* again!
3. Exit and walk left to ride *The Many Adventures of Winnie the Pooh*.
4. Turn left at the exit and ride *Peter Pan's Flight*, or get a FASTPASS and ride later if the wait is too long.
5. Turn right at the exit, cross to the right of *Cinderella's Golden Carrousel* and ride *Snow White's Scary Adventures*.
   Caution: This ride can frighten children age 6 and under. If your child is the squeamish type, skip the ride.
6. Across from *Peter Pan's Flight* is *"it's a small world."* If you have 15 minutes or more before the official opening time, enjoy the ride and the song.
7. After *"it's a small world,"* take some refreshment from one of the Fantasyland vendors.
8. When the park officially opens to the general public, ride *Cinderella's Golden Carrousel*.
9. Next, get in line for the first show of *Mickey's PhilharMagic* if it has opened.
10. Line up for the *Fantasyland Character Festival*. (If it's not yet open, return at the opening time; check your Times Guide). The entrance is at the far right end of the lagoon.
11. If your kids want more autographs (and what kids don't?), exit

and walk to the right of *Dumbo* and line up to meet Ariel at *Ariel's Grotto* at the rear of Fantasyland on the lagoon. The queue passes by an interactive fountain. If you don't mind your kids getting wet, strip them down to their bathing suits or other essentials (hopefully you brought along dry clothes for them) and let them go crazy! If the line for *Ariel's Grotto* is short, get Ariel's autograph before loosing your kids in the fountain.

12. After 10 minutes or so in the fountain, dry the kids off. Then go to step 8 of the following plan and skip any steps you've already done today.

Families with Children
One-Day Plan for Non Early Entry Days

1. Rent strollers, if needed, past the entrance turnstiles to the right at the archway under the *Walt Disney World Railroad*.
2. Line up at the rope nearest Cinderella Castle. When the rope drops, or if the rope is not up, head up either walkway and through Cinderella Castle to Fantasyland. Ride *Dumbo the Flying Elephant*.
3. Exit and walk left to ride *The Many Adventures of Winnie the Pooh*.
4. Turn left at the exit and ride *Peter Pan's Flight*, or get a FASTPASS and ride later if the wait is too long now.
5. Turn right and line up for *Mickey's PhilharMagic* (next door) if it has opened. Ask the attendant how long the wait is for the next show. Someone in your party can acquire some refreshments if the wait is long enough.
6. Line up to meet Ariel at *Ariel's Grotto* at the rear of Fantasyland on the lagoon. The queue passes by an interactive fountain. If you don't mind your kids getting wet, strip them down to their bathing suits or other essentials (hopefully you brought along an extra set of clothes for them) and let them go crazy!
7. If your kids want more autographs (and what kids don't?), turn left along the lagoon and get in line for the *Fantasyland Character Festival* (if it's not open yet, return at opening time; check your Times Guide).
8. Exit right and leave Fantasyland for Liberty Square. Take a right after entering Liberty Square and ride *The Haunted Mansion*. The ride is not that scary, but the darkness and loud sounds may frighten some squeamish youngsters. Get a FASTPASS if the wait

is too long.

9.   If you have 25 minutes or more before your priority seating time for lunch, walk across Liberty Square and into Frontierland. Turn left into the passageway just past the *Frontierland Shootin' Arcade*. Enter Adventureland and turn right to ride *Pirates of the Caribbean*. *Tip:* Choose the left queue if it's open; it's often shorter.

10. If you haven't made plans for lunch, eat after *Pirates* at Pecos Bill Cafe in Frontierland, or better yet at The Crystal Palace Character Buffet if the wait isn't too long.

11. After lunch, leave the Magic Kingdom and return to your hotel for a swim and naps if you're staying on property. Have your hands stamped at the exit for re-entry and keep any parking and stroller receipts.

   Alternative: If you're not staying on property or if you can't bring yourself to leave the park, find a resting spot (such as the Liberty Square park across from Sleepy Hollow and behind Ye Olde Christmas Shoppe). Park your family for a respite and maybe even naps for the kids.

   Note: If the Magic Kingdom is too crowded for your comfort and your ticket allows, switch to a non Early Entry Disney park at this point and start with the afternoon or evening section of the appropriate touring plan.

12. Return to the Magic Kingdom at around 2:30 p.m. Acquire a stroller with your receipt and claim a position for the 3:00 p.m. parade. Find a shady spot along the rope in Frontierland. (One good place to stand is between the columns that line the covered walkway next to the Liberty Tree Tavern.) Ask a Disney cast member where the parade is starting from. If it begins at Main Street, you have 15 or more minutes after starting time before the parade hits Frontierland. Send someone for refreshments if you wish. While you're waiting for the parade, check your Times Guide for any live shows that interest you. Insert them into your post-parade touring plan as time permits.

   Warning: People can get a bit pushy at parade time, so protect your viewing spot to prevent any potential irritation.

13. After the parade, walk toward *Splash Mountain* and turn right onto the first bridge to the *Tom Sawyer Island* raft loading dock. Ride the raft to *Tom Sawyer Island* and spend 30 to 40 minutes or so exploring the island's caves, trails, bridges, and interactive playthings.

14. The MK may close early or late. Spend the last hour in the park at

Mickey's Toontown Fair. If you have time before the last hour, leave *Tom Sawyer Island*, turn left, and cross Frontierland and Liberty Square along the waterfront to Fantasyland. Ride *"it's a small world."*

15. Go to Adventureland. Enjoy *The Magic Carpets of Aladdin* (if the wait isn't too long) and then *The Enchanted Tiki Room* show.

16. Exit left and go through the passageway to Frontierland. Turn left and see the *Country Bear Jamboree* if the wait isn't too long (15 minutes or less).

    Your kids can meet Cinderella in the downstairs waiting lobby of Cinderella's Royal Table restaurant; just ask the hostess when she's due to appear next.

    Alternatively, if your kids have been asking about *Splash Mountain* and if they're tall enough (40" or more), go get in line or use "switching off." But be aware that the wait will be long. Use the FASTPASS option if it's available.

17. Whenever it's appropriate, honor any priority seating time you may have reserved for dinner.

18. Leave Fantasyland through Cinderella Castle and veer left to the main entrance (the second entrance) into Tomorrowland. Ride *Buzz Lightyear's Space Ranger Spin*, or get a FASTPASS and ride later if the wait is too long.

19. If your kids are intrigued by the loud car noises, check out the line for the *Tomorrowland Indy Speedway*. If it's not too long (10-minute wait or less), go ahead and ride. While in the car, a parent can work the foot pedal while the child steers.
    Tip: The right queue to the first loading area is a shorter distance and thus may have a shorter wait.
    Height alert: You must be at least 52" tall to ride alone.

20. Leave time to see the evening parade. Stake out a viewing spot 20 minutes before parade time along the ropes in Frontierland or on Main Street. Get some refreshments to enjoy while you wait.

21. In Tomorrowland, walk around *Astro Orbiter* and relax aboard the *Tomorrowland Transit Authority*.

22. Walk to Mickey's Toontown Fair. Visit *Mickey's Country House*. Pass through Mickey's backyard to a big tent to get Mickey Mouse's autograph and a picture of him with your kids.

23. Walk down the street a bit and visit *Minnie's Country House*.

24. Next stop is the *Toontown Hall of Fame* between Mickey's and Minnie's houses. Here your kids can meet more characters. They can choose one of three queues leading to three different sets of characters. If time allows, let the kids wait through all three lines if they're up for it.

25. After the characters, cross the street to *The Barnstormer at Goofy's Wiseacre Farm*. This short roller coaster may be too zippy for some young kids, but other kids 6 and older may like it.
     Height/age alert: You must be at least 35" tall and age 3 to ride.

26. The final stop in Mickey's Toontown Fair is *Donald's Boat*. Kids go wild in this interactive fountain, and they can get drenched. Hopefully, you're prepared for wet munchkins.

27. Plan to see the nightly fireworks show, *Fantasy in the Sky*. Just before the fireworks, Tinker Bell floats down from near the top of Cinderella Castle to a rooftop in Tomorrowland. You can enjoy the show from the street in Mickey's Toontown Fair.

28. After the fireworks, board the train to Main Street (retrieve your stroller if necessary) and leave the park with everyone else. Or shop on Main Street until the crowds thin out. If you dawdle, be sure to enjoy the Disney window scenes at the Emporium shop.

One-Day Touring Plans for Seniors

(See "A Special Note on Early Entry," page 51.)

These plans include no fast, scary, or spinning attractions. If you enjoy such rides, follow the touring plan for adults and teens.

This plan assumes you will arrive at opening time. If you want to sleep in, just pick up the non Early Entry plan around step five. If the park is crowded and you arrive late, consider skipping the afternoon break and use the time to visit attractions that usually have minimal waits; or consult your Times Guide for stage shows. Use FASTPASS or the singles line option (when available) for crowded attractions.

Note: I consider a wait of more than 15 to 20 minutes "too long."

Seniors
One-Day Plan for Early Entry Days

(WDW property guests only)

1. Line up at the rope nearest Cinderella Castle. When the rope drops, or if the rope is not up, head up either walkway and through Cinderella Castle to Fantasyland. Walk past *Snow White's Scary Adventures*, turn right, and ride *The Many Adventures of Winnie the Pooh*.

2. Turn left at the exit. Cross to the other side of Fantasyland and ride *Peter Pan's Flight*.

3. Turn right at the exit and ride *Snow White's Scary Adventures*.

4. Walk back towards *Peter Pan's Flight* and ride *"it's a small world."*

5. 15 minutes before the official opening time, line up at the rope between Fantasyland and Liberty Square. If you have a few minutes, buy some coffee or refreshments to enjoy while you wait at the rope.

6. When the rope drops, walk at a leisurely pace into Liberty Square. Pass under the overpass and turn right to ride *The Haunted Mansion*.

7. Pick up the following plan at step 6. Skip any steps you've already done today.

Seniors
One-Day Plan for Non Early Entry Days

1. Line up at the rope nearest Cinderella Castle. When the rope drops, or if it is not up, head up either walkway and through Cinderella Castle to Fantasyland. Walk past *Snow White's Scary Adventures*, turn right, and ride *The Many Adventures of Winnie the Pooh*.

2. Turn left at the exit. Cross to the other side of Fantasyland and ride *Peter Pan's Flight*.

3. Turn right at the exit and ride *Snow White's Scary Adventures*.

4. Cross into Liberty Square. Grab some refreshment in Liberty Square or Frontierland and take a break.

5. When you're hydrated and rested, visit *The Haunted Mansion* in Liberty Square. Get a FASTPASS if the wait's too long.

6. Walk across Frontierland to the *Country Bear Jamboree* on your left

and enjoy the show.

7. Turn right at the exit. Walk to the *Liberty Square Riverboat* and board at the next departure. On the *Riverboat,* listen to the overhead spiel for some humorous Mark Twain aphorisms.

8. Consider an early lunch and show at *"The Diamond Horseshoe Saloon Revue"* in Liberty Square. You can wander in anytime for sandwiches.

9. Cross to Adventureland through the passageway next *to "The Diamond Horseshoe Saloon Revue."* Ride *Pirates of the Caribbean.* **Tip:** Choose the left queue if it's open; it's often shorter.

10. Exit *Pirates of the Caribbean* and turn left. Pass by *Splash Mountain* and turn left to *Walt Disney World Railroad.* Ride the train around the entire park and exit at Mickey's Toontown Fair on your second pass.

11. Visit *Mickey's Country House* and *Minnie's Country House.* Enjoy the colorful details of Mickey's neighborhood.

12. If you're staying on Disney property and you start feeling tired, consider leaving the park (via the train to Main Street) to refresh yourself at your hotel for a while. Have your hand stamped at the exit for re-entry and keep any parking receipts. Return to the park when you feel re-energized and pick up the touring plan where you left off. If the timing is right, eat an early dinner in your hotel or at the park and resume the touring plan after dinner if the park is open late.

    Alternative: If you are staying off property or just don't feel like leaving the park, rest in a shady spot for a while in mid-afternoon (like the park across from the Sleepy Hollow eatery behind Ye Olde Christmas Shoppe in Liberty Square).

    Note: If the Magic Kingdom is too crowded for your comfort and your ticket allows, switch to a non Early Entry Disney park after your break and start with the afternoon or evening section of the appropriate touring plan.

13. Walk through Mickey's Toontown Fair toward *Mad Tea Party* and turn left into Tomorrowland. Enjoy the show at *Walt Disney's Carousel of Progress.*

14. See *The Timekeeper* (or its replacement), across from *Alien Encounter.*

15. Turn left at the exit. Leave Tomorrowland and walk through or around the central hub on the right. Enter Liberty Square and catch the next show at *The Hall of Presidents.*

16. Turn right at the exit and walk past Columbia Harbour House

eatery to Fantasyland. Walk to *Mickey's PhilharMagic* on your right. Enjoy the show if has opened and the line is not too long.

17. Ride *"it's a small world"* across from *Peter Pan's Flight*. The wait for *"it's a small world"* is usually not too long.

18. Leave Fantasyland through Cinderella Castle and enjoy the elaborate mosaic mural inside on the Castle wall. Turn left and walk to the second entrance to Tomorrowland. Walk past *The Timekeeper* (or its replacement) and *Astro Orbiter* on your left to *Tomorrowland Transit Authority*. While you're enjoying the *Transit Authority*, consider your dinner options if you don't have priority seating reservations already. The Crystal Palace Buffet is a good bet (Disney characters visit your table), as is Cinderella's Royal Table in Cinderella Castle if you can get there early.

19. See the show at *The Enchanted Tiki Room* in Adventureland.

20. Ride *Jungle Cruise* in Adventureland. If the wait is long, use a FASTPASS if available. Or if two evening parades are scheduled, get in line during the early evening parade.

21. Plan to see one of the evening parades and the fireworks show. Find a viewing spot in Frontierland 20 to 30 minutes before parade time. Ask a Disney cast member where the parade is starting from. If it begins at Main Street, you have 15 or more minutes after starting time before the parade hits Frontierland. Send someone for refreshments if you wish.

    Later, watch the fireworks from the middle of the main bridge to Tomorrowland. Just before the fireworks, Tinker Bell floats down from near the top of Cinderella Castle to a rooftop in Tomorrowland.

22. Close down the park with any last-minute attractions you want to see, and shop on Main Street on your way out. Enjoy the Disney window scenes at the Emporium shop.

You can get a FASTPASS for a second attraction one minute after your current FASTPASS time window begins. So if the time on the FASTPASS you're holding is 2:40 p.m. to 3:40 p.m., you can pick up a second FASTPASS any time after 2:41 p.m.

Two-Day Touring Plans for Adults and Teens

(See "A Special Note on Early Entry," page 51.)

These plans assume you will arrive at opening time on both days. If you want to sleep in, just pick up the non Early Entry plan around step three or four. If the park is crowded and you arrive late, consider skipping the afternoon break and use the time to visit attractions that usually have minimal waits (see above), or consult your Times Guide for stage shows. Use FASTPASS or the singles line option (when available) for crowded attractions. Bear the following in mind:

• I consider a wait of more than 15 to 20 minutes "too long."

• Because guests generally take advantage of the Early Entry privilege (when available) only once at each park — or want to do the same popular rides again if they do two Early Entry days in the MK — the Early Entry tour plans are virtually the same for Days One and Two. I include them under both days so that you don't have to flip back and forth in the book.

• A few MK attractions are not included in this touring plan because they are not generally that popular with adults. If some of them appeal to you, check out one of the "Families with Children" touring plans to see when you might best fit them into your schedule.

Adults and Teens
Day One Plan for Early Entry Days

(WDW property guests only)

1. Ride *Space Mountain* (see "The Race to Space," page 82, for the fastest way to get there). Resist the urge to ride it again; there's a lot more fun stuff ahead. If *Space Mountain* is not open initially, ask a Tomorrowland attendant when it will open. Then continue with the touring plan and line up near *Space Mountain* about 15 minutes before opening.

2. Exit straight ahead, pass *Astro Orbiter* on your left, and ride *Alien Encounter*.

3. Exit *Alien Encounter*. Turn left and take the route to Fantasyland past *Tomorrowland Indy Speedway*. Walk into Fantasyland past *Mad*

Tea Party and ride *The Many Adventures of Winnie the Pooh.*

4. If you have more than 25 minutes before the official opening time, turn left, head past *Cinderella's Golden Carrousel* on your left, and ride either *Peter Pan's Flight* or *Snow White's Scary Adventures* if the wait is five minutes or less.

5. 15 minutes before the official opening time, line up at the rope between Fantasyland and Liberty Square. Ask the Disney rope attendant if the speaker is working so you can hear the park opening spiel. If there's any doubt, walk back through Fantasyland, turn right just before Cinderella Castle, pass by the Cinderella fountain, and line up at the rope on the small walkway to Liberty Square. If you have a few minutes, buy some coffee or refreshments to enjoy as you wait at the rope.

6. When the rope drops, hurry through Liberty Square to Frontierland. Or, if you're at the second rope by Cinderella Castle, go down the Liberty Square path and turn right at the Sleepy Hollow eatery and then left before the Liberty Tree to enter Frontierland. Hustle to the end of the Frontierland path, then get a FAST-PASS for *Splash Mountain* to ride later. Then turn left to the nearby entrance *to Big Thunder Mountain Railroad* and ride.

7. Exit *Big Thunder Mountain Railroad.* Return to ride *Splash Mountain* at your allotted time.

   Tip: The entry queue may split into lines, left and right. If both seem equally long, choose the left; it's shorter at the loading dock.

8. Pick up the following plan at step 4. Skip any steps you've already done today.

Adults and Teens
Day One Plan for Non Early Entry Days

1. Ride *Space Mountain* (see "The Race to Space," page 82, for the fastest way to get there).

2. Exit straight ahead. Pass *Astro Orbiter* on your left, and ride *Alien Encounter.*

3. Exit *Alien Encounter.* Turn left and take the route to Fantasyland past *Tomorrowland Indy Speedway.* Walk through Fantasyland past *Mad Tea Party* and *Dumbo the Flying Elephant* and ride *Peter Pan's Flight.* Get a FASTPASS if the wait is too long.

4. Exit and turn right to *Mickey's PhilharMagic.* Enjoy the show if it's

opened and the lines aren't too long.

5. Exit and turn left to Liberty Square. Make a hard right and experience *The Haunted Mansion*. Get a FASTPASS if the wait is too long.

6. Eat an early lunch to beat the crowds. A good bet is *"The Diamond Horseshoe Saloon Revue,"* which features sandwiches and a live comedy and dance performance at the times listed in your Times Guide. You can wander in anytime for sandwiches.

7. After lunch, go to the middle of Liberty Square to *The Hall of Presidents*. Consult the sign out front or ask the attendant at the door when the next show is. If it's more than 20 minutes away, walk to the *Liberty Square Riverboat* to find out if you can board within five minutes or so. If not, browse around the shops in Liberty Square and catch the next show of *The Hall of Presidents*.

8. At this point, if you're staying on property consider returning to your hotel for a rest or swim. Have your hand stamped at the exit for re-entry and keep any parking receipts. Return to the park when you feel re-energized and pick up the late afternoon or evening part of the touring plan.

   Alternative: If you need a rest but are staying off property, leaving may be more trouble than it's worth. Simply rest in a shady spot inside the park for a while. The park in Liberty Square, across the road from the Sleepy Hollow eatery, or the end of the cul-de-sac off Main Street behind the fruit stand are good resting spots.

   Note: If the Magic Kingdom is too crowded for your comfort and your ticket allows, switch to a non Early Entry Disney park at this point and start with the afternoon section of the appropriate touring plan.

9. At about 2:40 p.m. (20 minutes ahead of time), stake out a shady spot along the rope in Frontierland or along Main Street for the 3:00 p.m. afternoon parade. A good bet is to stand between the columns along the covered walkway next to the Liberty Tree Tavern. Ask a Disney cast member where the parade is starting from. If it begins at Main Street, you have 15 or more minutes after starting time before the parade hits Frontierland. Send someone for refreshments if you wish. Enjoy the parade.

10. After the parade, follow the Frontierland waterfront to the first bridge and on to the loading area for the raft to *Tom Sawyer Island*. Spend an hour or so enjoying the creative nooks and crannies scattered over the island. Get a lemonade or other refreshment at

Aunt Polly's Dockside Inn.

11. Return on the raft to Frontierland and keep to the right to enter Adventureland. Cross to the other end of Adventureland and visit the *Swiss Family Treehouse* on your right. This attraction requires some gentle stair climbing.

12. If you want to ride *Space Mountain* or *Splash Mountain*, get a FASTPASS if available (consult your Times Guide). Meanwhile...

13. Consider an early dinner or honor your priority seating schedule. The Liberty Tree Tavern has an entertaining character dinner.

14. Depending on when the park closes, you may be able to enjoy more attractions after dinner. During the two hours before closing, check out *Pirates of the Caribbean, The Magic Carpets of Aladdin*, the *Country Bear Jamboree*, or *Buzz Lightyear's Space Ranger Spin* (use FASTPASS if it's available; consult your Times Guide). Do not wait in any long lines. Check the Tip Board across from Casey's Corner for approximate attraction wait times (it's not always accurate). If the park is crowded and the lines seem long, check out the following attractions (which usually don't have long waits): *The Enchanted Tiki Room, "it's a small world," The Timekeeper* or its replacement, *Walt Disney's Carousel of Progress* (this attraction may close early), and *Tomorrowland Transit Authority*.

15. Check your Times Guide for any evening parades and fireworks. Line up at the ropes in Frontierland or along Main Street 20 to 30 minutes before parade time. Have someone fetch some refreshments while you wait. If two evening parades are scheduled, the later one is less crowded and you can stake out your position 10 to 15 minutes before parade time.

Adults and Teens
Day Two Plan for Early Entry Days

(WDW property guests only)

1. If you're up for more roller coasters, ride *Space Mountain* (see "The Race to Space," page 82, for the fastest way to get there). When you exit, take an about face and ride it again!

2. Exit straight ahead and ride *Astro Orbiter*. If it's not open yet, come back to ride it after step 4 if you have time.

3. Take the route to Fantasyland past *Tomorrowland Indy Speedway*. Ride *The Many Adventures of Winnie the Pooh* and then check out

Snow White's Scary Adventures if the line isn't too long.

4. If you still have more than 25 minutes before the official opening time, ride *Peter Pan's Flight* again if the wait is five minutes or so.

5. 15 minutes before the official opening time, line up at the rope between Fantasyland and Liberty Square. Ask the Disney rope attendant if the speaker is working so you can hear the park opening spiel. If there's any doubt, walk back through Fantasyland, turn right just before Cinderella Castle, pass by the Cinderella fountain, and line up at the rope on the small walkway to Liberty Square. If you have a few minutes, buy some coffee or refreshments to enjoy while you wait at the rope.

6. When the rope drops, hurry through Liberty Square to Frontierland. Or, if you're at the second rope by Cinderella Castle, go down the Liberty Square path and turn right at the Sleepy Hollow eatery and then left before the Liberty Tree to enter Frontierland. Hustle to the end of the Frontierland path, then get a FASTPASS to ride *Splash Mountain* later. Turn left to the nearby entrance to *Big Thunder Mountain Railroad* and ride.

7. When you return to ride *Splash Mountain*, the entry queue may split into two sides. If both lines seem about equally long, choose the left side; it's shorter at the loading dock.

8. Pick up the following plan at step 3. Skip steps you've done today.

Adults and Teens
Day Two Plan for Non Early Entry Days

1. Ride *Splash Mountain* (see "The Dash to Splash," page 83, for the fastest way to get there).
   Tip: The entry queue may split into two sides. If both lines seem about equally long, choose the left side; it's shorter at the loading dock.

2. Exit *Splash Mountain* and walk away from the *Walt Disney World Railroad* station. Turn left to the nearby entrance to *Big Thunder Mountain Railroad* (BTMR) and ride. (Alternatively, get a FASTPASS for *Splash Mountain*, ride BTMR, and return to ride *Splash Mountain* at your allotted time).

3. Exit and walk straight ahead past *Splash Mountain* to Adventureland. Ride *Jungle Cruise*. The queue may be getting long by now at *Jungle Cruise*, but unfortunately there's not another predictably

good time of day to enjoy this popular attraction. Nevertheless, skip it if the wait is longer than 15 minutes; a long wait in this line is energy-sapping (use FASTPASS if it's available; consult your Times Guide).

Alternative: Try *Jungle Cruise* later, 30 minutes before park closing. Just be aware that the line still may be too long!

4. If you haven't experienced *Country Bear Jamboree* yet, turn right past *The Enchanted Tiki Room*, then left through the passageway to Frontierland. Just to your left is *Country Bear Jamboree*. Enjoy the show.

5. Go back to Adventureland by turning left at the exit of *Country Bear Jamboree*. Ride *Pirates of the Caribbean*. Choose the left queue if it's open; it's often shorter.

6. Eat an early lunch. Try Pecos Bill Cafe in Frontierland or Columbia Harbour House in Liberty Square for fast food. You can get seated quickly if you show up at the Plaza Restaurant on Main Street near its 11:00 a.m. opening time. Also consider the character lunch at the Crystal Palace buffet restaurant if you can get there before its 11:30 a.m. opening time. While eating, review your Times Guide and note any live shows or parades you want to see. Work them into the touring plan.

7. Go to the closest *Walt Disney World Railroad* station (Main Street or Frontierland) and ride the train to Mickey's Toontown Fair. Visit *Mickey's Country House* and *Minnie's Country House*. Give yourself time to wander around and explore the interesting details of Mickey's neighborhood.

8. Re-board the *Walt Disney World Railroad* train and make a complete circuit of the Magic Kingdom.

9. Consider disembarking at Main Street Station and returning to your hotel for a rest or swim if you are staying on property. Have your hand stamped at the exit for re-entry and keep any parking receipts.

    Alternative: If you don't want to leave the park or you are staying off property, which makes leaving for a rest impractical, seek a shady place to relax for a while with refreshment. Among your options: the small alcove to the right of the entrance to *Pirates of the Caribbean*, the sitting area by the Sunshine Tree Terrace in Adventureland, or the shed at the edge of the rose garden between the two bridges to Tomorrowland.

    Note: If the Magic Kingdom is too crowded for your comfort and your ticket allows, switch to a non Early Entry Disney park at this point and start with the afternoon section of the appropriate touring plan.

10. In mid or late afternoon, after your rest, alternate FASTPASSes for *The Many Adventures of Winnie the Pooh* and *Buzz Lightyear's Space Ranger Spin*. Go to Liberty Square to ride the *Liberty Square Riverboat* (it sometimes closes at dusk) if you haven't enjoyed it already. On the *Riverboat*, listen to the overhead spiel for some humorous Mark Twain aphorisms.

11. Go to any of the following attractions that you haven't experienced yet: *The Enchanted Tiki Room*, *"it's a small world,"* *The Timekeeper* or its replacement, *Walt Disney's Carousel of Progress*, and the *Tomorrowland Transit Authority*. Check the Tip Board across from Casey's Corner for approximate attraction wait times (it's not always accurate).

12. Eat dinner or honor your priority seating schedule.

13. If you want to ride *Space Mountain* or *Splash Mountain* again, get a FASTPASS if available (consult your Times Guide). Meanwhile, consult your Times Guide and head for any attractions that you still want to ride before the park closes, especially if you haven't yet visited the *Country Bear Jamboree*, *Pirates of the Caribbean*, or *The Magic Carpets of Aladdin*. Remember that lines for popular attractions may remain long even at park closing time, especially during busy seasons.

14. Plan to see one of the evening parades and the fireworks if you haven't already done so.

15. Shop on Main Street in the late afternoon or on your way out. Enjoy the Disney window scenes at the Emporium shop.

Two-Day Touring Plans for Families with Children

(See "A Special Note on Early Entry," page 51.)

This plan assumes you will arrive at opening time on both days. If you want to sleep in, just pick up the non Early Entry plan around step four or five. If the park is crowded and you arrive late, consider skipping the afternoon break and use the time to visit attractions that usually have minimal waits; or consult your Times Guide for stage shows. For crowded attractions, use FASTPASS or the singles line option (if you and your children are comfortable with it) when available.

Note: I consider a wait of more than 15 to 20 minutes "too long."

Note, too, that because families generally take advantage of the Early Entry privilege only once at each park, the Early Entry tour plan is virtually the same for Day One and Day Two. I include it under both days so that you don't have to flip back and forth in your book.

Families with Children
Day One Plan for Early Entry Days

(WDW property guests only)

1. Rent strollers if necessary. You'll find them past the entrance turnstiles to the right at the archway under *Walt Disney World Railroad*.
2. Line up at the rope nearest Cinderella Castle. When the rope drops, or if the rope is not up, head up either walkway and through Cinderella Castle to Fantasyland. Ride *Dumbo the Flying Elephant*. Hey, this is Walt Disney World! Get back in line and soar on *Dumbo* again!
3. Exit and walk left to ride *The Many Adventures of Winnie the Pooh*.
4. Turn left at the exit and ride *Peter Pan's Flight*. Or get a FASTPASS to ride later if the wait is too long.
5. Turn right at the exit, cross to the right of *Cinderella's Golden Carrousel* and ride *Snow White's Scary Adventures*.
   Caution: Be aware that this ride can frighten children age 6 and younger. If your child is the squeamish type, skip the ride.
6. Across from *Peter Pan's Flight* is *"it's a small world."* If you have 15 minutes or more before the official opening time, enjoy the ride and the song.
7. After *"it's a small world,"* take some refreshment from one of the Fantasyland vendors.
8. When the park officially opens to the general public, ride *Cinderella's Golden Carrousel*.
9. Next, get in line for the first show of *Mickey's PhilharMagic* if it's opened.
10. Line up for the *Fantasyland Character Festival*. (If it's not open yet, return at opening time; check your Times Guide). The entrance is at the far right end of the lagoon.

11. If your kids want more autographs (and what kids don't?), exit and walk to the right of *Dumbo* and line up to meet Ariel at *Ariel's Grotto* at the rear of Fantasyland on the lagoon. The queue passes by an interactive fountain. If you don't mind your kids getting wet, strip them down to their bathing suits or other essentials (hopefully you brought along dry clothes for them) and let them go crazy! If the line for *Ariel's Grotto* is short, get Ariel's autograph before loosing your kids in the fountain.

12. After 10 minutes or so in the fountain, dry the kids off. Then go to the following plan and skip any steps you've already done today.

Families with Children
Day One Plan for Non Early Entry Days

1. Rent strollers if necessary past the entrance turnstiles to the right at the archway under the *Walt Disney World Railroad*.

2. Line up at the rope nearest Cinderella Castle. When the rope drops, or if the rope is not up, head up either walkway and through Cinderella Castle to Fantasyland and ride *Dumbo the Flying Elephant*.

3. Exit and walk left to ride *The Many Adventures of Winnie the Pooh*.

4. Turn left at the exit and ride *Peter Pan's Flight*. Or get a FASTPASS and ride later if the wait is too long.

5. Turn right and line up for *Mickey's PhilharMagic* next door (if it's opened). Ask the attendant how long the wait is for the next show. Someone in your party can acquire some refreshments if the wait in line is long enough.

6. Line up to meet Ariel at *Ariel's Grotto* at the rear of Fantasyland on the lagoon. The queue passes by an interactive fountain. If you don't mind your kids getting wet, strip them down to their bathing suits or other essentials (hopefully you brought along dry clothes for them) and let them go crazy!

7. If your kids want more autographs (and what kids don't?), turn left along the lagoon and get in line for the *Fantasyland Character Festival* (if it's not open yet, return at its opening time; check your Times Guide). The entrance is at the far right end of the lagoon.

8. Exit right and leave Fantasyland for Liberty Square. Take a right after entering Liberty Square and ride *The Haunted Mansion*. The ride is not all that scary, but the darkness and loud sounds may

frighten some squeamish youngsters.

9. If you have 25 minutes or more before your lunch priority seating time, walk across Liberty Square and into Frontierland. Turn left into the passageway just past the *Frontierland Shootin' Arcade*. Enter Adventureland and turn right to ride *Pirates of the Caribbean*. *Tip:* Choose the left queue if it's open; it's often shorter.

10. If you haven't made plans for lunch, eat after *Pirates* at Pecos Bill Cafe in Frontierland, or better yet at The Crystal Palace Character Buffet if the wait isn't too long.

11. If you are staying on property, leave the Magic Kingdom after lunch and return to your hotel for a swim and naps. Have your hands stamped at the exit for re-entry and keep any parking and stroller receipts.

    Alternative: If you're not staying on property or if you can't bring yourself to leave the park, find a resting spot to park your family for a respite and maybe even naps for the kids. One option: the shady park in Liberty Square across from Sleepy Hollow and behind Ye Olde Christmas Shoppe.

    Note: If the Magic Kingdom is too crowded for your comfort, switch to a non Early Entry Disney park after your rest (if your ticket allows) and start with the afternoon or evening section of the appropriate touring plan.

12. Claim a position for the 3:00 p.m. parade about 20 minutes before it starts. (If you left the MK for a rest, return at around 2:30 p.m. and re-acquire a stroller with your receipt.) Find a shady spot along the rope in Frontierland. One good place: between the columns along the covered walkway next to the Liberty Tree Tavern. Ask a Disney cast member where the parade is starting from. If it begins at Main Street, you have 15 or more minutes after starting time before the parade hits Frontierland. Send someone for refreshments if you wish.

    Warning: People can get a bit pushy at parade time, so protect your viewing spot to prevent any potential irritation.

    While you're waiting for the parade, check your Times Guide for any live shows that interest you. Remember you have two days to fit the live shows in. Insert the shows into the touring plan as time permits.

13. After the parade, walk toward *Splash Mountain* and turn right onto the first bridge to the *Tom Sawyer Island* raft loading dock. Ride the raft to *Tom Sawyer Island* and spend 45 minutes or so ex-

ploring the caves, trails, bridges, and other interactive playthings.

14. The Magic Kingdom may close early or late. If you have time before dinner, take in *Storytime* at Fairytale Garden in Fantasyland or a live show at the Castle Forecourt Stage or in Tomorrowland at the Galaxy Palace Theater (check your Times Guide). To get decent seats, arrive at the theater about 20 minutes before show time.

15. Leave Tomorrowland and go left around the central hub to Adventureland. Check the Tip Board across from Casey's Corner for approximate attraction wait times (it's not always accurate). Enjoy *The Enchanted Tiki Room* show.

16. Exit left and go through the passageway to Frontierland. Turn left and see the *Country Bear Jamboree*, if the wait isn't too long (15 minutes or less).

17. Whenever it's appropriate, honor any dinner priority seating times that you may have reserved.

18. Spend some time in Tomorrowland. Ride *Buzz Lightyear's Space Ranger Spin* (get a FASTPASS to ride later if the wait's too long).

19. If your kids are intrigued by the loud car noises, check out the line for the *Tomorrowland Indy Speedway*. If it's not too long (10-minute wait or less), go ahead and ride. While in the car, a parent can work the foot pedal while the child steers.
   Tip: The right queue to the first loading area is a shorter distance and thus may have a shorter wait.
   Height alert: You must be at least 52" tall to ride alone.

20. Leave time to see the evening parade. Stake a spot 20 minutes before parade time along the ropes in Frontierland or on Main Street. Get some refreshments to enjoy while you wait and watch. Meanwhile . . .

21. In Tomorrowland, walk around *Astro Orbiter* and relax aboard the *Tomorrowland Transit Authority*.

22. Wander over to Fantasyland and ride *Cinderella's Golden Carrousel* if the wait is 10 minutes or less. The *Carrousel* is especially beautiful at night.

23. Ride *"it's a small world"* if you haven't already.

24. Get some refreshments and relax until it's time for the *Fantasy in the Sky* fireworks. Walk to the middle of the main bridge to Tomorrowland. Just before the fireworks begin, Tinker Bell floats down from near the top of Cinderella Castle to a rooftop in Tomorrowland. After the fireworks, leave the park with everyone

else or shop on Main Street until the crowds thin out. If you dawdle, be sure to enjoy the Disney window scenes at the Emporium shop.

Families with Children
Day Two Plan for Early Entry Days

(WDW property guests only)

1. Rent strollers if necessary past the entrance turnstiles to the right at the archway under the *Walt Disney World Railroad*.
2. Line up at the rope nearest Cinderella Castle. When the rope drops, or if the rope is not up, head up either walkway and through Cinderella Castle to Fantasyland and ride *Dumbo the Flying Elephant*. If your kids want to ride it again, get in line for another go!
3. Exit and walk left to ride *The Many Adventures of Winnie the Pooh*.
4. Turn left at the exit and ride *Peter Pan's Flight*. Or get a FASTPASS and ride later if the wait is too long.
5. Next ride *Snow White's Scary Adventures* or *"it's a small world."* **Caution:** *Snow White's Scary Adventures* can frighten children ages 6 and under. If your child is the squeamish type, skip the ride.
6. Now take some refreshment from one of the Fantasyland vendors.
7. 15 minutes or so before official opening time, walk past the *Mad Tea Party* ride and line up at the rope across the path to Mickey's Toontown Fair.
8. When the rope drops, walk to Mickey's Toontown Fair and pick up the following touring plan at step 4.

Families with Children
Day Two Plan for Non Early Entry Days

1. Rent strollers if necessary. You'll find them past the entrance turnstiles to the right at the archway under *Walt Disney World Railroad*.
2. Line up at the rope across the second entrance to Tomorrowland near Cinderella Castle. This leads to the most direct route to Mickey's Toontown Fair.
3. When the rope drops, walk straight past Cosmic Ray's Starlight Cafe in Tomorrowland and then to the right of the *Mad Tea Party*

to Mickey's Toontown Fair. If Mickey's Toontown Fair doesn't open until later in the morning (check your Times Guide), ride *Dumbo the Flying Elephant, The Many Adventures of Winnie the Pooh, Peter Pan's Flight,* and any other attractions in Fantasyland with short lines. Use FASTPASS to your advantage. Enter Mickey's Toontown Fair as soon as it opens.

4. Go to *The Barnstormer at Goofy's Wiseacre Farm.* This short roller coaster may be too zippy for some young kids, but other kids 6 and older may like it.

   Age/height alert: You must be at least 3 years old and 35" tall to ride *The Barnstormer.*

5. Next enjoy *Mickey's Country House,* then walk through his backyard and line up to meet Mickey for autographs and photos.

6. Now stop at the *Toontown Hall of Fame* between Mickey's and Minnie's houses. Here your kids can meet more characters. They can choose one of three queues leading to three different sets of characters. Let the kids wait through all three lines if they're up for it.

7. Next meander through *Minnie's Country House.*

8. The final stop in Mickey's Toontown Fair is *Donald's Boat.* Kids go wild in this interactive fountain, and they can get drenched. Hopefully, you're prepared for wet munchkins.

9. Eat an early lunch. If you don't have plans, pick up some fast food at Cosmic Ray's Starlight Cafe. Better yet, meet Cinderella for autographs and photos inside the waiting area for Cinderella's Royal Table Restaurant in Cinderella Castle. You must have priority seating reservations (see "Where to Eat" in *Chapter One*) on most days or you're out of luck for lunch. Show up 15 minutes before your seating time and ask the receptionist when Cinderella is next scheduled to appear. When the time arrives, stand near the center of the room to greet her early on.

10. If you're staying on property, leave the Magic Kingdom after lunch and return to your hotel for a swim and naps. Have your hands stamped at the exit for re-entry and keep any parking and stroller receipts.

    Alternative: If you're staying off property, or if you can't bring yourself to leave the park, find a resting spot to park your family for a respite and maybe even naps for the kids. The small alcove with benches to the right of the entrance to *Pirates of the Caribbean* in Adventureland makes a good resting place.

Note: If the Magic Kingdom is too crowded for your comfort, switch to a non Early Entry Disney park after your rest break (if your ticket allows) and start with the afternoon or evening section of the appropriate touring plan.

11.   If you've left the MK for a rest, return at around 2:30 or 2:40 p.m. and reclaim your stroller(s) with your receipt. If your kids want to meet more characters, check the Times Guide for "Character Greeting" areas. Get on the *Walt Disney World Railroad* train at the Main Street station.

Note: Only collapsible strollers are allowed on the train; leave a noncollapsible stroller at the station and retrieve it later. Or get a replacement stroller with your rental receipt at your destination. To meet the "Song of the South" characters, get off at the Frontierland station and walk to the *Splash Mountain* exit area. To meet other assorted characters, go to the *Pirates of the Caribbean* attraction building, where you will usually find them outside, on the *Splash Mountain* side of the building. Or disembark at Mickey's Toontown Fair and walk to Fantasyland to the *Mad Tea Party* ride area.

Note: These character areas may change. The Times Guide and the separate "Character Greeting Location Guide" (if available) will provide current information.

12.   Catch a show circa 4:00 p.m. — at the Castle Forecourt Stage, the Galaxy Palace Theater, or the Fairytale Garden. Claim your seats about 15 to 20 minutes before show time.

13.   Go to Tomorrowland and see *Walt Disney's Carousel of Progress.*

14.   Then check out *The Timekeeper* (or its replacement).

15.   The Magic Kingdom may close early or late. Plan to ride *Jungle Cruise* and *The Magic Carpets of Aladdin* during the hour before closing or during the evening parade (during the early parade if there are two scheduled). Alternatively, use the FASTPASS option for *Jungle Cruise* if it's available.

16.   Whenever it's appropriate, honor any dinner priority seating times you may have reserved. The character dinner at Liberty Tree Tavern is worthwhile. Or sit with sandwiches and watch *"The Diamond Horseshoe Saloon Revue"* (check your Times Guide for show times).

17.   Ride the Liberty Belle around *Tom Sawyer Island* if it is still running (the *Riverboat* attraction sometimes shuts down at dusk.)

18.   Plan to see any attractions you haven't yet visited or want to see

again. For approximate wait times, consult the Tip Board on Main Street. It's across from Casey's Corner and not always accurate.

Also, schedule any last-minute shopping you may want to do. Don't forget periodic refreshments.

Tip: Lines tend to be shortest during the evening parades.

19. In the hour before park closing, ride *Jungle Cruise* or *The Magic Carpets of Aladdin.* Alternatively, if your kids have been asking about *Splash Mountain* and if they're tall enough (40" or more), go get in line or use "switching off." But be aware that the wait will be long. Use FASTPASS (if available).

    Tip: The entry queue may split into two sides, left and right. If both lines seem about equally long, choose the left side; it's shorter at the loading dock.

20. Enjoy the *Swiss Family Treehouse* if time permits.

21. Watch the evening fireworks, *Fantasy in the Sky,* from the main bridge to Tomorrowland or from the end of Main Street near the central hub. Or leave the park before the fireworks if you want to beat the exit crowds.

Two-Day Touring Plans for Seniors

(See "A Special Note on Early Entry," page 51.)

This plan includes no fast, scary, or spinning attractions. If you enjoy such rides, follow the touring plans for adults and teens.

This plan assumes you will arrive at opening time on both days. If you want to sleep in, just pick up the non Early Entry plan around step 5. If the park is crowded and you arrive late, you might consider skipping an after lunch break and using the time to visit attractions that usually have minimal waits; or consult your Times Guide for stage shows you would enjoy seeing. Use FASTPASS or the singles line option (when available) to minimize your waits for crowded attractions.

Note: Because visitors generally take advantage of the Early Entry privilege only once at each Disney park they visit, the Early Entry tour plan is virtually the same for Day One and Day Two. I include it under both days so that you don't have to flip back and forth in your guidebook. Moreover, because this Two-Day plan for mature visitors anticipates that the young-at-heart may want to spend the early morning hours elsewhere on at least one of their two Magic Kingdom days, steps one through five of the Day One and Day Two non Early Entry plans are also virtual duplicates.

It's been my observation that seniors visiting WDW on their own tend to spend only one day at the Magic Kingdom, saving their two-day visits for Epcot and Disney-MGM Studios.

This Two-Day Plan caters to mature visitors who want to see more of the MK than they could in a single day, but prefer to see it at a more leisurely pace.

Note: I consider a wait of more than 15 to 20 minutes too long. Don't wait; go on to the next step and come back later. Pick up a FASTPASS (if available) for the attraction you are skipping.

Seniors
Day One Plan for Early Entry Days

(WDW property guests only)

1. Line up at the rope nearest Cinderella Castle. When the rope drops, or if the rope is not up, head up either walkway and through Cinderella Castle to Fantasyland. Walk past *Snow White's Scary Adventures*, turn right and ride *The Many Adventures of Winnie the Pooh*.
2. Turn left at the exit. Cross to the other side of Fantasyland and ride *Peter Pan's Flight*.
3. Turn right at the exit and ride *Snow White's Scary Adventures*.
4. Walk back towards *Peter Pan's Flight* and ride *"it's a small world."*
5. 15 minutes before the official opening time, line up at the rope between Fantasyland and Liberty Square. If you have a few minutes, buy some coffee or refreshments to enjoy while you wait for the rope to drop.
6. When the rope drops, take your time walking into Liberty Square. Pass under the overpass and turn right to ride *The Haunted Mansion*.
7. Pick up the following plan at step 6. Skip any steps you've already done today.

Seniors
Day One Plan for Non Early Entry Days

1. Line up at the rope nearest Cinderella Castle. When the rope drops, or if the rope is not up, head up either walkway and through Cinderella Castle to Fantasyland. Walk past *Snow White's Scary Adventures*, turn right and ride *The Many Adventures of Winnie the Pooh*.

2. Turn left at the exit. Cross to the other side of Fantasyland and ride *Peter Pan's Flight*.

3. Turn right at the exit and ride *Snow White's Scary Adventures*.

4. Cross into Liberty Square. Grab some refreshment in Liberty Square or Frontierland and take a break.

5. When you're hydrated and rested, visit *The Haunted Mansion* in Liberty Square. Get a FASTPASS if the wait's too long.

6. Walk across Frontierland to the *Country Bear Jamboree* on your left and enjoy the show.

7. Turn right at the exit. Walk to the *Liberty Square Riverboat* and board at the next departure. On the *Riverboat*, listen to the overhead spiel for some humorous Mark Twain aphorisms.

8. Consider an early lunch and show at *"The Diamond Horseshoe Saloon Revue"* in Liberty Square. You can wander into the theater anytime and eat before or during the show.

9. Cross to Adventureland through the passageway next to *"The Diamond Horseshoe Saloon Revue."* Ride *Pirates of the Caribbean*. *Tip:* Choose the left queue if it's open; it's often shorter.

10. Exit *Pirates of the Caribbean* and turn left. Pass by *Splash Mountain* and turn left to *Walt Disney World Railroad*. Ride it around the entire park and exit at Mickey's Toontown Fair on your second pass.

11. Visit *Mickey's Country House* and *Minnie's Country House* and enjoy the colorful details of Mickey's neighborhood.

12. If you're staying on Disney property and you start feeling tired, consider leaving the park (via the train to Main Street) to refresh yourself at your hotel for a while. Have your hand stamped at the exit for re-entry and keep any parking receipts. Return to the park when you feel re-energized and pick up the touring plan where you left off. If the timing is right, eat an early dinner in your hotel or at the park and resume the touring plan after dinner if the park is open late.

Alternative: If you are staying off property or just don't feel like leaving the park, rest in a shady spot for a while in mid-afternoon (like the park across from the Sleepy Hollow eatery behind Ye Olde Christmas Shoppe in Liberty Square).

Note: If the Magic Kingdom is too crowded for your comfort and your ticket allows, switch to a non Early Entry Disney park after your rest and start with the afternoon or evening section of the appropriate touring plan.

13. Walk through Mickey's Toontown Fair toward *Mad Tea Party* and turn left into Tomorrowland. Enjoy the show at *Walt Disney's Carousel of Progress.*

14. See *The Timekeeper* (or its replacement), across from *Alien Encounter.*

15. Turn left at the exit. Leave Tomorrowland and walk through or around the central hub on the right. Enter Liberty Square and catch the next show at *The Hall of Presidents.*

16. Turn right at the exit and walk past Columbia Harbour House eatery to Fantasyland. Walk to *Mickey's PhilharMagic* on your right. Enjoy the show if it is open and the line is not too long. Use FASTPASS (if available) if the wait is long.

17. Ride *"it's a small world"* across from *Peter Pan's Flight.* The wait for *"it's a small world"* is usually not too long.

18. Leave Fantasyland through Cinderella Castle and enjoy the elaborate mosaic mural inside on the Castle wall. Turn left and walk to the second entrance to Tomorrowland. Walk past *The Timekeeper* (or its replacement) and *Astro Orbiter* on your left to *Tomorrowland Transit Authority.* While you're enjoying the *Tomorrowland Transit Authority,* consider your dinner options if you don't have priority seating reservations already. The Crystal Palace Buffet is a good bet (Disney characters visit your table), as is Cinderella's Royal Table in Cinderella Castle if you can get there early.

19. See the show at *The Enchanted Tiki Room* in Adventureland.

20. Ride *Jungle Cruise* in Adventureland. If the wait is long, use a FASTPASS if available. Or if two evening parades are scheduled, get in line during the early evening parade.

21. Plan to see one of the evening parades and the fireworks show. Find a viewing spot in Frontierland 20 to 30 minutes before parade time. Ask a Disney cast member where the parade is starting from. If it begins at Main Street, you have 15 or more minutes after starting time before the parade hits Frontierland. Send some-

one for refreshments if you wish.

Later, watch the fireworks from the middle of the main bridge to Tomorrowland. Just before the fireworks, Tinker Bell floats down from near the top of Cinderella Castle to a rooftop in Tomorrowland.

22. Close down the park with any last-minute attractions you want to see, and shop on Main Street on your way out. Enjoy the Disney window scenes at the Emporium shop.

Seniors
Day Two Plan for Early Entry Days

(WDW property guests only)

1. Line up at the rope nearest Cinderella Castle. When the rope drops, or if the rope is not up, head up either walkway and through Cinderella Castle to Fantasyland. Walk past *Snow White's Scary Adventures*, turn right and ride *The Many Adventures of Winnie the Pooh*.

2. Turn left at the exit. Cross to the other side of Fantasyland and ride *Peter Pan's Flight*.

3. Turn right at the exit and ride *Snow White's Scary Adventures*.

4. Relax for a while at a table near *Ariel's Grotto*. Then 15 minutes before the official opening time, line up at the rope between Fantasyland and Liberty Square. Buy some coffee or refreshments to enjoy while you wait at the rope.

5. When the rope drops, walk at a leisurely pace into Liberty Square. Pass under the overpass then turn right to ride *The Haunted Mansion*.

6. Pick up the following plan at step 6. Skip any steps you've already done today or yesterday.

Seniors
Day Two Plan for Non Early Entry Days

1. Line up at the rope nearest Cinderella Castle. When the rope drops, or if it is not up, head up either walkway and through Cinderella Castle to Fantasyland. Walk past *Snow White's Scary Adventures*. Turn right and ride *The Many Adventures of Winnie the Pooh*.

2. Turn left at the exit. Cross to the other side of Fantasyland and ride *Peter Pan's Flight.*

3. Turn right at the exit and ride *Snow White's Scary Adventures.*

4. Cross into Liberty Square. Grab some refreshment in Liberty Square or Frontierland and take a break.

5. When you're hydrated and rested, visit *The Haunted Mansion* in Liberty Square. Get a FASTPASS if the wait is too long.

6. Walk through Frontierland and ride *Mike Fink Keelboats* (or their replacement).

7. Go to the raft to *Tom Sawyer Island.* Ride the raft to the island and enjoy a sandwich and lemonade for lunch on the riverside porch at Aunt Polly's Dockside Inn. Then explore *Tom Sawyer Island* all the way back to Fort Sam Clemens.

8. If you're staying on Disney property and feel tired, consider leaving the park (via the train from Frontierland station to Main Street) to refresh yourself at your hotel for a while. Have your hand stamped at the exit for re-entry and keep any parking receipts. Return to the park when you feel re-energized and pick up the touring plan where you left off.

   Alternative: If you are staying off property or don't want to take the time to leave and return, an alternative is to rest in a shady spot for a while in mid-afternoon (like the benches in the small alcove to the right of the entrance to *Pirates of the Caribbean*).

   Note: If the Magic Kingdom is too crowded for your comfort, switch to a non Early Entry Disney park after your rest (if your ticket allows) and start with the afternoon or evening section of the appropriate touring plan.

9. Return to the Magic Kingdom at about 2:30 p.m. to get a viewing position along Main Street or in Frontierland for the 3:00 p.m. afternoon parade. Enjoy the parade.

10. Walk through one of the passageways to Adventureland and ride *Jungle Cruise* if you didn't ride it yesterday (or if you want to ride it again). If the line for *Jungle Cruise* is long, get a FASTPASS and return later to enjoy the boat ride.

11. Check the Times Guide for the next available shows at the Castle Forecourt Stage (in front of Cinderella Castle) and/or the Galaxy Palace Theatre in Tomorrowland.

12. If you don't have priority seating reservations for dinner, consider an early dinner at Liberty Tree Tavern, Tony's Town Square Restaurant, or The Plaza Restaurant. Disney characters visit your

table at the Liberty Tree Tavern.

13. Enjoy *Mickey's PhilharMagic* in Fantasyland if it is open and you haven't yet seen the show.

14. Revisit any of your favorite attractions where the waiting lines aren't too long. Check the Tip Board next to Casey's Corner on Main Street for approximate current waiting times (it's not always accurate).

15. Browse through the shops on Main Street.
    Caution: Avoid Main Street if a parade has just ended.

16. If you're up for more fun, enjoy the evening parade and the fireworks show.
    Tip: If two parades are scheduled, the second one is less crowded.

Remember, all the shops in the park will send bulky purchases to "package pickup" near the exit at no extra charge.

CHAPTER THREE:

Epcot

Walt Disney's "experimental prototype community of tomorrow," or "Epcot" for short, never materialized into the grand self-sustaining city of the future he had envisioned. Instead, since his death, it has become one of the most unique entertainment parks anywhere. Epcot is a more adult-oriented park than the Magic Kingdom and is more than twice as large as either the MK or Disney-MGM Studios — which gives you room to spread out even on busy days.

Epcot shelters two "Worlds," Future World and World Showcase. Future World is a collection of pavilions that house rides and attractions showcasing technology and progress. World Showcase offers visitors a glimpse of the cultures of eleven different countries, with samples of their characteristic foods, goods (many for sale), and attractions. Each "country" is housed in its own pavilion, and the pavilions are set along a wide promenade surrounding a lagoon. Bridges connect the two worlds and wind around the Odyssey Center, a large facility used for special events.

Future World

You enter Future World after passing through the main (front) entrance turnstiles to Epcot. Directly in front of you is the awesome *Spaceship Earth* geosphere, the first of nine pavilions you'll find in this world of gleaming silver, futuristic designs, and bright colors.

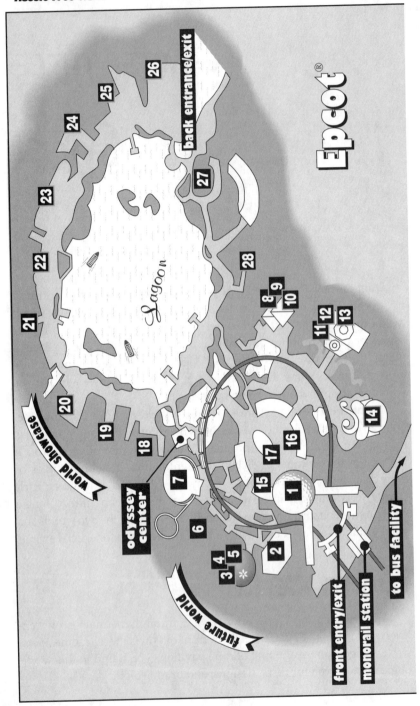

WORLD SHOWCASE

18 Mexico:
　　El Rio del Tiempo

19 Norway:
　　Maelstrom

20 China:
　　Wonders of China

21 Germany

22 Italy

23 U.S.A. The American Adventure:
　　The American Adventure Show

24 Japan

25 Morocco

26 France:
　　Impressions de France

27 United Kingdom

28 Canada:
　　O Canada!

FUTURE WORLD

1 Spaceship Earth Pavilion

2 Universe of Energy Pavilion

Wonders of Life Pavilion

3 Body Wars

4 Cranium Command

5 The Making of Me

6 Mission: SPACE Pavilion

7 Test Track Pavilion

Imagination! Pavilion

8 Honey, I Shrunk the Audience

9 Journey Into Imagination with Figment

10 ImageWorks

The Land Pavilion

11 Living with the Land

12 The Circle of Life

13 Food Rocks

14 The Living Seas Pavilion

15 Innoventions East Side

16 Innoventions West Side

17 Innoventions Plaza

Spaceship Earth

Rating: ✴ ✴ ✴ ✴ ✴
Type: Educational "dark ride"
Time: 16 - 17 minutes
Steve says: History can be fun! Visually stunning

This huge aluminum geosphere houses a ride that carries you past Audio-Animatronics scenes depicting the evolution of communications. Your car begins at the dawn of language and alphabets and takes you forward through the centuries — past the Age of Rome, Gutenberg's printing press, the invention of movies and television, and other landmark achievements — to the current age of virtual reality and the Internet.

At the exit of the ride is the **Global Neighborhood**, a large area with interactive games. Skip this area in the morning. Return and have fun here in the early evening when you're visiting Innoventions nearby.

Tip: Global Neighborhood stays open during **IllumiNations**, the evening fireworks show. You can access it without taking the ride by walking in a side door below the geosphere.

Universe of Energy

Rating: ✴ ✴ ✴ ✴
Type: Indoor theater show and "dark ride"
Time: 27 minutes (plus pre-show of up to 8 minutes)
Steve says: A bit ponderous but the dinosaur segment is fun

Huge theater cars travel slowly between large rooms for a series of entertaining presentations about energy. Bill Nye, the Science Guy, preps Ellen DeGeneres for a *Jeopardy* game show competition with Jamie Lee Curtis. In the middle of the show, your car accompanies Ellen and Bill back in time to a prehistoric forest for some relatively close encounters with convincing Audio-Animatronics allosauruses, pteranodons, velociraptors, a tyrannosaurus rex, and other reptilian cousins. While you're waiting to enter the theater, a pre-show prepares you for Ellen's *Jeopardy* adventure.

Wonders of Life Pavilion

In addition to the three main attractions detailed below, this pavilion houses various interactive experiences (in the Fitness Fairgrounds) and two theaters that let you come and go as you please. In one, *Goofy about Health*, an eight-minute movie, shows Goofy concerned about the poor state of his health and then doing something about it. At the other, the **"Wonders of Laugh"** comedians use interactive comedy to address questions about health.

In the **Fitness Fairgrounds**, computerized stationary bicycles with video screens let you peddle through different venues such as Disneyland and the Rose Bowl Parade. Numerous hands-on exhibits dealing with touch, vision, hearing, and balance await you in the **Sensory Funhouse**, and you can input your vital statistics and habits into a computer to get advice about how to get healthier at the **Lifestyle Revue**. **Coach's Corner** offers a computer analysis of your golf, tennis, or baseball swing, while the **Frontiers of Medicine** presents serious educational exhibits on contemporary medical topics.

Body Wars

Rating: * * * * *

Type: Flight simulator thrill ride

Time: About 5 minutes

Steve says: Exhilarating fun

This flight simulator ride takes you through a human's blood vessels, heart, lung, and brain. You're miniaturized along with your copassengers in a vessel designed to navigate through the human body. Your mission is to rescue a stranded scientist as she's hauled headlong through the bloodstream. The result is a furiously paced, bouncing ride alongside red blood cells that ends in the brain, where a neuron fires just in time to send your energy-depleted vehicle back to the safety of the research lab.

The technology in these rides is similar to the technology in the flight simulators real pilots train on.

Height restriction: Kids must be 40" or taller to ride. Switching off is available.

Caution: Flight simulator rides can be problematic for those folks prone to motion sickness. Since *Body Wars* involves realistic anatomic scenes, it has caused more vomiting episodes among passengers than other less "bloody" flight simulator rides. For those of us who can enjoy it, *Body Wars* is great fun. If you feel queasy during the ride, take your eyes off the screen and stare elsewhere for the duration. Better yet, take an over-the-counter motion-sickness remedy before you enter the park if you are the least bit prone to motion sickness.

Cranium Command

Rating: ★★★★★
Type: Theater show
Time: 18 - 20 minutes
Steve says: One of a kind; don't miss it!

This theater-style presentation with video screens and Audio-Animatronics is one of the most entertaining attractions at WDW. The animated pre-show outside the theater humorously explains the set-up for the amusing story inside. Watching it will add to your enjoyment of what's to come. Inside, you enter the mind of a 12-year-old boy during a school day that turns adventurous. His brain, heart, stomach, and adrenal glands are represented by various well-known comedians. He accidentally starts a fire in science lab, launches a food fight in the cafeteria, shows courage in defending a girl's honor, and has to choose between honesty and dishonesty in front of the school principal. In the classic style of most Disney attractions, you leave *Cranium Command* smiling and feeling uplifted.

The Making of Me

Rating: ★★★
Type: Indoor movie in a sit-down theater
Time: 14 minutes
Steve says: Lighthearted view of the birds and the bees

This movie offers a sensitive look at pregnancy and childbirth. Actor Martin Short goes back in time to the birth of his parents and their later decision to marry and then have a child: him. He watches his own birth and, throughout the film, marvels at the whole process of human conception, pregnancy, and birth.

Note: The theater is small and waiting lines are often long in the late morning and early afternoon.

Mission: SPACE

Rating: Not open at press time
Type: Simulator ride
Steve says: Another choice ride for Future World

Wonder what it would be like to experience weightlessness? *Mission: SPACE* will let you simulate that experience, along with the "liftoff" from planet earth. The ride is scheduled to open sometime in 2003. When it does, check for a review on www.TheOtherOrlando.com, in the Updates section of the site.

Test Track

Rating: ✻ ✻ ✻ ✻ ✻
Type: Simulation of an automobile test track
Time: 4 - 5 minutes
Steve says: Unique track ride with a high-speed section

This fast-moving ride is a combination roller coaster and flight simulator. As you approach it, your queue winds past displays on automobile testing — the brake test, corrosion test, and even the "seat squirm test" among others. These displays feature the testing equipment complete with convincing video and sound effects. You end up in a briefing room where you are prepared for your ride in a six-seater test vehicle. Then it's on to the "proving grounds" for high-speed tests on straightaways and curves, over bumpy terrain, and through hot and cold temperatures and near-collisions. Two sudden braking sequences test the difference between regular and antilock brakes. More displays of automotive technology await you at the ride exit, including an interactive video area where you can drive a vehicle on a simulated test track. You'll walk away with a visceral appreciation of the extensive testing to which car components are subjected along with firsthand knowledge of the benefits of antilock brakes and other safety features.

Height restriction: You must be 40" or taller to ride.

Imagination! Pavilion

Outside this pavilion is an **"upside-down waterfall,"** which is especially colorful at night. Inside are two attractions, *Honey, I Shrunk the Audience* and *Journey Into Imagination with Figment.* You'll find a series of unusual fountains with jumping and leaping water effects at the exit of *Honey, I Shrunk the Audience.* It's fun to spend a few minutes here, especially when Dreamfinder (a jolly, red-headed adventurer) and Figment (a small, happy purple dragon) drop by. These two characters have been popular with visitors, but don't be too disappointed if you don't see them. Their appearances are usually unscheduled and Disney has apparently retired Dreamfinder, at least for the time being.

Honey, I Shrunk the Audience

Rating: ✻ ✻ ✻ ✻ ✻
Type: 3-D movie in a sit-down theater
Time: 17 - 18 minutes
Steve says: The audience squeals with delight through this one

This 3-D film has some of the best special effects anywhere. Rick Moranis and company are back to introduce some of the Professor's new inventions, including a duplicator machine that copies a mouse and inadvertently releases hundreds of mice into the audience! You also get to meet a cat, a lion, and a snake up close and personal. The new deluxe model shrinking machine accidentally miniaturizes the entire theater audience, and the result is quite believable. In the final big scene, imagine a face-to-face encounter with a snotty-nosed dog who lets loose with a huge sneeze.

Tip: Avoid the first few rows; the 3-D effects may be diluted.

Journey Into Imagination with Figment

Rating: * * *
Type: "Dark ride"
Time: 8 - 9 minutes
Steve says: Whimsical ride, relaxing, but not worth a long wait

A gently moving vehicle takes you through the sensory testing labs of the Imagination Institute, where you experience some amazing demonstrations of sound, sight, and smell (your nose will get a jolt!). Figment (the small, purple dragon from a previous attraction at this site) accompanies you through the ride and shows off his upside-down house.

Tip: At one point you'll feel a strong wind, so take off your hat before you ride!

ImageWorks

Rating: * * *
Type: Interactive exhibit area
Time: As long as you want, but 15 minutes at a minimum
Steve says: These unusual exhibits can be enjoyed by folks of all ages

This interactive playground has stations where you can experiment with photography, colors, and music. You can conduct an orchestra of sounds by raising and lowering your hands, step among splotches of light on the floor to cause a cacophony of animal and other noises, and create a unique photograph of yourself that you can send immediately by email to your home or someone else's computer. And that's just for starters.

Caution: It's easy to lose track of time at *ImageWorks* and children often don't want to leave.

The Land Pavilion

This pavilion contains several attractions and one of the best food courts in WDW. It's also a choice place to get out of the rain.

Living with the Land

Rating: * * * *
Type: Indoor, gentle boat ride
Time: 12 - 14 minutes
Steve says: More proof that education (in this case, science) can be fun

The first part of this boat ride takes you past Audio-Animatronics scenes of various ecosystems: rain forest, prairie, desert, and a family farm complete with crops and farm animals. You then float through a series of active greenhouses lush with edible plants (used in meals at WDW restaurants), followed by research areas for aeroponics, fish farming, and even experimental moon-soil gardening. Along the way, your boat guide offers an informative spiel.

The Circle of Life

Rating: * * *
Type: Indoor movie in a sit-down theater
Time: 13 minutes
Steve says: Entertaining movie about a serious subject

Characters from *The Lion King* (Simba, Timon, and Pumbaa) are the stars in a film about the potential dangers of mankind's mishandling of the environment. Timon and Pumbaa dam a river to create a lake for a new resort. Simba teaches them about the unfortunate consequences their for-profit venture creates in nature. The theater is comfortable and the presentation lighthearted but educational. Television monitors in the pre-show area flash interesting ecological facts about our earth and how we treat (and mistreat) it.

Food Rocks

Rating: * * *
Type: Indoor sit-down theater show
Time: 13 - 14 minutes
Steve says: Lighthearted musical show will have you humming and tapping along

Food items assume the personas of famous performers (the "Peach

Boys," "Chubby Cheddar," and others) and sing classic rock and roll songs to present an entertaining overview of nutrition. The comfortable theater seats face a large kitchen on stage. The song lyrics have been cleverly changed to ring out their nutritional message. It's fun to sing along with the well-known melodies, even though the words are a bit different. If you have time before or after the show, enjoy the historical food facts printed artfully along the walls in the pre-show area.

The Living Seas

Rating: * * * *
Type: Combination movie, ride, and gigantic aquarium
Time: Movie: 7 minutes; Ride: about 3 minutes; Exhibits: as long as you want, but a minimum of 15 minutes depending on the crowds
Steve says: An awesome and beautiful oceanic experience

This pavilion houses a huge saltwater aquarium teeming with fish and coral reefs. Following a short pre-show, a film about the oceans shows what they provide for us and how much we still don't know about them. Then a simulated elevator descent takes you to a slow-moving car for a short ride through the aquarium, which re-creates the environment of the Caribbean Sea. After the ride, you enter a large area where you can spend more time gazing into the aquarium (including a section devoted to manatees) and explore exhibits about sea life, marine research, and current ocean exploration techniques. You can stay as long as you want but you can't enter this area directly from the outside. You have to re-experience the ride (but can bypass the film) if you want to get back to the exhibit area.

Note: The ride portion may not be operating when you visit. If it is out of service, you will go directly to the exhibits after the film.

Innoventions East Side and West Side

Rating: * * * *
Type: Indoor exhibits
Time: As long as you want, but allow a minimum 10 minutes per building for a walk-through, more if you interact with the exhibits
Steve says: These new, cutting-edge products can occupy you for an afternoon or an entire day

Two large buildings, one on the east side of Future World and one on the west, curve gently away from *Spaceship Earth*. These buildings house a series of walk-through exhibits that will keep technology buffs happy for hours on end. The Innoventions buildings showcase new and developing consumer products. Companies proudly display their latest technologies in interactive games, Internet and email exhibits, and computers galore. Among the interesting sights you may encounter: a walk-through house of the future (how about a toilet with a heated seat!), the newest home theater designs, and a large area in Innoventions West Side that's filled with video games — free to play and quite a few of them not yet on the market.

Tip: Unless you plan to spend at least two days at Epcot, use your daylight hours to experience the park's other attractions and return to Innoventions in the early evening.

Innoventions Plaza

As you pass by *Spaceship Earth*, you'll spot a large electronic Tip Board in the middle of the square between the two Innoventions buildings. The board gives approximate wait times for Epcot attractions. Further along in the plaza, the large Fountain of Nations comes to life every 15 minutes with a beautiful water ballet, complete with a rousing musical score. The ballet is worth a stop.

Caution: The water shoots high in the air, so consider the wind direction if you want to assure yourself a dry viewing spot.

Past the Innoventions buildings on the right side of the middle path to World Showcase is a small interactive fountain. Random spurts of water in different formations emanate from a flat, circular padded area, drawing kids like bees to honey. It's delightful to watch the young folks cavorting carefree.

Note: This fountain has proven so popular that similar ones are showing up all over WDW. In fact, your kids may have already spotted the colorful interactive fountain outside Innoventions East Side on the walkway to *Mission: SPACE.*

World Showcase

Surrounding a large lagoon are eleven individual areas representing specific countries. Each re-creates some of that country's classic characteristics and landmarks in fascinating detail. The shops, food, architecture, and attractions reflect the particular country, as do the live performers and shows. Adding to the feeling of authenticity, the Disney cast members employed in each country are natives or descendants of it. The overall effect provides a convincing, cosmopolitan experience for the tourist strolling from one country to the next along the Showcase's wide promenade.

Note for Kids: Only some of the countries offer traditional theme park attractions, such as rides or movies, but each one offers a **Kidcot Fun Stop** and a **Passport Center**. Kids can make masks and do other crafts free of charge at the *Fun Stops* under the supervision of a Disney cast member. They can also get their "Passports" stamped by a cast m-ember and endorsed with a handwritten foreign phrase (there's a $9.95 charge for the Passports, none for the stamping and endorsement). *Fun Stops* open around 1:00 p.m. (sometimes earlier) and close around 8:00 p.m. (Check your Times Guide for Fun Stop times.)

Tip: Shopping is especially fun in this part of Epcot.

Mexico

A great pyramid enveloped in lush vegetation greets you at the Mexico Pavilion. Just inside is a collection of valuable **cultural artifacts**. Further along you will find a beautiful shopping plaza. Walk through it to reach the entrance to *El Rio del Tiempo* (just after the last shop on the left) and the San Angel Inn restaurant.

Tip: As you walk away from the pyramid entrance toward Norway, say hello to the colorful parrots sometimes perched in a tree to your left.

El Rio del Tiempo

Rating: * *
Type: Indoor boat ride
Time: 7 - 8 minutes
Steve says: Pleasant and relaxing, but not worth a long wait

A boat floats you gently past scenes of Mexico past and present, from ancient Mayan culture to current city life, including holiday fireworks, cliff divers, and vendors who bargain with you for their wares. Some of the Audio-Animatronics figures are reminiscent of those in the Magic Kingdom's *"it's a small world"* ride.

Norway

The central courtyard is surrounded by replicas of architectural landmarks of Norway: a wooden stave church (which contains a gallery of artifacts), the 14th-century Akershus Castle, and other historic buildings. A statue of legendary marathoner Grete Waitz stands behind the bakery (toward the Mexico Pavilion). Near the statue is a Viking ship that kids can climb on and explore. Norway, like several other countries in World Showcase, offers guided tours at posted times during the day (consult your Guidemap).

Maelstrom

Rating: ＊＊＊＊
Type: Indoor boat ride
Time: 12 - 14 minutes (5-minute boat ride, 2 - 4 minutes to explore a Norwegian fishing village, 5-minute movie)
Steve says: Ride soon after World Showcase opens or you're in for a long wait (or a FASTPASS)

A Viking longboat takes you along Norwegian waterways past a maelstrom (giant whirlpool), a waterfall, a deep-sea oil rig, and menacing trolls. After the boat journey, you get to explore a seaside Norwegian village and then watch an informative film about Norway.

Tip: You can skip the film by walking across the theater and out the exit doors on the far side, but the movie is worth watching to get the full Disney-style experience of Norway and its interesting culture.

China

An archway of good fortune welcomes you to a scaled-down replica of Beijing's Temple of Heaven. Beautiful gardens filled with rosebushes and reflecting ponds add to the quiet, relaxing atmosphere of this pavilion. There's usually an interesting exhibit relating to Chinese art or culture on offer. Various acrobats stage appealing shows; check your Times Guide for performance times.

Wonders of China

Rating: ＊＊＊
Type: Indoor movie in Circle-Vision
Time: About 20 minutes
Steve says: A collage of spectacular scenes

The Temple of Heaven houses this informative movie about the mysterious country of China. Disney filmed Beijing's Forbidden City, the Great Wall, and areas of China such as vast Mongolia. The film is in

"Circle-Vision 360 degrees"; the screens encircle you and you have to stand to watch.

Warning: Wheelchairs are welcome, but there are no seats in the theater. If you can't stand for 20 minutes (and aren't using a wheelchair), you should give this one a skip.

Germany

Architecturally diverse buildings border the courtyard here and are sure to impress visitors. The beer hall at the rear of the square houses a restaurant that comes alive with meal time entertainment. The shops around the square contain abundant items of interest, including Hummel figurines and a huge assortment of cuckoo clocks. An elaborate **G scale miniature railroad**, complete with farms and villages, is located on the side of the pavilion toward Italy.

Italy

Like Germany, the Italy Pavilion has a courtyard surrounded by examples of diverse Italian architectural styles, including a replica of the fourteenth-century Doge's Palace in Venice. The sea god Neptune watches over the fountain at the rear of the piazza, and Venetian gondolas are moored in the lagoon. Shops contain popular items such as Armani collectibles and Venetian glass. The entertainment here is unique. Especially notable: the group of musicians in 18th-century dress playing classical melodies.

U.S.A. The American Adventure

A huge Colonial-style mansion sits at the southernmost part of World Showcase in America (i.e., the United States), the central country of the Epcot eleven. On the lagoon side of the World Showcase promenade is the **America Gardens Theater**, a large open-air venue for live entertainment. Flower beds in front of the theater are planted with red, white, and blue blossoms.

The American Adventure Show

Rating: * * * * *
Type: Indoor historical theater presentation
Time: About 30 minutes

Steve says: Patriotic for Americans, compelling history experience for others

This show is staged in a theater inside the mansion. You get to sit in comfortable seats for the show, which uses Audio-Animatronics, animation, and photo collages to take you on a journey through American history. The experience is much more than a dry history lesson; it's a wonderfully entertaining view of American heritage. Mark Twain and Ben Franklin are the main narrators. They review the uplifting (Thomas Jefferson, Alexander Graham Bell, Susan B. Anthony, John Muir, Jackie Robinson, Will Rogers, and many others) as well as some of the sobering aspects of U.S. history. Some folks will have moist eyes after the Civil War segment.

Between the holding area and the theater is the **Hall of Flags** corridor, which displays 44 historic flags. You may also see an American flag recovered from the World Trade Center debris hanging on the right lobby wall. Try to catch the **Voices of Liberty**, a terrific a cappella choir that performs just inside the entrance, usually late morning through late afternoon (check your Times Guide for performances).

Japan

A five-story pagoda sits at the entrance to this pavilion. Behind it is a garden with walking paths that wind among streams, flowers, and trees. Brightly colored koi fish dart in the pools. You can enter the garden via a path from the promenade on the America Pavilion side of the pagoda. As you walk up this path, look to your right and you'll see a monkey puzzle tree, the only tree monkeys can't climb because of the small sharp spines sticking out of the bark (the tree label says "Bunya-Bunya" tree). A gallery in the rear of the pavilion displays interesting cultural items. The large building across from the pagoda on the other side of the pavilion was modeled after the Imperial Palace at Kyoto.

Serene is the word for the Japan Pavilion. It's a perfect place to sit and relax. Enjoy one of the **Japanese drumming routines**; your Times Guide lists performance times.

Morocco

Ocher-colored stuccoed buildings and archways encompass the central courtyard and market area of the Morocco Pavilion. A replica of the prayer tower in Marrakesh stands at its entrance, and beautifully colored tile decorates the indoor walls of the shops and the museum of Moroccan culture. If you'd like to explore the pavilion, consider taking a free guided walking tour. Your Guidemap offers information about it, or enter the courtyard and ask for information at the greeting podium or at the Moroccan National Tourist Office on the right side.

France

A model of the Eiffel Tower overlooks the streets and buildings of this pavilion. The architecture of the front part of the pavilion is reminiscent of Parisian architecture in the Belle Epoque ("beautiful age," 1870 to 1910). On the promenade you'll find kiosks covered with advertisements for artists and museums Parisians might have seen during that era. The shops sell perfume, jewelry, and other luxury items. At the far side of the pavilion, near the waterway to the Epcot resort hotels, is a beautiful and peaceful garden — a perfect spot to relax and get away from the crowds. The influence of Impressionist French artists is visible both in the rose-colored dresses the hostesses wear and in one of the shops; it sells gift items (such as umbrellas and mugs) covered with scenes from famous paintings.

Impressions de France

Rating: * * * *
Type: Indoor movie
Time: 18 minutes
Steve says: Delicious, like fine wine

This beautiful, lyrical film is shown in a theater with comfortable seats. The movie is projected on a wide screen (not 360 degrees) and accompanied by a wonderful classical music score. You visit many French landmarks (including the Eiffel Tower, Versailles, Cannes, the French Alps), as well as some lesser known scenic areas. Many sites were filmed from the air, including one filmed from a balloon. Like the France Pavilion in general, the film is enchanting and relaxing.

United Kingdom

The variety of historic architectural styles in this pavilion is fascinating to behold. You stroll past a cottage modeled on Anne Hathaway's (William Shakespeare's wife), past a panoply of changing historical architectural styles (including formal Tudor and Victorian) to a quiet, serene park reminiscent of the beautiful parks of London. Behind the facades are shops aplenty, all of them connected but each designed to match the exterior "architecture." Even the pub on the lagoon side of the promenade retains the focus; it's built in a combination of historical pub styles. Behind the shops is a scenic path through traditional English flower and herb gardens.

Canada

This pavilion has a refreshing outdoor atmosphere. A giant totem pole greets you at the entrance and a large Rocky Mountain rises up at the rear of the pavilion. Winding paths bring you to a waterfall, a gurgling stream, and an expansive hillside flower garden modeled after the Butchart Gardens in Victoria, British Columbia.

O Canada!

Rating: ★ ★ ★
Type: Indoor movie in Circle-Vision
Time: 18 minutes
Steve says: Energetic tribute to our northern neighbor

The "Great White North" is displayed in all its splendor in this "Circle-Vision 360 degree" film. In other words, you must stand during the movie. Along with the beautiful rivers, mountains, and wildlife of this vast country, the film introduces you to the Royal Canadian Mounted Police, chuck wagon racers at the annual Calgary Stampede, skiers, skaters, dog sledders, and hockey players. The theater is inside the pavilion's "Rocky Mountain."

Warning: Give this a skip if standing 18 minutes is too much for you. There are no seats in the theater. Wheelchairs are welcome.

Attractions with Minimal Waits (Usually)

- *Cranium Command.* The wait is usually the time until the next show, especially in the afternoon or evening.
- *Fitness Fairgrounds.* This interactive area in the Wonders of Life Pavilion generally has room for more guests, as do the *Wonders of Laugh* theater show and the *Goofy About Health* movie.
- *The Circle of Life.* The wait is usually the time until the next show, especially in the afternoon or evening.
- *Food Rocks.* The wait is usually the time until the next show, espe-

cially in the afternoon or evening.

- *The Living Seas.* This attraction often has a short wait in the afternoon or evening.
- Innoventions. Some exhibits are accessible any time in the Innoventions buildings.
- *El Rio del Tiempo.* The wait is usually short, except on very crowded days.
- *Wonders of China.* The wait is usually the time until the next show.
- *The American Adventure.* The wait is usually the time until the next show.
- *Impressions de France.* The wait is usually the time until the next show, except on very crowded days.
- *O Canada!* The wait is usually the time until the next show.

Attractions That May Frighten Children

Remember that switching off is available at some of these attractions (see *Chapter One,* "Good Things to Know About").

- *Universe of Energy.* The realistic dinosaur segment can frighten preschoolers.
- *Body Wars.* This intense flight simulator ride may frighten young children and can cause motion sickness in anyone. Switching off is available.
- *Test Track.* This fast, intense car ride can frighten anyone. Switching off is available.
- *Honey, I Shrunk the Audience.* 3-D visual effects and loud noises may frighten young children.
- *Journey Into Imagination with Figment.* Loud noises in the dark may frighten young children.
- *Maelstrom.* Angry looking trolls can frighten young children.

Least Crowded Restrooms

- The restrooms in the Wonders of Life Pavilion near *Cranium Command.*
- The outside restrooms to the right of the Imagination! Pavilion.
- The restrooms at the Odyssey Center, located between Future World and World Showcase.
- The restrooms on the right side of Germany.

Resting Places

- The benches in the small alcove on the side of France to the right of the Guerlain Boutique.
- The benches in the park at the rear of the United Kingdom.

Hidden Mickeys

Here are just a few of the hidden Mickeys you may want to look for in Epcot:

- *Spaceship Earth.* When you pass by the sleeping monk, look back at the document he is working on. You'll find an ink blot shaped like Mickey's frontal silhouette in the upper far corner.
- *Body Wars* in the Wonders of Life Pavilion. Before you reach the entrance to the ride, look up at the colorful mural on the wall above you. Walk back about 20 feet to the left side of the mural and stare at the green nerve tissue; part of it looks like broccoli buds. Mickey's face is here, gazing up and to your left. This is a tough hidden Mickey to find. If you can't see it, look for the closest Disney cast member and ask him or her to help you. Chances are, you will be guided to the hidden Mickey.
- *Living with the Land* ride in The Land Pavilion. When you reach the greenhouses in your boat, begin to look for a large window in front of you that looks into a laboratory. Inside the laboratory room on the right side is a white disc tilted upward with test tubes resting in holes in the disc. The test tubes form a pattern: the frontal silhouette of Mickey Mouse.
- *Maelstrom* at the Norway Pavilion. Stare at the left side of the large wall mural at the loading area where you enter the boats. One of the Vikings on the ship deck has Mickey ears for a helmet.

Touring Epcot

Epcot is one of the largest of the WDW theme parks and feels relatively spacious even on busy days. Compared with the Magic Kingdom, it's a cinch to enter and leave. Nonetheless, it pays to know the lay of the land.

Entrances

Epcot has two entrances, the main entrance in front and another in the rear. The front entrance opens into Future World, the rear into World Showcase. The parking lot is at the front and it's here that the WDW monorail and buses stop. The rear entrance opens out onto a walkway to the Epcot resort hotels and a dock for the boat that carries visitors to and from the Epcot hotels and Disney-MGM Studios.

If you plan to arrive first thing in the morning (recommended), you'll want to head for the front entrance if possible. World Showcase doesn't open until 11:00 a.m., and visitors who arrive at the rear entrance have to trek first to Future World. By the time they get there, they are usually at the back of the pack of early arrivals who came in the front way.

Getting to and from Epcot

By car. The quickest way to get to Epcot's front entrance is by car, even if you are staying within walking distance at an Epcot resort hotel. Drive in, park in the main parking lot, and head for the entrance turnstiles. Later in the day, if you decide to leave to spend the afternoon in the Magic Kingdom, you can take the monorail from Epcot (about a 30-minute trip one way) and then return by monorail in the evening to retrieve your car. If you want to go anywhere else, you can drive there.

Insider Tip 1: If you plan to spend the entire day at Epcot, consider moving your car in the afternoon to an Epcot resort hotel (especially if you're staying in one). You'll avoid the mass exodus through the front gates when Epcot closes and simply stroll out the rear exit to your hotel or car. The Swan and Dolphin don't have guard gates yet.

Insider Tip 2: If you arrive by car in the afternoon, try to wend your way to the front of the parking lot to cut your distance to the entrance turnstiles.

Without a car. You can walk from any of the Epcot resort hotels in five to ten minutes (see *Chapter One*, "WDW Lodging"), but you have to enter through the rear entrance. That's a major disadvantage in the early morning, as noted above. Don't be dismayed if it's your only choice, however. Epcot is a large park and the touring plans below will give you an advantage over most visitors. Car-less guests at other WDW properties can take the monorail or bus to the front entrance (check your Transportation Guide). Off-property visitors without cars will have to depend on cabs (expensive), hotel shuttles (if available), and public transportation (also if available). All three tend to be inconvenient. Ask at your hotel Guest Services how long it will take you to get to the Epcot front entrance.

Note: If you don't have a car and decide to switch from Epcot to another Disney theme park in the afternoon, take a WDW bus or monorail (or 25- to 35-minute boat ride to Disney-MGM Studios). Consult your WDW Transportation Guide for schedules or ask a Disney attendant at one of the Epcot exits.

Tip: Remember to have your hand stamped at the exit when you leave in case you decide to return later.

When to Arrive

Come early in the day, preferably before opening time, so that you can experience some of the major attractions with minimal waits. Be at the front entrance turnstiles about 35 to 40 minutes before the official opening time. Add 10 minutes if you have to buy your admission tickets. Pick up a Guidemap and Times Guide as you enter (at the turnstiles or just inside).

Note: Walkers from Epcot resort hotels should be at the rear entrance turnstiles 15 minutes earlier than the above times. Then walk to Future World as quickly as you can without straining yourself.

If the morning lines are long at all entrance turnstiles, line up in an outside queue. Sometimes, an attendant will open up a nearby turnstile at the last minute, and you may be positioned to move with other excited guests to the new and shorter queue.

Note: All the touring plans below assume you will arrive at or before opening time. If you want to sleep in, simply pick up the appropriate non Early Entry plan later in the day. Use FASTPASS or the singles line option (if available) to minimize your wait at crowded attractions. I consider a wait of more than 15 to 20 minutes too long.

Start with Priority Seating Reservations

Unless you plan to eat fast food all day, or to leave the park to eat, be sure you make priority seating reservations for lunch and dinner. The food in Epcot is good and the restaurants tend to fill up fast. So if you don't already have priority seating plans, make them as soon as you clear the entrance turnstiles. Walk quickly around the left side of

Spaceship Earth to Guest Relations. Among your options: lunch at San Angel Inn Restaurant in Mexico or great seafood at Restaurant Akershus in Norway, and dinner at Coral Reef restaurant at The Living Seas Pavilion or The Garden Grill Restaurant's Disney character meal in The Land Pavilion. If you come back for a second day, consider lunch at Rose & Crown Restaurant in the United Kingdom or a bit more exotic fare at Restaurant Marrakesh in Morocco, and dinner at Chefs de France in France or L'Originale Alfredo di Roma Ristorante in Italy.

Tip: Try for lunch at around 11:30 a.m. and dinner around 5:30 p.m. to minimize your waiting time and get the best possible tables. If most of Future World closes at 7:00 p.m. (check your Times Guide), make dinner priority seating reservations for around 7:00 to allow for optimal touring.

Note: *Body Wars* and *Test Track* are simulator rides. If you are prone to motion sickness but want to give them a try, take an over-the-counter remedy before you enter the park.

One-Day Touring Plans for Adults, Teens and Seniors

(See "A Special Note on Early Entry," page 51.)

Be sure to check the entrance, arrival, priority seating, and other important recommendations above before you start your tour.

You won't be able to experience every attraction in Epcot in a day, but following this plan will ensure that you experience the best Epcot has to offer adults, teens, and seniors.

Note: These plans do not include an afternoon break. If you're flagging after lunch, return to your hotel for a swim and rest (or rest awhile at the small alcove in France behind the shops). Return to the park in mid-afternoon and take up the touring plan in Japan or France.

Adults, Teens and Seniors One-Day Plan for Early Entry Days

(WDW property guests only)

Note: Most of the attractions in Future World lie east (to your left from the front entrance) and west of *Spaceship Earth* and Innoventions Plaza. Only one side may be open during the Early Entry period. Thus the alternatives below.

1. Ask a Disney attendant what attractions are open for Early Entry guests (this list changes periodically) and then make your priority seating reservations if you haven't already done so (see above).

2. Walk into Innoventions Plaza and through Innoventions West Side (to your right). Then veer left toward the tall pyramids (Imagination! Pavilion) and see *Honey, I Shrunk the Audience* (avoid the first few rows). Don't dally at the exit; the unusual water effects here can be enjoyed later.

3. Ride *Spaceship Earth*. Don't dally at the exhibits at the exit.

4. Walk to The Land Pavilion. Enjoy the *Living with the Land* ride.
    Alternative: If the west side of Future World is not open for Early Entry, go through Innoventions East Side and get a FASTPASS (if available) for *Mission: SPACE*, then ride *Test Track* and *Spaceship Earth*. (If *Test Track* is crowded, try the singles line.) If time permits, ride *Body Wars* or *Universe of Energy*.
    Note: Seniors may want to avoid the jerky simulator experiences of *Test Track* and *Body Wars*.

5. Get some light refreshments at the Food Court in The Land Pavilion (or at the "Pure and Simple" food area in the Wonders of Life Pavilion). Carry them with you back through Innoventions Plaza. Stroll across to the opposite Innoventions walkway and line up at the rope. When the rope drops at the official opening time, or if the rope is already down, proceed to step 2 or 3 below. Skip any attractions you've already experienced today.

Adults, Teens and Seniors
One-Day Plan for Non Early Entry Days

1. On your way in, ask the turnstile attendant if *Test Track* and *Mission: SPACE* will open immediately. Before you head for them, go to Guest Relations and make priority seating reservations for lunch and dinner if you haven't already done so (see above).

2. Go to the walkway through Innoventions East Side. When the rope is down, continue through to get a FASTPASS for *Mission: SPACE* or *Test Track* (follow the crowd) if they are open. (Or use the singles line at *Test Track* if it is crowded.) Ride one then the other.

If they are not yet open, come back and ride them after step 4.

Note: Seniors may want to skip the roller coaster-simulator ride, *Test Track.*

3. Cross back through Innoventions East Side and West and bear left to the Imagination! Pavilion. See *Honey, I Shrunk the Audience* (avoid the first few rows).

    Tip: Use FASTPASS if eligible if the wait is too long. Don't dally at the exit; the unusual water effects here can be enjoyed later.

4. Walk to your left and experience the *Journey Into Imagination with Figment* ride.

    Caution: Take off your hat before the ride!

5. Cross back through both Innoventions buildings to the east side of Future World. Veer left to the Wonders of Life Pavilion and ride *Body Wars.*

    Note: Seniors may want to skip this rough flight simulator ride.

6. At the Wonders of Life Pavilion, enjoy *Cranium Command.*

7. Exit left from the Wonders of Life Pavilion and walk past *Test Track* onto the bridges to World Showcase. These bridges pass around the Odyssey Center building. Once on the bridges, keep left to access the bridge to Mexico. World Showcase usually opens at 11:00 a.m. When the opening rope drops, or if it's already down, walk fast past Mexico to the Norway Pavilion and ride *Maelstrom.* Use FASTPASS if the wait is already too long.

    Note: The Norway film is worth watching.

9. Go to your lunch restaurant if you have 11:30 a.m. priority seating times. If you have no reservations, try fast food at Cantina de San Angel at the Mexico Pavilion. Or try to get seated anyway at Restaurant Akershus in Norway (if you like seafood) since this restaurant sometimes has tables available. While there, consult your Times Guide for any outdoor or stage performances or parades in World Showcase or Future World you may want to see.

10. Head for *El Rio del Tiempo* in the Mexico Pavilion. Walk through the interior plaza to the far left corner to the ride entrance. Enjoy.

11. Exit Mexico and head left to China. Browse the shops and exhibits for a short while.

12. Stroll through Germany. Spend a few minutes at the elaborate outdoor miniature G scale train on the right side of the pavilion.

13. Stroll through the Italy Pavilion.

14. Walk left to the America Pavilion. Check your Times Guide for the next performance of the singing group *Voices of Liberty* or one

of the other a cappella groups. They sing inside the main building at the entrance to the show, *The American Adventure.* The main show is a must (sit toward the front of the auditorium), but try to find time for the singers, too, if possible. If you have time before or after the shows, grab some refreshments from the outside vendors or at the Liberty Inn on the left side of the pavilion.

15. Walk left to Japan and wander amidst the beautiful gardens and streams.

16. Go next to Morocco and stroll through the shops.

17. Walk left to France and see the movie *Impressions de France.*
    Note: This theater has comfortable seats.

18. Head to the United Kingdom. If you're thirsty for a beer, order one at the Rose & Crown pub. Wander through the UK's shops and gardens.

19. Walk past the entrance to the new conference center and on to Canada. Stroll the pathways along its beautiful streams and gardens.

    Walk along the stream in Japan and find the wooden water lever, which emits a repetitive, soothing sound.

20. Return to Future World via the first path to your left past the Refreshment Port. Walk to the end of Innoventions West Side to Ice Station Cool to enjoy exotic, refreshing soft drinks from foreign countries.
    Note: These drinks are on Epcot; you don't pay a thing for them.

21. Get a FASTPASS for *Living with the Land,* then go left to The Living Seas Pavilion and enjoy the show and ride. Then spend some time in the exhibit area.
    Tip: Hold back as you enter the sit-down theater for the show so that you can position yourself to sit on the far right benches. That will put you among the first on the elevators (stand toward the rear) and the subsequent ride to the exhibit area.

22. Exit and walk toward Innoventions West Side. Before reaching Innoventions, turn to your right and enjoy the "talking drinking fountains" in front of the nearby restrooms. Walk through Innoventions West Side and turn left to ride *Spaceship Earth* (if you haven't already). Check the Tip Board in Innoventions Plaza for approximate attraction wait times (it's not always accurate).

23. Consult your Times Guide for any outdoor or stage performances or parades in World Showcase or Future World you may

still want to see and program them into your touring plan.

24. Walk to the *Universe of Energy*. Enjoy the show.
    Tip: Stand near the left front entry door in the pre-show area. When the doors open, walk to the front row of the front car on your left for the best vantage point.

25. Walk back through the Innoventions buildings and enjoy the *Living with the Land* ride if you haven't already. (Or ride it at your FASTPASS time.) Also entertaining are the two shows at The Land Pavilion: *The Circle of Life* sit-down movie and the *Food Rocks* sit-down show. Each show takes about 25 minutes including the wait.

26. Keep your priority seating reservations for dinner. If you don't have reservations, eat at the Food Court in The Land Pavilion. If you have time before dinner, enjoy the water ballet at the huge Fountain of Nations between the Innoventions buildings. The water dances to music every 15 minutes.

27. If you have more than 30 minutes before the *IllumiNations* fireworks show, spend some time with the exhibits inside the Innoventions buildings (check your Guidemap for details) or head toward the *ImageWorks* interactive area at the Imagination! Pavilion (if open) to take in some lighthearted and interesting sensory exhibits. Then enjoy the "jumping fountains" area outside the Imagination! Pavilion.

28. Claim a viewing spot for the *IllumiNations* fireworks display 20 to 30 minutes before show time, which is usually 9:00 p.m. If you want to leave quickly through the front entrance after the show, find an open spot near the water along the wide promenade between Future World and World Showcase. If you can linger after the show, or if you're leaving Epcot through the rear entrance, seek less congested areas along the waterfront in Italy, between Morocco and France, or on the bridges between France and the United Kingdom.
    Tip: If you feel a steady, strong wind, choose a spot where the wind is not directly in your face to avoid smoke from the fireworks.

Don't lug your purchases around. Shops in the park will send purchases to "package pickup" near the exit at no extra charge. If you're staying on property and not checking out for at least another day, they will deliver right to your hotel room.

One-Day Touring Plans for Families with Children

(See "A Special Note on Early Entry," page 51.)

Note: Be sure to check the entrance, arrival, priority seating, and other important recommendations on pages 138 to 140 before you start your tour.

You won't be able to experience every attraction in Epcot in a day, but following these plans will ensure that you experience the best Epcot has to offer families with children.

Families with Children One-Day Plan for Early Entry Days

(WDW property guests only)

Note: Most of the attractions in Future World lie east (to your left from the front entrance) and west of *Spaceship Earth* and Innoventions Plaza. Only one side may be open during the Early Entry period. Thus the alternatives below.

1. Rent strollers if necessary. You'll find them on the left (east) side of the main entrance plaza near *Spaceship Earth* and on the left side of the rear entrance plaza.

2. Ask a Disney attendant what attractions are open for Early Entry guests today (this list changes periodically) and then go to Guest Relations to make your priority seating reservations for lunch and dinner if you need them (see above).

3. Walk into Innoventions Plaza and through Innoventions West Side (to your right from the front entrance). Then veer left toward the tall pyramids (Imagination! Pavilion) and see *Honey, I Shrunk the Audience* (avoid the first few rows). Don't dally at the exit; the unusual water effects here can be enjoyed later.
   Caution: This 3-D show has a few loud, convincing special effects that may frighten some young children.

4. Ride *Spaceship Earth*. Don't dally at the exhibits at the exit.

5. Walk to your left to The Land Pavilion. Enjoy the *Living with the Land* ride. (Get a FASTPASS if the wait is too long.)
   Alternative: If the west (right) side of Future World is not open

for Early Entry, get a FASTPASS for either *Mission: SPACE* or *Test Track* then ride the other followed by *Spaceship Earth*. If time allows, ride *Body Wars* or *Universe of Energy*.

Height/fright alert: Test Track and *Body Wars* are too intense for many small children. Switching off is available at both. Kids must be 40" or taller to ride either one.

6. Get some light refreshments at the Food Court in The Land Pavilion (or at the "Pure and Simple" food area in the Wonders of Life Pavilion). Carry them with you back through Innoventions Plaza. Stroll across to the Innoventions walkway and line up at the rope. When the rope drops at the official opening time, or if the rope is already down, proceed to step 3 or 4 below. Skip any attractions you've already experienced today.

Families with Children
One-Day Plan for Non Early Entry Days

1. Rent strollers if necessary on the left (east) side of the main entrance plaza near *Spaceship Earth*, or on the left side of the rear entrance plaza.
2. Ask the turnstile attendant if *Mission: SPACE* and *Test Track* will open immediately and then go quickly to Guest Relations (around the left side of *Spaceship Earth*) to make priority seating reservations for lunch and dinner if you don't already have them (see above).
3. Go to the walkway through Innoventions East Side. When the rope is down, continue through to get a FASTPASS for either *Mission: SPACE* or *Test Track* (follow the crowd) if they are open; then ride the other. If they are not open, come back and ride one or both of them after step 5.

    Height/fright alert: Test Track can be too intense for small children; switching off is available. Kids must be 40" or taller to ride.
4. Cross back through Innoventions East Side and West and bear left to the Imagination! Pavilion. See *Honey, I Shrunk the Audience* (avoid the first few rows). Use FASTPASS if eligible if the wait is too long. Don't dally at the exit; the unusual water effects here can be enjoyed later.

    Caution: This 3-D show has a few loud, convincing special effects that may frighten some young children.

5. Walk to your left and experience the *Journey Into Imagination with Figment* ride.
    Tip: Take off your hat before the ride!

6. Cross back through the Innoventions buildings to the east side of Future World. Veer left to the Wonders of Life Pavilion and enjoy *Cranium Command*.

7. If the time is 10:30 a.m. or earlier, see the movie *The Making of Me* or ride *Body Wars* in the Wonders of Life Pavilion.
    Height/fright alert: Kids must be 40" or taller to ride *Body Wars* and able to handle a rough simulator ride; switching off is available.

8. Exit left from the Wonders of Life Pavilion and walk past *Test Track* onto the bridges to World Showcase. (These bridges pass around the Odyssey Center building.) Once on the bridges, keep left to access the bridge to Mexico. The World Showcase usually opens at 11:00 a.m. When the opening rope drops, or if it's already down, walk fast past Mexico to the Norway Pavilion and ride *Maelstrom*. Then watch the Norway film if your kids are up for a movie. Otherwise, walk through the theater to the exit.

9. Go to your lunch restaurant if you have 11:30 a.m. priority seating times. If you have no reservations, try fast food at Cantina de San Angel at the Mexico Pavilion. Or try to get seated anyway at Restaurant Akershus in Norway (if you like seafood); it sometimes has tables available.

10. Ride *El Rio del Tiempo* in the Mexico Pavilion. Walk through the interior plaza to the far left corner to the ride entrance. After the ride, check out the *Kidcot Fun Stop* in Mexico (there's one in every country) if your children are interested; it's free!
    Note: The *Fun Stops* may not open until 1:00 p.m. or so.

11. Head back to your hotel for a rest or swim. If you leave World Showcase via the central bridge in front of Showcase Plaza, your kids will pass by an interactive fountain on their left. If you're prepared, let the kids go crazy and get soaked! Dry them off then walk to Ice Station Cool at the end of Innoventions West Side and enjoy free exotic soft drinks from foreign countries before you leave the park.
    Caution: The temperature of the entrance walkway is quite cool and may be uncomfortable if you're wet.
    Have your hands stamped at the exit for re-entry and keep any parking or stroller receipts.
    Alternative: If you're not staying on property or if you can't bring

yourself to leave the park, find a resting spot (such as the small alcove in France behind the shops) to park your family for a respite and maybe even naps for the kids. Consult your Times Guide for any outdoor or stage performances or parades in World Showcase or Future World you may want to see.

Solar panels on the rooftop of the Universe of Energy Pavilion generate part of the energy that powers the attraction inside.

12. Return to Epcot at about 3:00 p.m. and retrieve strollers if necessary. Get a FASTPASS for *Living with the Land*, then walk to The Living Seas Pavilion and enjoy the show, ride, and exhibit area.
Tip: Hold back as you enter the sit-down theater for the show so that you can position yourself to sit on the far right benches. That will put you among the first on the elevators (stand toward the rear) and the subsequent ride to the exhibit area. Enjoy the exhibits.

13. Exit and walk toward Innoventions West Side. Before reaching Innoventions, turn to your right and enjoy the "talking drinking fountains" in front of the nearby restrooms. Now cross through both Innoventions buildings and turn left to the *Universe of Energy*. Enjoy the show.
Tip: Stand near the left front entry door in the pre-show area. When the doors open, walk to the front row of the front car on your left for the best vantage point.

14. If you have more than 30 minutes before your dinner priority seating reservations, go back through Innoventions East Side and turn right to ride *Spaceship Earth*. Check the Tip Board in Innoventions Plaza for approximate attraction wait times (it's not always accurate). If you've already been on *Spaceship Earth*, turn left from the *Universe of Energy* and spend some time with the interactive exhibits in the Wonders of Life Pavilion.

15. Cross through the Innoventions buildings and walk to The Land Pavilion. Enjoy the *Living with the Land* ride if you haven't already. Or ride it at your FASTPASS time.

16. See *The Circle of Life* in the sit-down theater on the upper floor to the right.

17. Go back downstairs and see the *Food Rocks* sit-down show.

18. Exit The Land Pavilion and turn right to the Imagination! Pavilion. Spend 20 minutes or so in the *ImageWorks* interactive playground. Then enjoy the "jumping fountains" area outside the pa-

vilion. Otherwise, shop awhile in Future World.

19. Keep your priority seating reservations for dinner. If you don't have reservations, eat at the Food Court in The Land Pavilion or at one of the restaurants in Innoventions.

    Tip: If you still have time before dinner, enjoy the water ballet at the huge Fountain of Nations between the Innoventions buildings. The water dances to music every 15 minutes.

20. After dinner, visit a *Kidcot Fun Stop* in a World Showcase country. While the kids are busy, consult your Times Guide for any outdoor or stage performances or parades in World Showcase or Future World you may want to see.

21. If you have more than 40 minutes before the *IllumiNations* fireworks display, spend some time wandering through the Innoventions buildings. Both sides have kid-friendly, free interactive games.

22. Claim a viewing spot for *IllumiNations* 20 to 30 minutes before show time, which is usually 9:00 p.m. If you want to leave quickly through the front entrance after the show, find an open spot near the water along the wide promenade between Future World and World Showcase. If you can linger after the show or if you're leaving Epcot through the rear entrance, seek less congested areas along the waterfront in Italy, between Morocco and France, or on the bridges between France and the United Kingdom.

    Tip: If you feel a steady, strong wind, choose a spot where the wind is not directly in your face, to avoid smoke from the fireworks.

Two-Day Touring Plans for Adults and Teens

(See "A Special Note on Early Entry," page 51.)

Note: Be sure to check the entrance, arrival, priority seating, and other important recommendations on pages 138 to 140 before starting.

These plans assume you will arrive at or before opening time. If you want to sleep in, simply pick up the touring plan several steps down to match your arrival time. Later in the day, use FASTPASS or the singles line option (if available) to minimize waits at crowded attractions. Bear the following in mind:

- I consider a wait of more than 15 to 20 minutes "too long."
- Because guests generally take advantage of the Early Entry privilege (when available) only once at each park — or want to do the same popular rides again if they do two Early Entry days — the Early Entry touring plans are virtually the same for Days One and Two. I include them under both days so that you don't have to flip back and forth in your book.
- Most of the attractions in Future World lie east (to your left from the front entrance) and west of *Spaceship Earth* and Innoventions Plaza. Only one side may be open early in the day. Thus the alternatives offered in the touring plans that follow.

Adults and Teens
Day One Plan for Early Entry Days

(WDW property guests only)

1. Ask a Disney attendant what attractions are open for Early Entry guests (this list changes periodically). Then quickly make your priority seating reservations for meals if you haven't yet done so.
2. Walk into Innoventions Plaza and through Innoventions West Side on your right. Then veer left toward the tall pyramids (Imagination! Pavilion) and see *Honey, I Shrunk the Audience* (avoid the first few rows). Don't dally at the exit; the unusual water effects here can be enjoyed later.
3. Ride *Spaceship Earth*. Don't dally at the exhibits at the exit.
4. Walk to The Land Pavilion. Enjoy the *Living with the Land* ride.
   Alternative: If the west side of Future World is not open for Early Entry, get a FASTPASS for *Mission: SPACE* or *Test Track*, then ride the other, followed by *Spaceship Earth*. If time permits, ride *Body Wars* or *Universe of Energy*. Be sure to use the *Test Track* singles line to your advantage.
   Caution: *Body Wars* is an exhilarating but rough simulator ride. Take a motion-sickness remedy before you enter the park if you are prone to that malady.
5. Get some light refreshments at the Food Court in The Land Pavilion (or at the "Pure and Simple" food area in the Wonders of Life Pavilion). Carry them with you back through Innoventions Plaza. Stroll across to the opposite Innoventions walkway and line up at the rope. When the rope drops at the official opening time, or if

the rope is already down, proceed to step 2 or 3 below. Skip any attractions you've already experienced today.

Adults and Teens
Day One Plan for Non Early Entry Days:

1. Ask the turnstile attendant if *Test Track* and *Mission: SPACE* will open immediately. Then quickly make priority seating reservations for lunch and dinner if you don't already have them.
2. Go to the walkway through Innoventions East Side. When the rope is down, continue through to get a FASTPASS for *Mission: SPACE* or *Test Track* (follow the crowd) if they are open, then ride the other one. Or use the singles line at *Test Track* if lines are long. If they are not open, come back and ride them after step 4.
3. Cross back through Innoventions East Side and West and bear left to the Imagination! Pavilion. See *Honey, I Shrunk the Audience* (avoid the first few rows). Use FASTPASS if eligible if the wait is too long. Don't dally at the exit; the unusual water effects here can be enjoyed later.
4. Walk to your left and experience the *Journey Into Imagination with Figment* ride. (Take your hat off before the ride!)
5. Cross back through the Innoventions buildings to the east side of Future World. Veer left to the Wonders of Life Pavilion and ride *Body Wars*.
    Caution: *Body Wars* is an exhilarating but rough simulator ride. Be prepared. Take a motion sickness remedy before the ride if you need to.
6. At the Wonders of Life Pavilion, enjoy *Cranium Command*.
7. Exit left from the Wonders of Life Pavilion and walk past *Test Track* onto the bridges to World Showcase. (These bridges pass around the Odyssey Center building.) Once on the bridges, keep left to access the bridge to Mexico. The World Showcase usually opens at 11:00 a.m. When the opening rope drops, or if it's already down, walk fast past Mexico to the Norway Pavilion and ride *Maelstrom*. (Use FASTPASS if the wait is already too long.)
    Note: The Norway film at the end is worth watching.
8. Exit and head for your lunch restaurant if you have 11:30 a.m. priority seating. If you have no reservations, try fast food at Cantina de San Angel at the Mexico Pavilion. Or try to get seated anyway

at Restaurant Akershus in Norway (if you like seafood); this restaurant isn't always booked up.

9. After lunch ride *El Rio del Tiempo* in the Mexico Pavilion. Walk through the interior plaza to the far left corner to the ride entrance.

10. Return to your hotel for a rest or swim. If you plan to leave via the front exit, walk to the end of Innoventions West Side to enjoy exotic soft drinks from foreign countries at Ice Station Cool on your way out. (They're free!) Have your hands stamped at the exit for re-entry and keep any parking receipts.

    Alternative: If you're not staying on property or if you can't bring yourself to leave the park, find a resting spot (such as the small alcove in France behind the shops) and sit down for a respite and maybe a nap.

11. Return to Epcot at about 3:00 p.m. Get a FASTPASS for *Living with the Land*, then walk to The Living Seas Pavilion and enjoy the show, ride, and exhibits.

    Tip: When you enter the sit-down theater, hold back and then sit on the far right of the benches, so you can be among the first on the elevators (stand toward the rear) and subsequent ride to the exhibits.

12. Walk toward Innoventions West Side. Before reaching it, turn to your right and enjoy the "talking drinking fountains" in front of the nearby restrooms. Now cross through both Innoventions buildings and turn left to the *Universe of Energy*. Enjoy the show.

    Tip: Stand near the left front entry door in the pre-show area. When the doors open, walk to the front row of the front car on your left for the best vantage point.

13. Cross through the Innoventions buildings and walk to The Land Pavilion. Enjoy the *Living with the Land* ride if you haven't already, or visit it at your FASTPASS time.

14. See *The Circle of Life* in the sit-down theater on the upper floor to the right.

15. Go back downstairs and see the *Food Rocks* sit-down show.

16. Exit The Land Pavilion and turn right to the Imagination! Pavilion. Spend 20 minutes or so in the *ImageWorks* interactive playground.

17. If you have more than 30 minutes before your dinner priority seating reservations, go back through Innoventions East Side and turn right to ride *Spaceship Earth* if you wish, or spend some time with the interactive exhibits in the Wonders of Life Pavilion.

Check the Tip Board in Innoventions Plaza for approximate attraction wait times (it's not always accurate).

18.   Keep your priority seating reservations for dinner. If you don't have reservations, eat at the Food Court in The Land Pavilion or one of the restaurants in Innoventions. If you have time before dinner, enjoy the water ballet at the huge Fountain of Nations between the Innoventions buildings. The water dances to music every 15 minutes.

19.   Visit Innoventions East Side or West.

20.   Claim a viewing spot for the *IllumiNations* fireworks display 30 minutes before show time, which is usually 9:00 p.m. If you want to leave quickly through the front entrance after the show, find an open spot near the water along the wide promenade between Future World and World Showcase. If you can linger after the show or if you're leaving Epcot through the rear entrance, seek less congested areas along the waterfront in Italy, between Morocco and France, or on the bridges between France and the United Kingdom.

Tip: If you feel a steady, strong wind, choose a spot where the wind is not directly in your face to avoid smoke from the fireworks.

Adults and Teens
Day Two Plan for Early Entry Days

(WDW property guests only)

Consider skipping the afternoon break today to spend more time in the countries of World Showcase. Consult your Times Guide early in the day for any outdoor or stage performances or parades that interest you and work them into the touring plan.

1.   Ask a Disney attendant what attractions are open for Early Entry guests (this list changes periodically). Then make priority seating reservations for lunch and dinner if you need them (see above).

2.   Ride *Spaceship Earth*. Spend a short while with the exhibits at the exit.

3.   Walk into Innoventions Plaza and through Innoventions West Side on your right. Veer left toward the tall pyramids (Imagination! Pavilion) and see *Honey, I Shrunk the Audience* (avoid the first few rows). At the exit, spend 10 minutes or so enjoying the "jumping

fountains" outside.

Alternative: If this side of Future World is not open for Early Entry, ride *Mission: SPACE* and *Test Track* (get a FASTPASS for one of them if the lines are long.) Then ride *Spaceship Earth* and/or *Body Wars*. Be sure to use the *Test Track* singles line to your advantage. *Caution: Body Wars* is an exhilarating but rough simulator ride. Be prepared. Take a motion sickness remedy before coming to the park if you need to.

4. Get some light refreshments at the Food Court in The Land Pavilion (or at the "Pure and Simple" food area in the Wonders of Life Pavilion). Carry them with you back through Innoventions Plaza. Stroll across to the opposite Innoventions walkway and line up at the rope. When the rope drops at the official opening time, or if the rope is already down, proceed to step 2 or 3 below. Skip any attractions you've already experienced today.

Adults and Teens
Day Two Plan for Non Early Entry Days

1. Ask the turnstile attendant if *Test Track* and *Mission: SPACE* will open immediately, then make lunch and dinner priority seating reservations at Guest Relations if you need them (see above).

2. Go to the walkway through Innoventions East Side. When the rope is down, continue through and get a FASTPASS for either *Mission: SPACE* or *Test Track* (follow the crowd) if they are open and then ride the other. Or use the singles line at *Test Track* if it is crowded. If they aren't yet open, come back and ride them after step 3.

3. Cross back through the Innoventions buildings and bear left to the Imagination! Pavilion. See *Honey, I Shrunk the Audience* (avoid the first few rows). Use FASTPASS if the wait is too long. At the exit, spend 10 minutes or so enjoying the "jumping fountains."

4. Check your Times Guide to see if the *JAMMitors* are performing. If exact showtimes aren't listed, ask a cast member near Innoventions Plaza when the *JAMMitors* will be entertaining. Try to catch a show.

5. After their show, cross back through the Innoventions buildings to the east side of Future World. Veer left to the Wonders of Life Pavilion and ride *Body Wars*.

Caution: Body Wars is an exhilarating but rough simulator ride. Be prepared. Take a motion sickness remedy before coming to the park if you need to.

6.   Explore the interactive exhibits inside the Wonders of Life Pavilion.

7.   Exit left from the Wonders of Life and walk past *Test Track* onto the bridges to World Showcase, which usually opens at 11:00 a.m. When the opening rope drops or if it's already down, walk to Mexico and explore the pavilion.

8.   Go to your lunch restaurant if you have 11:30 a.m. priority seating times. If you have no reservations, try fast food at Cantina de San Angel in Mexico or the Kringla Bakeri og Kafe in Norway.

9.   Walk to Norway and explore.

10. Go next to China and watch the movie *Wonders of China*. After the film, visit the exhibits.

11. Consider returning to your hotel for a rest or swim. If you leave via the front exit, walk to the end of Innoventions West Side to enjoy exotic refreshment, soft drinks from foreign countries at Ice Station Cool (they're free!). Have your hands stamped at the exit for re-entry and keep any parking receipts.

     Alternative: If you're not staying on property or if you can't bring yourself to leave the park, find a resting spot (such as the small park at the rear of the United Kingdom) to park yourself for a respite and maybe a nap.

     During your break, consult your Times Guide for any performances or parades you may want to see.

12. Return to Epcot at around 3:00 p.m. Go to Germany and browse the shops. Spend a few minutes at the elaborate outdoor miniature G scale train on the right side of the pavilion.

13. Next stop is Italy. Enjoy the shops and the decor.

14. Go left to the America Pavilion. Check your Times Guide for the next performance of the singing group *Voices of Liberty* or one of the other a cappella groups. They sing inside the main building at the entrance to the show *The American Adventure*. The main show is a must (sit toward the front of the auditorium), but try to find time for the singers, too, if possible. If you have time before the shows (or after the shows), grab some refreshments from the outside vendors or at the Liberty Inn on the left side of the pavilion.

15. Walk to Japan and wander among the beautiful gardens and streams. Visit the exhibit in the gallery.

16. Honor your priority seating reservations for dinner. If you have

no reservations, try the Yakitori House fast food in Japan, Tangier-ine Cafe in Morocco, fish and chips in the United Kingdom, or the Food Court in The Land Pavilion.

17. Go next to Morocco and stroll through the shops.

18. Walk left to France and see the movie *Impressions de France*. This theater has comfortable seats. Wander around France after the movie, and enjoy any outdoor or stage performances you can conveniently work in to your touring schedule (check your Times Guide for times).

If you're a natural ham, volunteer for the audience participation comedy show with the World Showcase Players.

19. Go next to the United Kingdom. Wander through the shops and gardens. The musical show in the park at the rear of the pavilion is entertaining (check your Times Guide for times). If you're thirsty for a beer, order one at the Rose & Crown pub.

20. Walk next door to Canada and see the movie *O Canada!* After the show, stroll along the streams and gardens.

21. Consult your Times Guide for any outdoor performances or parades in World Showcase or Future World that you may still want to see.

22. You have a few more options now: Spend as much time as you want at the exhibits in the Innoventions buildings; explore the *Global Neighborhood* exhibits at the exit of *Spaceship Earth*, see the movie *The Making of Me* in the Wonders of Life Pavilion (it sometimes closes at 7:00 p.m.); shop in World Showcase or Future World, or revisit any attractions you want, if they have a short wait.

23. Claim a viewing spot for the *IllumiNations* fireworks display 30 minutes before show time, which is usually 9:00 p.m. If you want to leave quickly through the front entrance after the show, find an open spot near the water along the wide promenade between Future World and World Showcase. If you can linger after the show or if you're leaving Epcot through the rear entrance, seek less congested areas along the waterfront in Italy, between Morocco and France, or on the bridges between France and the United Kingdom.
Tip: If you feel a steady, strong wind, choose a spot where the wind is not directly in your face, so you can avoid smoke from the fireworks.

Two-Day Touring Plans for Families with Children

(See "A Special Note on Early Entry," page 51.)

Note: Be sure to check the entrance, arrival, priority seating, and other important recommendations on pages 138 to 140 before you start your tour.

These plans assume you will arrive at or before opening time. If you want to sleep in, simply pick up the touring plan several steps down to match your arrival time. Later in the day, use FASTPASS or the singles line option (if available) to minimize waits at crowded attractions. Bear the following in mind:

• I consider a wait of more than 15 to 20 minutes "too long."

• Because guests generally take advantage of the Early Entry privilege (when available) only once at each park — or want to do the same popular rides again if they do two Early Entry days — the Early Entry touring plans are virtually the same for Days One and Two. I include them under both days so that you don't have to flip back and forth in your book.

• Most of the attractions in Future World lie east (to your left from the front entrance) and west of *Spaceship Earth* and Innoventions Plaza. Only one side may be open early in the day. Thus the alternatives offered in the touring plans that follow.

Families with Children Day One Plan for Early Entry Days

(WDW property guests only)

1. Rent strollers if necessary. You'll find them on the left (east) side of the main entrance plaza near *Spaceship Earth* and on the left side of the rear entrance plaza.

2. Ask a Disney attendant what attractions are open for Early Entry guests (this list changes periodically) and then quickly visit Guest Relations to make your priority seating reservations for lunch and dinner if you haven't already done so (see above).

3. Walk into Innoventions Plaza and through Innoventions West Side on your right. Then veer left toward the tall pyramids (Imagina-

tion! Pavilion) and see *Honey, I Shrunk the Audience* (avoid the first few rows). Don't dally at the exit; the unusual water effects here can be enjoyed later.

Caution: This 3-D show has a few loud, convincing special effects that may frighten young children.

4. Ride *Spaceship Earth*. Don't dally at the exhibits at the exit.

5. Walk to your left to The Land Pavilion. Enjoy the *Living with the Land* ride. (Get a FASTPASS if the wait is too long.)

    Alternative: If the west (right) side of Future World is not open for Early Entry, head left and get a FASTPASS for *Mission: SPACE* or *Test Track* (switching off is available), then ride the other, followed by *Spaceship Earth*. If time allows, ride *Body Wars* or *Universe of Energy*.

    Height/fright alert: *Body Wars* and *Test Track* are too intense for many small children. Switching off is available at both rides. Kids have to be 40" or taller to ride either one.

6. Get some light refreshments at the Food Court in The Land Pavilion (or at the "Pure and Simple" food area in the Wonders of Life Pavilion). Carry them with you back through Innoventions Plaza. Stroll across to the opposite Innoventions walkway and line up at the rope. When the rope drops at the official opening time, or if the rope is already down, proceed to step 3 or 4 below. Skip any attractions you've already experienced today.

Families with Children
Day One Plan for Non Early Entry Days

1. Rent strollers if necessary. They are on the left (east) side of the main entrance plaza near *Spaceship Earth* and on the left side of the rear entrance plaza.

2. Ask the turnstile attendant if *Mission: SPACE* and *Test Track* will open immediately, then quickly make your priority seating reservations for lunch and dinner if you don't have them (see above).

3. Go to the walkway through Innoventions East Side. When the rope is down, continue through to get a FASTPASS for *Mission: SPACE* or *Test Track* (follow the crowd) if they are open. Then ride the other one. If they are not yet open, come back and ride them after step 5.

    Height/fright alert: *Test Track* can be too intense for small children; switching off is available. Kids must be 40" or taller to ride.

4. Cross back through Innoventions East Side and West and bear left to the Imagination! Pavilion. See *Honey, I Shrunk the Audience* (avoid the first few rows). Use FASTPASS if eligible if the wait is too long. Don't dally at the exit; the unusual water effects here can be enjoyed later.

   Caution: This 3-D show has a few loud and convincing special effects that may frighten young children.

5. Walk to your left and experience the *Journey Into Imagination with Figment* ride.

   Tip: Take off your hat before the ride!

6. Cross back through the Innoventions buildings to the east side of Future World. Veer left to the Wonders of Life Pavilion and enjoy *Cranium Command*.

7. If the time is 10:30 a.m. or before, see the movie *The Making of Me* or ride *Body Wars* in the Wonders of Life Pavilion.

   Height/fright alert: Kids must be 40" or taller to ride *Body Wars* and able to handle a rough simulator ride; switching off is available.

8. Exit left from the Wonders of Life Pavilion and walk past *Test Track* onto the bridges to World Showcase. (These bridges pass around the Odyssey Center building.) Once on the bridges, keep left to access the bridge to Mexico. The World Showcase usually opens at 11:00 a.m. When the opening rope drops, or if it's already down, walk fast past Mexico to the Norway Pavilion and ride *Maelstrom*. (Use FASTPASS if the wait is already too long.) Watch the Norway film at the end if your kids are up for a movie. Otherwise, walk through the theater to the exit.

9. Go to your lunch restaurant if you have 11:30 a.m. priority seating. If you have no reservations, try fast food at Cantina de San Angel at the Mexico Pavilion. Or try to get seated anyway at Restaurant Akershus in Norway (if you like seafood); it is not always fully booked.

10. Exit and head for *El Rio del Tiempo* in the Mexico Pavilion. The ride entrance is in the far left corner of the interior plaza. Then check out the *Kidcot Fun Stop* in Mexico if your kids are interested.

    Note: There's a *Kidcot Fun Stop* in every country in World Showcase, but they may not open until 1:00 p.m. or so.

11. Head back to your hotel for a rest or swim. If you leave World Showcase via the central bridge in front of Showcase Plaza, your kids will pass by an interactive fountain on their left. If you're

prepared, let the kids go crazy and get soaked! Dry them off, then walk to Ice Station Cool at the end of Innoventions West Side and enjoy free exotic soft drinks from foreign countries before you leave the park. Have your hands stamped at the exit for re-entry and keep any parking or stroller receipts.

Caution: The temperature of the entrance walkway to Ice Station Cool is quite cool; you're likely to feel chilly if you're wet.

Alternative: If you're not staying on property or you can't bring yourself to leave the park, find a resting spot (such as the small park in France behind the shops) to park your family for a respite and maybe even naps for the kids.

12. Return to Epcot at about 3:00 p.m. and retrieve strollers if necessary. Get a FASTPASS for *Living with the Land*, then walk to The Living Seas Pavilion and enjoy the show, ride, and exhibits.

    Tip: When you enter the sit-down theater for the show, hold back and then sit on the far right of the benches, so you can be among the first on the elevators (stand toward the rear) and subsequent ride to the exhibits.

13. Walk toward Innoventions West Side. Before reaching Innoventions, turn to your right and enjoy the "talking drinking fountains" in front of the nearby restrooms. Now cross through both Innoventions buildings and turn left to *Universe of Energy*. Enjoy the show.

    Tip: Stand near the left front entry door in the pre-show area. When the doors open, walk to the front row of the front car on your left for the best vantage point.

14. Cross through the Innoventions buildings and walk to The Land Pavilion. Enjoy the *Living with the Land* ride if you haven't already. Or ride it at your FASTPASS time.

15. See *The Circle of Life* in the sit-down theater on the upper floor to the right.

16. Go back downstairs and see the *Food Rocks* sit-down show.

17. Exit The Land Pavilion and turn right to the Imagination! Pavilion. Spend 20 minutes in the *ImageWorks* interactive playground, then enjoy the "jumping fountains" area outside the pavilion.

18. If you have more than 30 minutes before your dinner priority seating reservations, go back through Innoventions East Side and turn right to ride *Spaceship Earth*. Check the Tip Board in Innoventions Plaza for approximate attraction wait times (it's not always accurate).

If you've already been on *Spaceship Earth,* turn left from the *Universe of Energy* and spend some time with the interactive exhibits in the Wonders of Life Pavilion.

19. Keep your priority seating reservations for dinner. If you don't have reservations, eat at the Food Court in The Land Pavilion or at one of the restaurants in Innoventions. If you have time before dinner, enjoy the water ballet at the huge Fountain of Nations between the Innoventions buildings. The water dances to music every 15 minutes.

20. Visit Innoventions East Side or West. The video games (no charge!) are in the West Side building, and you'll find other interactive kid-friendly games in the East Side building.

21. Claim a viewing spot for the *IllumiNations* fireworks display 30 minutes before show time, which is usually 9:00 p.m. If you want to leave quickly through the front entrance after the show, find an open spot near the water along the wide promenade between Future World and World Showcase. If you can linger after the show, or if you're leaving Epcot through the rear entrance, seek less congested areas along the waterfront in Italy, between Morocco and France, or on the bridges between France and the United Kingdom.

Tip: If you feel a steady, strong wind, choose a spot where the wind is not directly in your face to avoid fireworks smoke.

Families with Children
Day Two Plan for Early Entry Days

(WDW property guests only)

Note: Consider skipping the afternoon break today (or simply resting in the park for a while) so that you can spend more time in the countries of World Showcase and include *Kidcot Fun Stops* and passport signings for the kids (see step 7 of the "Non Early Entry Plan" below). Also, be sure to consult your Times Guide early in the day for any outdoor shows, stage performances, parades, or character greetings you want to work in.

1. Rent strollers if necessary, on the left (east) side of the main entrance plaza near *Spaceship Earth* or on the left side of the rear entrance plaza.

2. Ask a Disney attendant what attractions are open for Early Entry

guests (this list changes periodically), then quickly make any priority seating reservations you may need at Guest Relations.

3.   Ride *Spaceship Earth*. If your kids are interested, spend a short while with the exhibits at the exit.

4.   Walk into Innoventions Plaza and through Innoventions West Side on your right. Then veer left toward the tall pyramids (Imagination! Pavilion) and see *Honey, I Shrunk the Audience* (avoid the first few rows). At the exit, spend 10 minutes or so enjoying the "jumping fountains."

   Caution: This 3-D show has a few loud special effects that may frighten some young children.

   Alternative: If the west (right) side of Future World is not open for Early Entry, get a FASTPASS for either *Test Track* or *Mission: SPACE*, then ride the other, followed by *Spaceship Earth* and/or *Body Wars*. Otherwise, have fun with the interactive exhibits in the Wonders of Life Pavilion or in one of the Innoventions buildings.

   Caution: Test Track and *Body Wars* can be too intense for small children. Kids must be at least 40" tall to ride either one. Switching off is available at both rides.

5.   Get some light refreshments at the Food Court in The Land Pavilion (or at the "Pure and Simple" food area in the Wonders of Life Pavilion). Carry them with you back through Innoventions Plaza. Stroll across to the opposite Innoventions walkway and line up at the rope. When the rope drops at the official opening time, or if the rope is already down, proceed to step 3 or 4 below. Skip any attractions you've already experienced today.

Families with Children
Day Two Plan for Non Early Entry Days

1.   Rent strollers if necessary, on the left (east) side of the main entrance plaza near *Spaceship Earth* or on the left side of the rear entrance plaza.

2.   Ask the turnstile attendant if *Test Track* and *Mission: SPACE* will open immediately and quickly make any priority seating reservations you may need (see above) at Guest Relations.

3.   Go to the walkway through Innoventions East Side. When the rope is down, continue through to get a FASTPASS for either *Mission:*

SPACE or *Test Track* (follow the crowd) if they are open. Then ride the other one. If they are still closed, come back and ride them after step 4.

Height/fright alert: Test Track can be too intense for small children; switching off is available. Kids must be 40" or taller to ride.

4. Cross back through Innoventions East Side and West Side and bear left to the Imagination! Pavilion. See *Honey, I Shrunk the Audience* (avoid the first few rows). Get a FASTPASS if eligible if the wait is too long. At the exit, spend 10 minutes or so enjoying the "jumping fountains."

   Caution: This 3-D show has a few loud, convincing special effects that may frighten some young children.

5. Check your Times Guide to see if the *JAMMitors* are performing. If exact show times aren't listed, try to find out from a cast member near Innoventions.

6. After their show, cross back through the Innoventions buildings to the east side of Future World. Veer left to the Wonders of Life Pavilion. If the time is 10:30 a.m. or before, see the movie *The Making of Me* or ride *Body Wars*. Afterwards, explore the shows and interactive exhibits inside the pavilion.

   Height/fright alert: To ride *Body Wars*, kids must be 40" or taller and able to handle a rough simulator ride; switching off is available.

7. If your kids enjoyed the World Showcase on the first day, consider buying them "passports" ($9.95 each) to add to their fun today. Ask an employee in the Wonders of Life Pavilion where the passports can be purchased or buy them in any World Showcase country.

8. Exit left from the Wonders of Life Pavilion and walk past *Test Track* onto the bridges to World Showcase, which usually opens at 11:00 a.m. When the opening rope drops, or if it's already down, walk to Mexico to get the passports signed and stamped. Then go to Norway and climb on the ship on the left side of the pavilion. The kids can get their passports signed and stamped and have some interactive fun at the *Kidcot Fun Stop* in Norway if it's open.

9. Go to your lunch restaurant if you have 11:30 a.m. priority seating times. If you have no reservations, try fast food at Cantina de San Angel in Mexico or the Kringla Bakeri og Kafe in Norway.

10. Return to your hotel for a rest or swim. On your way out the main entrance, walk to the end of Innoventions West Side to enjoy exotic (free) soft drinks from foreign countries at Ice Station Cool. Have your hands stamped at the exit for re-entry and keep any

parking and stroller receipts.

Alternative: If you're not staying on property or if you can't bring yourself to leave the park, find a resting spot (such as the small park at the rear of the United Kingdom) to park your family for a respite and maybe even naps for the kids.

11. Return to Epcot at about 3:00 p.m. and retrieve strollers if necessary. Walk to China to begin the passport and *Kidcot Fun Stop* rounds. In Germany, spend a few minutes at the elaborate outdoor miniature G scale train on the right side of the pavilion. Make stops in any or all of the following countries (depending on your and your kids' stamina):

At the rear of the plaza above the restaurant entrance is an elaborate glockenspiel, which chimes on the hour.

Italy, America, Japan, Morocco, France, the United Kingdom, and Canada. Shop whenever you feel the urge. If your kids are interested, check your Times Guide for character greeting times in these countries.

Note: The movies in World Showcase are not included in this touring plan because they're not generally popular with children.

12. Consult your Times Guide for any other outdoor performances, stage performances, or parades you may want to see in World Showcase or Future World. Imaginum (Living Statues) in France and the acrobats in China are worthwhile shows.

13. Interrupt the *Fun Stop* tour for any priority dinner seating reservations you hold. If you have no reservations, try the Tangierine Cafe in Morocco or fish and chips in the United Kingdom.

14. After dinner, check out the United Kingdom musical show in the park at the rear of the UK Pavilion; your Times Guide lists show times. Then complete the *Fun Stop* and passport tour of any remaining countries your kids want to visit.

Note: The *Fun Stops* often close at 8:00 p.m.

15. Spend time before the *IllumiNations* fireworks display with the Innoventions exhibits. If you don't want to see *IllumiNations* a second time, finish your stay in Epcot at Innoventions. Some folks can easily spend 30 to 60 minutes or more there. Also check out the *Global Neighborhood* (behind *Spaceship Earth*) which is open during *IllumiNations*.

Two-Day Touring Plans for Seniors

(See "A Special Note on Early Entry," page 51.)

Note: Be sure to check the entrance, arrival, priority seating, and other important recommendations on pages 138 to140 before you start. These plans include no fast, scary, or spinning rides. If you enjoy such attractions, follow the two-day touring plan for adults and teens.

These plans assume you will arrive at or before opening time. If you want to sleep in, simply pick up the touring plan several steps down to match your arrival time. Later in the day, use FASTPASS or the singles line option (if available) to minimize waits at crowded attractions. Bear the following in mind:

• I consider a wait of more than 15 to 20 minutes "too long."

• Because guests generally take advantage of the Early Entry privilege (when available) only once at each park — or want to do the same popular rides again if they do two Early Entry days — the Early Entry touring plans are virtually the same for Days One and Two. I include them under both days so that you don't have to flip back and forth in your book. I also anticipate that you will probably take a more leisurely pace on one day than the other. So steps two through five of the non Early Entry plans are similar to allow choices.

• Most of the attractions in Future World lie east (to your left from the front entrance) and west of *Spaceship Earth* and Innoventions Plaza. Only one side may be open early in the day. Thus the alternatives offered in the touring plans that follow.

Seniors
Day One Plan for Early Entry Days

(WDW property guests only)
1. Head for Guest Relations to make priority seating reservations for lunch and dinner if you don't yet have them (see above).
2. Ride *Spaceship Earth*. Don't dally at the exhibits at the exit. Ask a Disney attendant what other attractions are open for Early Entry guests (this list changes periodically).

3. Walk into Innoventions Plaza and through Innoventions West Side on your right. Then veer left toward the tall pyramids (Imagination! Pavilion) and see *Honey, I Shrunk the Audience* (avoid the first few rows). Don't dally at the exit; the unusual water effects here can be enjoyed later.

4. Walk to your left to The Land Pavilion. Enjoy the *Living with the Land* ride. Get a FASTPASS if the wait is too long.
    Alternative: If the west (right) side of Future World is not open for Early Entry substitute *Universe of Energy, Mission: SPACE,* or *Cranium Command* (in the Wonders of Life Pavilion) for the attractions in steps 3 and 4. (Use FASTPASS if available and if necessary.)

5. Get some light refreshments at the Food Court in The Land Pavilion (or at the "Pure and Simple" food area in the Wonders of Life Pavilion). Carry them with you back through Innoventions Plaza. Stroll across to the opposite Innoventions walkway and line up at the rope. When the rope drops at the official opening time, or if the rope is already down, proceed to step 3 or 4 below, depending on what was open early. Skip any attractions you've already experienced today.

Seniors
Day One Plan for Non Early Entry Days:

1. Make your priority seating reservations for lunch and dinner if you haven't already done so (see above).

2. Ride *Spaceship Earth*. Don't dally at the exhibits at the exit.

3. If you're up for it, ride *Mission: SPACE*. Get a FASTPASS (if available) if the wait is too long.

4. Walk back through Innoventions West Side and bear left to the Imagination! Pavilion. See *Honey, I Shrunk the Audience* (avoid the first few rows). Don't dally at the exit; the unusual water effects here can be enjoyed later.

5. Walk to your left and experience the *Journey Into Imagination with Figment* ride.
    Tip: Take off your hat before the ride!

6. Cross back through the Innoventions buildings to the east side of Future World. Veer left to the Wonders of Life Pavilion and enjoy the *Cranium Command* show.

7. Exit left from the Wonders of Life Pavilion and walk past *Test Track* onto the bridges to World Showcase. (These bridges pass around the Odyssey Center building.) Once on the bridges, keep left to access the bridge to Mexico. The World Showcase usually opens at 11:00 a.m.

    Make same-day reservations at the Green Thumb Emporium for a one-hour guided tour of The Land greenhouses (adults about $6, kids, $4).

    When the opening rope drops, or if it's already down, walk past the Mexico Pavilion to the Norway Pavilion and ride *Maelstrom.* Use FASTPASS if the wait is too long. Enjoy the Norway film at the end.

8. Exit and head for your lunch restaurant if you have 11:30 a.m. priority seating times. If you have no reservations, try fast food at Cantina de San Angel at the Mexico Pavilion. Or try for a table at Restaurant Akershus in Norway (if you like seafood); it's not always booked up.

9. After lunch, ride *El Rio del Tiempo* in the Mexico Pavilion. The ride entrance is at the far left corner of the interior plaza.

10. Return to your hotel for a rest or swim. If you leave via the front exit, walk to the end of Innoventions West Side to enjoy exotic soft drinks from foreign lands at Ice Station Cool (the drinks are free!). Have your hands stamped at the exit for re-entry and keep any parking receipts.

    Alternative: If you're not staying on property or if you can't bring yourself to leave the park, find a resting spot (such as the small alcove in France behind the shops) for a respite and maybe a nap.

11. Return to Epcot at about 3:00 p.m. Get a FASTPASS for *Living with the Land,* then walk to The Living Seas Pavilion and enjoy the show, ride, and exhibits.

    Tip: When you enter the sit-down theater for the show, hold back and then sit on the far right of the benches, so you can be among the first on the elevators (stand toward the rear) and subsequent ride to the exhibits.

12. Walk toward Innoventions West Side. Before reaching Innoventions, turn to your right and enjoy the "talking drinking fountains" in front of the nearby restrooms.

13. Now cross through both Innoventions buildings and turn left to the *Universe of Energy.* Enjoy the show.

Tip: Stand near the left front entry door in the pre-show area. When the doors open, walk to the front row of the front car on your left for the best vantage point.

14. Cross through the Innoventions buildings and walk to The Land Pavilion. Enjoy the *Living with the Land* ride if you haven't already. Or ride it at your FASTPASS time.

15. See *The Circle of Life* in the sit-down theater on the upper floor to the right.

16. Go back downstairs and see the *Food Rocks* sit-down show.

17. Exit The Land Pavilion and turn right to the Imagination! Pavilion. Spend 20 minutes or so in the *ImageWorks* interactive playground for adults and kids.

18. If you have more than 30 minutes before your dinner priority seating reservations, go back through Innoventions East Side and turn right to ride *Spaceship Earth*. Check the Tip Board in Innoventions Plaza for approximate attraction wait times (it's not always accurate). If you've already been on *Spaceship Earth*, turn left from *Universe of Energy* and spend some time with the interactive exhibits in the Wonders of Life Pavilion.

19. Keep your priority seating reservations for dinner. If you don't have reservations, eat at the Food Court in The Land Pavilion or at one of the restaurants in Innoventions.

    Note: If you have time before dinner, enjoy the water ballet at the huge Fountain of Nations between the Innoventions buildings. The water dances to music every 15 minutes.

20. Visit one of the Innoventions buildings and enjoy the exhibits.

21. Claim a viewing spot for the *IllumiNations* fireworks display 30 minutes before show time, which is usually 9:00 p.m. If you want to leave quickly through the front entrance after the show, find an open spot near the water along the wide promenade between Future World and World Showcase. If you can linger after the show or if you're leaving Epcot through the rear entrance, seek less congested areas along the waterfront in Italy, between Morocco and France, or on the bridges between France and the United Kingdom.

    Tip: If you feel a steady, strong wind, choose a spot where the wind is not directly in your face to avoid smoke from the fireworks.

Seniors
Day Two Plan for Early Entry Days

(WDW property guests only)

Note: Consider skipping the afternoon break today to spend more time in the countries of World Showcase. Consult your Times Guide for any outdoor or stage performances or parades that interest you and fit them in to the touring plan. Remember, most of the attractions in Future World lie east (to your left from the front entrance) and west of *Spaceship Earth* and Innoventions Plaza. Only one side may be open during the Early Entry period. Thus the alternatives offered in the touring plans below.

1. Make priority seating reservations for lunch and dinner if you haven't already done so (see above).

2. Ride *Spaceship Earth*. Spend a short while with the exhibits at the exit.

3. Next walk into Innoventions Plaza and on through Innoventions West Side on your right. Then veer left toward the tall pyramids (Imagination! Pavilion) and see *Honey, I Shrunk the Audience* (avoid the first few rows). At the exit, spend 10 minutes or so enjoying the "jumping fountains."

    Alternative: If this side of Future World is not open for Early Entry, substitute *The Making of Me* show at the Wonders of Life Pavilion for step 3.

4. Get some light refreshments at the Food Court in The Land Pavilion (or at the "Pure and Simple" food area in the Wonders of Life Pavilion). Carry them with you back through Innoventions Plaza. Stroll across to the opposite Innoventions walkway and line up at the rope. When the rope drops at the official opening time, or if the rope is already down, proceed to step 3 or 4 below. Skip any attractions you've already experienced today or yesterday (unless you want to enjoy them again).

Seniors
Day Two Plan for Non Early Entry Days

1. Make priority seating reservations if you need them (see above).
2. Ride *Spaceship Earth*. Spend a short while with the exhibits at the exit.

3. If you're up for it, ride *Mission: SPACE*. Get a FASTPASS (if available) if the wait is too long.

4. Cross back through the Innoventions buildings and bear left to the Imagination! Pavilion. See *Honey, I Shrunk the Audience* (avoid the first few rows). At the exit, spend 10 minutes or so enjoying the "jumping fountains".

5. Enjoy *Journey Into Imagination with Figment*. Take off your hat before the ride!

6. Check your Times Guide to see if the *JAMMitors* are performing. If so, see them now. If exact show times aren't listed, try to find out from a cast member near Innoventions.

7. After the show, spend some time in the Innoventions buildings.

8. Next, cross to the east side of Future World. Veer left to the Wonders of Life Pavilion to see *The Making of Me* movie and explore the interactive exhibits inside.

9. Exit left from the Wonders of Life Pavilion. Walk past *Test Track* onto the bridges to World Showcase, which usually opens at 11:00 a.m. When the opening rope drops, or if it's already down, walk to Mexico and explore the pavilion.

10. Exit and go to your lunch restaurant if you have 11:30 a.m. priority seating times. If you have no reservations, try fast food at Cantina de San Angel in Mexico or the Kringla Bakeri og Kafe in Norway.

11. After lunch explore Norway.

12. Go next to China and watch the movie *Wonders of China*. After the film, visit the exhibits.

13. Consider returning to your hotel for a rest or swim. If you leave via the front exit, walk to the end of Innoventions West Side for a round of exotic soft drinks from foreign countries served free at Ice Station Cool. Have your hands stamped at the exit for re-entry and keep any parking receipts.
    Alternative: If you're not staying on property or if you can't bring yourself to leave the park, find a resting spot (such as the small park at the rear of the United Kingdom) for a respite and maybe a little nap. Check your Times Guide for shows or parades.

14. Return to Epcot at around 3:00 p.m. Go to Germany and browse the shops. Spend a few minutes at the elaborate, outdoor miniature (G scale) train on the right side of the pavilion.

15. Your next stop is Italy. Enjoy the shops and the decor.

16. Exit left to the America Pavilion. Check your Times Guide for the next performance of the singing group *Voices of Liberty* or one of

the other a cappella groups. They sing inside the main building at the entrance to the show, *The American Adventure*. The main show is a must (sit toward the front of the auditorium), but try to find time for the singers, too. If you have time before the shows (or after the shows), grab some refreshments from the outside vendors (or at the Liberty Inn on the left side of the pavilion).

17. Walk to Japan and wander among the beautiful gardens and streams. Visit the exhibit in the gallery.

18. Go on to Morocco and stroll through the shops.

19. Honor your priority seating reservations for dinner. If you have no reservations, try the Yakitori House fast food in Japan, the Tangierine Cafe in Morocco or fish and chips in the United Kingdom.

20. Exit left and walk to France. See the movie *Impressions de France*, where you can sink into comfortable theater seats.

21. Wander around France after the movie, and enjoy any outdoor or stage performances you can conveniently catch (check the performance schedules in your Times Guide).

> *If you like to be in the spotlight, volunteer for the audience participation comedy show with Cyranose de Bergerac.*

22. Visit the United Kingdom. Wander through the shops and gardens. If you're thirsty for a beer, order one at the Rose & Crown pub.

23. Walk next door to Canada and watch the movie *O Canada!* After the show, stroll along the streams and gardens.

24. If the timing is right, enjoy any outdoor performances in World Showcase or Future World that catch your interest (check your Times Guide for show times). Some options that are worth your while are the acrobats in China, musicians in Italy, the Fife and Drum Corps in the America Pavilion, Matsuriza drumming in Japan, and the Statue Act in France.

25. After the performance(s), you'll have to make some choices. In the time remaining before the *IllumiNations* fireworks, you can explore the exhibits in either the Innoventions buildings or the *Global Neighborhood* at the exit of *Spaceship Earth*. Or shop. If you saw the fireworks last night and don't want to see them again, you can leave Epcot during the show to beat the crowds or continue to enjoy the exhibits and shops. *Global Neighborhood* remains

open during *IllumiNations*.

26.   If you haven't yet seen *IllumiNations* (or want to see it again), claim your viewing spot 30 minutes before show time, which is usually 9:00 p.m. If you want to leave through the front entrance immediately after the show, find an open spot near the water along the wide promenade between Future World and World Showcase. If you can linger after the show or if you're leaving Epcot through the rear entrance, seek less congested areas along the waterfront in Italy, between Morocco and France, or on the bridges between France and the United Kingdom.

Tip: If you feel a steady, strong wind, choose a spot where the wind is not directly in your face to avoid smoke from the fireworks.

CHAPTER FOUR:

Disney-
MGM Studios

Disney-MGM Studios is a combination theme park and working movie and television production facility. It's filled with exciting rides, stellar shows, and entertaining tours. As you approach the entry turnstiles, the architecture, overhead music, and Art Deco colors create the illusion that you are walking onto a Hollywood movie set of the past. Perhaps that's one reason why repeat visitors tend to refer to the park as "the Studios."

Attractions Described & Rated

"Disney's The Hunchback of Notre Dame" — A Musical Adventure

Rating: * * * *
Type: Outdoor live musical show
Time: 32 - 34 minutes
Steve says: Great show, picturesque sets and costumes

The Backlot Theater hosts this live performance based on the Disney animated movie. A colorful troupe of gypsies relates the story of Quasimodo and Esmeralda with music, puppets, and dance. Victor, Hugo, and Laverne are amusing gargoyles who serve as Quasimodo's conscience. During the show, characters come down into the audience.

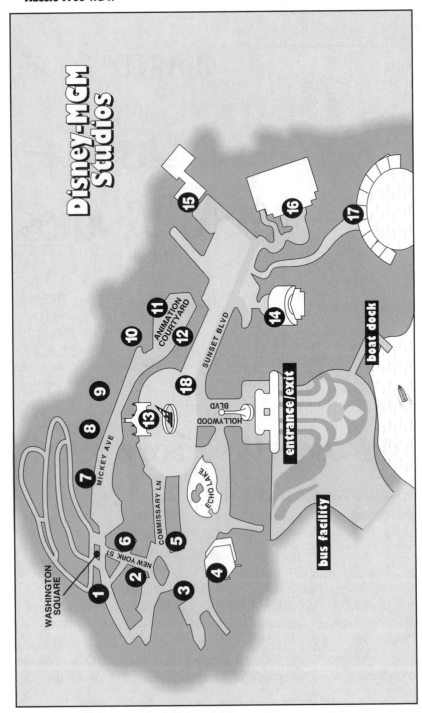

Disney-MGM Studios

1. Disney's The Hunchback of Notre Dame
2. Jim Henson's MuppetVision 3D
3. Star Tours
4. Indiana Jones™ Epic Stunt Spectacular
5. Sounds Dangerous — Starring Drew Carey
6. "Honey, I Shrunk the Kids" Movie Set Adventure
7. Disney-MGM Studios Backlot Tour
8. Backstage Pass
9. Who Wants to Be a Millionaire — Play It!
10. Voyage of The Little Mermaid
11. The Magic of Disney Animation
12. Playhouse Disney — Live on Stage!
13. The Great Movie Ride
14. Beauty and the Beast
15. Rock 'n' Roller Coaster Starring Aerosmith
16. The Twilight Zone Tower of Terror™
17. Fantasmic!
18. Guest Information Board

Note: The theater is covered by a canopy but can become very hot in the afternoon during warmer months. It is located past *Jim Henson's MuppetVision 3D* attraction and one block to the left of the Washington Square monument arch. The show may not run every day; consult your Times Guide.

Jim Henson's MuppetVision 3D

Rating: ★ ★ ★ ★
Type: 3-D movie in a sit-down theater
Time: About 18 minutes
Steve says: A real gas, from start to finish

This show is a convincing 3D movie with special effects added inside the theater. The comedy stars the Muppets (on-screen and live) and an odd prankster called "The Spirit of 3D," a creation of the Muppet Labs' Dr. Bunsen Honeydew. Miss Piggy performs a romantic solo, which is turned into a hilarious fiasco by Bean Bunny. The jokes and one-liners are plentiful. Thanks to a short pre-show on TV monitors (mounted in a large room outside the main theater), you'll be laughing even before you sit down.

Note: This attraction is located under the big green and yellow Kermit balloon. To get to the entrance, cross New York Street in front of the Empire State Building facade and walk past the Miss Piggy fountain.

Caution: Lines can get long at midday, and cannon shots and fireworks in the theater are loud enough to shock toddlers.

Star Tours

Rating: ★ ★ ★ ★ ★
Type: Flight simulator thrill ride
Time: 7 - 8 minutes
Steve says: A winner that will have you smiling throughout

This flight simulator ride is a perennial favorite at the Studios. The pre-show on overhead TV monitors briefs you on the tour you're about to take to the Moon of Endor. Once on board, however, something goes awry and your rookie robot pilot barely escapes tragedy, over and over again. Your craft flies among ice crystals, through a comet. Then it is suddenly in the midst of a space battle between the good rebels and the evil Empire. Along the way, you meet familiar Star Wars movie characters. All ends well, and you end the trip feeling a lot more cheerful than when you started.

Note: Star Tours is past *Sounds Dangerous* on the left side of the park.

Height restriction: Kids must be 40" or taller to ride.

Caution: This attraction is similar to *Body Wars* at Epcot (both are flight simulator rides), but more folks seem to get nauseated and lose their cookies during *Body Wars*. If you are prone to motion sickness but want to give it a try, take an over-the-counter motion-sickness remedy before you enter the park (follow the directions on the label).

Indiana Jones Epic Stunt Spectacular

Rating: * * * *
Type: Stunt show in open-air theater
Time: About 30 minutes
Steve says: Fun to see how some action-movie stunts are done

Professional stunt men and women demonstrate action sequences along the lines of those used in the *Indiana Jones* movies. A stunt man avoids booby traps to find a golden treasure in a temple. Then, he and his woman friend fight bad guys on the streets of Cairo and dodge Nazi bullets in the desert. Volunteers are chosen from the audience to be extras in the show.

Tip: If you want to be picked, sit toward the front of the theater in any of the sections (and near the center), then stand up, wave your arms, and make noise when the casting director is choosing volunteers. You just might get lucky! To stake out these front seats, arrive early: queue up 20 minutes ahead of show time for the first show and up to 45 minutes ahead of show time for later shows (especially during busy seasons). Or use FASTPASS.

Note: This stunt demonstration show is staged in a huge open-air, canopied theater at the far side of Echo Lake just past the big green dinosaur (Dinosaur Gertie's Ice Cream of Extinction).

Sounds Dangerous—Starring Drew Carey

Rating: * * *
Type: Indoor sound effects movie
Time: 12 - 13 minutes
Steve says: Humorous plot and acting

Undercover agent Drew Carey dons a microphone and a small movie camera to track down diamond smugglers in this movie short. You experience the action firsthand as you watch his video transmission and listen through earphones to his broadcast. Then his movie camera fails, the theater turns pitch black, and your earphones become your only link to Mr. Carey's movements. That's when you discover that the realistic sound effects give you all the clues you need to interpret the frantic action even though you can't see a thing.

At the exit, you enter **SoundWorks**, a small, interactive sound-effects area. Here you can dub your voice into short film clips, listen to amazingly realistic sounds through headphones in a soundproofed room, and enjoy other adventures with your ears.

Tip: This small area can get crowded as guests pour into it after the *Sounds Dangerous* show. For a less crowded experience, enter Sound-Works directly from outside and time your visit 10 to 15 minutes before the next sound effects studio show (see Tip Board or Times Guide) to give guests from the previous show time to have moved on. Better yet, visit in the evening.

Note: The ABC Sound Studio is across the plaza from *Star Tours*.

"Honey, I Shrunk the Kids" Movie Set Adventure

Rating: * * *
Type: Imaginative outdoor playground
Time: As long as you want, minimum 15 minutes
Steve says: Great place for energetic kids to let off steam

This creative playground at the end of New York Street is filled with oversized blades of grass, ants, toys, and anything else you might find in your backyard if you were shrunk to the size of an ant's antenna. The playground is strewn with slides, tunnels, rope ladders, and things to climb on; most surfaces are padded. One area has an oversized leaky hose that randomly squirts water onto the wet kids below. The blades of grass are as tall as trees and provide some protection from the sun.

Caution: The playground can get crowded by late morning. On summer afternoons, the lack of good ventilation combined with all those little bodies having fun can turn this adventure area into a hot and humid place to play.

Disney-MGM Studios Backlot Tour

Rating: * * * *
Type: Guided tram and walking tour
Time: 25 - 30 minutes
Steve says: Let's you in on some secrets of movie-making

A large water tank special-effects area is the first stop on this entertaining tour of film production techniques. Several guests are chosen from the tour group to help demonstrate how storms and battles at sea are reproduced for movies and television. Then you board trams for a guided tour past the huge Disney wardrobe department; television and movie sets; a residential street with facades of famous movie and television homes (such as "The Golden Girls" house); and a collection of cars, boats, and other vehicles from well-known movies. Next stop is the highlight, the aptly named **Catastrophe Canyon**. Here your tram is subjected to an earthquake, an explosion with fire, and a flash flood (folks on the left side of the tram can get wet). Then the tram guide takes you behind the huge canyon set to explain how some of the special effects were created. In the final segment, the tram turns past New York Street for a good view of the "forced perspective" of the Empire State and other buildings (in other words, it's an optical illusion: the buildings are constructed and painted to make them seem taller than they really are).

Note: The entrance to the *Backlot Tour* is toward the end of Mickey Avenue near the entrance to *Backstage Pass*.

Backstage Pass

Rating: ★ ★ ★ ★
Type: Guided walking tour
Time: 25 - 30 minutes
Steve says: More secrets of movie and television production

This walking tour provides an entertaining and informative introduction to some aspects of movie and television development that aren't covered in the *Backlot Tour*. To make its points, *Backstage Pass* focuses on a specific movie or TV show. Recently, the subject was ABC's *Home Improvement*.

The tour starts with a video on the production aspects of the show, after which you enter a large room called **Jim Henson's Creature Shop**. There, a Disney cast member demonstrates some of the props used in the show. Then it's on to the **Special Effects Stage**, where a volunteer previously chosen from the tour group "rides" a bicycle or other vehicle in front of a blue screen so the video crew can insert him or her into a chase scene. Afterward, you walk on soundproof paths above the soundstages (the buildings along Mickey Avenue) where they actually film movies and TV shows. You may get to watch a *Millionaire — Play it!* game in progress. If you're lucky, movie or TV filming may be in progress during your visit. Finally, you stroll past actual sets and props from the highlighted show or movie.

Tip: If you'd like to tour while filming is in progress, ask the cast member at the entrance to the attraction if any filming or production is scheduled for the soundstages today (or ask at Guest Relations, to your left just inside the entrance to the park). Time your visit accordingly. And try not to be too disappointed if nothing is scheduled; there's still plenty to see.

Note: Enter *Backstage Pass* on Mickey Avenue next to *Backlot Tour.*

Who Wants To Be A Millionaire — Play It!

Rating: ★ ★ ★ ★
Type: Quiz show with audience participation
Time: 25 - 30 minutes
Steve says: If you like quiz shows, don't miss this one

The indoor set for this attraction is modeled after the set of the prime time TV show. Everyone in the audience can compete to get to the Hot Seat, where you can win prizes (pins, clothing, etc.). The more questions the Hot Seat player answers correctly, the more prizes he or she can win. The Hot Seat player gets to use up to three lifelines: "Fifty-Fifty" (two of the four answers are deleted by the computer), "Ask the Audience," and "Phone a Complete Stranger" (a guest in front of the building or in the *Backstage Pass* tour above the set). Fifteen correct answers nets the Hot Seat player one million points, which means lots of prizes, including a trip for two to New York City to be in the audience of the TV show. You don't have to be in the Hot Seat to play, however. There's an answer pad in front of each seat in the WDW auditorium that lights up after each question is asked on the overhead video screens. Guests in the WDW audience who want to participate can press A, B, C, or D as soon as the pad lights. If the Hot Seat player loses before the session is over (each lasts about 25 minutes), the audience member with the highest score may be called upon to take his or her place.

Note: Audience members can't win prizes, but the ten with the highest scores have the satisfaction of seeing their scores (listed by seat number) posted at the end of the session.

Tip: Keep your fingers close to the answer pad if you hope to be one of them. Bonus points are awarded for quickness, and you have to be really fast to get a high score. Watch the answer pad and punch in your answer as soon as it lights up.

The Making of . . .

Rating: ★ ★
Type: Walking tour with sit-down presentation

Time: As long as you want

Steve says: Interesting if you have the time

This attraction comes and goes, depending on what the Disney movie-makers are up to. When open, it combines a short tour of more movie production facilities with a sit-down theater presentation on the making of a recent live-action Disney movie. The theater presentation is similar to cable channel documentaries that show how certain movies were filmed. Props, makeup, special effects, and the musical score may be discussed, and the director and actors interviewed.

Note: The entrance is down Mickey Avenue from the *Voyage of The Little Mermaid*. Recently this area hosted "Walt Disney: One Man's Dream," a walk-through documentary tribute to the great man himself, including artifacts and video clips of his life and works.

Voyage of The Little Mermaid

Rating: * * * *

Type: Indoor musical stage show

Time: About 15 minutes

Steve says: A feast for the eyes and ears

At the front of the Animation Courtyard, on the left side, is this perennially popular attraction. You sit in a comfortable theater and watch a multimedia show that includes animation, puppetry, and live acting. Ariel, Eric, Flounder, Sebastian, Ursula, and other characters from the animated movie act and sing to tell the dramatic and uplifting story. Special effects in the theater, such as laser lights and falling sheets of water, add to the experience. The rendition of the song "Under the Sea" is truly memorable.

The Magic of Disney Animation

Rating: * * * *

Type: Guided walking tour plus sit-down presentations

Time: 36 - 38 minutes

Steve says: Fascinating, enriching, amusing

At the rear of the Animation Courtyard is the "Animation Tour" building. After a short introduction, you're admitted to a theater with comfy seats to watch a humorous film about the animation process starring Walter Cronkite and Robin Williams. If you wonder just how they do it, you can ask at your next stop, a room where an animator is usually available to answer questions. (Warning: they generally won't say what their salaries are.) Then it's on your feet for a walk through the animators' work area. If you visit weekdays before 5:00 p.m., you'll be able to watch them at their computer drawing boards through the glass windows that separate you. They're generally busy with a future movie or television production. After viewing video clips of animators discussing their work, your tour ends in another theater where you sit and enjoy a montage of short takes from Disney animated movies.

Note: The animators work weekdays until 5:00 or 6:00 p.m., but the tour is quite enjoyable even without them.

Playhouse Disney – Live on Stage!

Rating:	* *
Type:	Musical children's theater show
Time:	About 20 minutes
Steve says:	Especially fun for younger fans of Disney TV characters

Past the Hollywood Brown Derby Restaurant is the archway that leads to the Animation Courtyard. Just inside the archway on the right is the entrance to the *Playhouse Disney* stage show. Bear, Tutter, Shadow, Rolie Polie Olie, Pooh, and other characters from the Disney Channel kids' shows sing, dance, and have fun. You sit on a carpeted floor and enjoy the performance with your happy kids, who quickly realize that they're not confined by chairs, lap bars, or anything else! They can join in the dancing at times during the show and usually do.

Note: The show in this theater changes from time to time and may not run every day; consult your Times Guide.

The Great Movie Ride

Rating:	* * * *
Type:	"Dark ride" past movie sets
Time:	20 - 22 minutes
Steve says:	Lose yourself in some classic movie scenes

You enter *The Great Movie Ride* through a replica of Hollywood's Chinese Theater and join an inside queue. A montage of short takes from famous movies plays on a large screen in front of you to keep you entertained until you board a tram-like vehicle for a gentle ride past Audio-Animatronics scenes from — what else? — more movies. *Mary Poppins, Alien, Casablanca, Raiders of the Lost Ark, The Wizard of Oz*, and other big-screen classics are given the robotic treatment, along with such stars as Gene Kelly, Clint Eastwood, Harrison Ford, James Cagney, John Wayne, Julie Andrews, Dick Van Dyke, Judy Garland (as

Dorothy) and Margaret Hamilton (as Dorothy's nemesis, the Wicked Witch). Your ride ends with a fast-paced series of classic movie clips.

"Beauty and the Beast" — Live on Stage

Rating: ★ ★ ★ ★
Type: Outdoor live musical show
Time: About 30 minutes
Steve says: Timeless story, terrific show

The first major attraction you approach on Sunset Boulevard is the Theater of the Stars on your right. The *Beauty and the Beast* musical stage show comes to life at this open-air theater at times listed in your Times Guide. Belle, Gaston, Mrs. Potts, the Beast, and the rest of the cast entertain you with the well-known story. The "Be Our Guest" song is especially delightful.

Caution: The show is an uplifting experience, unless you're at the theater on a hot afternoon, when the heat and sweat can dampen your mood.

Note: This show isn't always open; consult your Times Guide.

Rock 'n' Roller Coaster Starring Aerosmith

Rating: ★ ★ ★ ★ ★
Type: Indoor roller coaster
Time: 2 - 3 minute pre-show; 1.5-minute ride
Steve says: Join in with everyone else and scream from start to finish!

Coaster junkies should love this high speed jaunt (0 to 60 mph in 2.8 seconds) in the dark with twists and turns, two loops, and a corkscrew — all to a background beat of rock-and-roll music. You meet the rock band Aerosmith and their manager during a pre-show. Then your super-stretch limo zips through nighttime Los Angeles streets to get Aerosmith to its concert on time!

Tip: If you want to ride in the front seats, queue up at the very front of the loading area after you pass through the last turnstile.

Height restriction: Riders must be 48" or taller.

The Twilight Zone Tower of Terror

Rating: ★ ★ ★ ★ ★
Type: Indoor ride with more than one drop
Time: 2 - 3 minute pre-show; 3 - 4 minute ride
Steve says: An elevator ride like none other

As you approach the old, out-of-service Hollywood Tower Hotel at the end of Sunset Boulevard, you can hear the screams from the elevator shafts. But intrepidly, you walk through the dusty lobby into the hotel library, where you watch Rod Serling narrate a television re-enactment of that terrible night years ago when lightning struck the hotel and the elevator fell 13 stories with five helpless people inside. Undeterred, you join the queue through the boiler room to line up for the elevator, which takes you past eerie audiovisual special effects and then up 13 stories for a bird's eye view of the Studios. Suddenly the cable breaks and you drop. In the nick of time, you feel the elevator stabilize, but just when you think you're safe . . .

Note: The precise sequence of elevator ups and downs is computer-programmed by Disney's Imagineers. It changes from time to time to keep the ride fresh for repeat visitors.

Height restriction: Kids must be 40" or taller to ride.

Fantasmic!

Rating:	*****
Type:	Outdoor live amphitheater show
Time:	25 minutes

Steve says: A perfect way to wind up your day in the Studios

This multimedia production is performed on an island and a lagoon in front of a huge amphitheater located behind *The Twilight Zone Tower of Terror*. Getting to a seat is cumbersome, but the performance is well worth the effort. Mickey Mouse, as the Sorcerer's Apprentice from *Fantasia*, has a nightmare in which he struggles against classic Disney villains. The scenes are staged with lasers, fireworks, music, live action, flames on the lagoon, and images projected onto a wall of water mist.

Tip 1: Center front seats provide the best view, but you generally have to arrive 60 to 90 minutes before showtime to claim them. That's a long time to sit and wait on hard benches, especially with restless children. So be aware that seats in the outer sections of the amphitheater provide good views of the action and can usually be had if you arrive 30 minutes or so before the first (or only) show of the evening. If two shows are scheduled, the later show is always less crowded. To ease the discomfort of waiting, a comedian often regales the audience before the show.

Tip 2: If you have blow-up seat cushions, bring them along. You'll be a whole lot more comfortable.

Caution: You may get damp from the water mist if you sit in the first 13 rows or so.

Note: This show may be cancelled in bad weather.

Attractions with Minimal Waits (Usually)

- *Disney-MGM Studios Backlot Tour.* The wait is often relatively short, except on busy days.
- *The Making of [Disney's Latest Movie].* The wait is usually the time until the next show. Recently, "Walt Disney: One Man's Dream" has been here.

Attractions That May Frighten Children

Remember that switching off is available at some of these attractions (see *Chapter One*, "Good Things to Know About").

- *Star Tours.* This intense flight simulator ride may frighten young children and can cause motion sickness in anyone. Switching off is available.
- *Sounds Dangerous Starring Drew Carey.* The theater goes completely black during part of the show. That and the startling, realistic sound effects may frighten young children.
- *Disney-MGM Studios Backlot Tour.* Prepare children for the Catastrophe Canyon segment during which an earthquake, fire, and flash flood are simulated.
- *The Great Movie Ride.* Some of the realistic displays can frighten young children.
- *Rock 'n' Roller Coaster Starring Aerosmith.* Unless your kids (48" or taller) happen to relish fast roller coasters. Switching off is available.
- *The Twilight Zone Tower of Terror.* The elevator drop can frighten anyone, especially children. Switching off is available.
- *Fantasmic!* Some special effects, such as gunshots and an explosion, may frighten young children.

Least Crowded Restrooms

- To the left of the entrance to The Hollywood Brown Derby restaurant is a door that leads to inside restrooms not noted on the Guidemap.
- Walk into the Tune-In Lounge and turn left to some usually uncrowded restrooms (not noted on the Guidemap).

Resting Places

- The benches in the trees between the Sci-Fi Dine-In Theater Restaurant and *Star Tours*.
- The benches at the edge of Echo Lake across from the 50s Prime Time Cafe, but there's not much shade.
- The chairs under cover (in the shade) at the Studio Catering Company, but it's often noisy because of the nearby *"Honey, I Shrunk the Kids" Movie Set Adventure* playground.

Hidden Mickeys

Here are just a few of the hidden Mickeys you may want to look for in the Studios:

- *The Great Movie Ride*. As you pass through the *Indiana Jones* movie set, look at the wall to your left near the corner past the last statue. Mickey is etched into the wall design, sitting on a chair facing left. Opposite Mickey is Donald Duck.
- *The Twilight Zone Tower of Terror*. During the pre-show film in the library, the little girl in the elevator holds a plush Mickey Mouse doll.
- Find Mickey in the fountain in front of *Jim Henson's MuppetVision 3D* below the character with the megaphone. Mickey's eyes and snout bulge out.

Touring Disney–MGM Studios

Whether you are staying on property or off, the fastest way to get to Disney-MGM Studios (aka "the Studios") is to drive your car to the main parking lot. Otherwise take a bus or boat (check your Transportation Guide). Buses run from all the WDW properties and some off-property lodgings as well. The boat brings guests from Epcot and the Epcot resort hotels. Bear in mind, however, that taking the bus is nowhere near as convenient as driving, and the boat is rather slow-loading and slow-moving (taking up to 35 minutes one way); so you should drive from the Epcot resort hotels to the Studios if you have a car. Ask at your hotel Guest Services how long it will take you to get to the Studios entrance.

Dining recommendations: Before you come, or shortly after you arrive, you may want to make priority seating reservations for lunch and/or dinner. Among the possibilities for lunch: Sci-Fi Dine-In for an entertaining meal or Hollywood & Vine for a Disney character buffet. For dinner consider: The Hollywood Brown Derby for an elegant setting or the 50s Prime Time Cafe for an entertaining meal. Eat an early lunch to beat the crowds (11:15 to 11:30 a.m.) and plan to eat a later dinner (7:00 p.m.) to allow for early shows and optimal touring.

When to Arrive

Plan to arrive early in the day, preferably before opening time, so that you can experience the major rides and attractions with minimal waits. You'll want to be at the front entrance turnstiles about 35 to 40 minutes before the official opening time. Allow an additional 10 minutes to get from the parking lot to the turnstiles and another 10 minutes if you have to buy your admission tickets.

Tip: If the morning lines are long at all entrance turnstiles, line up in an outside queue. Sometimes, an attendant will open up a nearby turnstile at the last minute, and you may be positioned to move with other excited guests to the new and shorter queue.

One- and Two-Day Touring Plans for All

(See "A Special Note on Early Entry," page 51.)

You probably won't be able to experience every attraction in Disney-MGM Studios in one day. If possible, return a second morning to complete the tour, especially if you take an afternoon break on the first day. I recommend taking a break if the park is open late (7:00 p.m. or later) so that you have the energy to enjoy every minute of your visit. If you want to sleep in, pick up the non Early Entry plan later in the day.

Note: At the end of Hollywood Boulevard near the Starring Rolls Bakery is a chalk Tip Board ("Guest Information Board") which lists approximate wait times for the attractions and start times for the shows. I consider a wait of more than 15 to 20 minutes "too long." If the wait is longer, use FASTPASS or the singles line option (if available) or move on to the next attraction and come back later.

Tip: If you arrive by car in the afternoon, try to wend your way to the front of the parking lot to cut your walk to the entrance turnstiles and speed your exit.

One-Day (or Day One) Plan for Early Entry Days

(WDW property guests only)

1. Pick up a Guidemap and Times Guide at the turnstiles or just inside at a vendor. Check to see if a "Star of the Day" (an entertainment celebrity) is scheduled to appear. If so and you're interested, make time for this special event in the touring plan. Then find out what attractions are open for Early Entry. Plan to skip attractions you don't want to experience.

2. Rent strollers, if needed, at Oscar's Super Service inside the entrance turnstiles on the right.

3. If you like fast roller coasters, make *Rock 'n' Roller Coaster Starring Aerosmith* your first ride. Walk to the end of Hollywood Boulevard. If a rope is up, line up at the rope with the other guests. When the rope drops, you may be asked not to jog or run, but to follow several Disney attendants to your first attraction. Turn right on Sunset Boulevard and follow the attendants down the right sidewalk. (If the rope is already down, head for the coaster at the fastest pace that's comfortable for you.) Before you get in line, stop and get a FASTPASS for *Tower of Terror*. Now line up and ride the coaster.

   Height restriction: Kids must be 48" or taller to ride. Switching off is available (see *Chapter One*, "Good Things to Know About").

4. Turn left at the exit and ride *The Twilight Zone Tower of Terror* at your FASTPASS time.

   Height/fright alert: Kids must be 40" or taller to ride, but the elevator drop can frighten even adults. Don't force unwilling members of your party onto this ride. You'll all be unhappy. Again, switching off is available.

5. Walk back down Sunset Boulevard and turn right to Mickey Avenue. Get in line for *Who Wants to Be A Millionaire — Play It!* Or visit any other attractions open for Early Entry.

6. Now calm down with some refreshments; a good bet is the Starring Rolls Bakery on Sunset Boulevard just past the Guest Information Tip Board. After your break, continue with step 4 of the

following plan. Skip any attractions you've already experienced.

One-Day (or Day One) Plan for Non Early Entry Days

1. Pick up a Guidemap and Times Guide at the turnstiles or just inside at a vendor. Check to see if a "Star of the Day" (an entertainment celebrity) is scheduled to appear. If so and you're interested, make time for this special event in the touring plan. Skip any attractions you don't want to experience.

2. Rent strollers, if needed, at Oscar's Super Service inside the entrance turnstiles on the right.

3. Walk fast to the end of Hollywood Boulevard. Turn right on Sunset Boulevard and get a FASTPASS for *Tower of Terror*. Then ride *Rock 'n' Roller Coaster.*
   Height/fright alert: Children must be 48" or taller to ride. Don't force unwilling children or seniors to ride the coaster. Use switching off instead.

4. Ride *The Twilight Zone Tower of Terror* at your FASTPASS time. Use switching off if some members of your party want to skip it.
   Height/fright alert: Children must be 40" or taller to ride.

5. If the first *Voyage of The Little Mermaid* show is soon (check your Times Guide for shows), walk back down Sunset Boulevard, turn right in front of the Starring Rolls Bakery and right again along the curving sidewalk in front of The Hollywood Brown Derby restaurant. Pass under the arch, turn left, and get in line for the show. Otherwise, return later for the first show. Send someone for coffee or refreshments if your wait in line is long enough.
   Tip: When you're admitted to the pre-show area, stand close to the left or middle doors at the side of the room. After the doors open, pick a row in the middle or rear (your left) of the theater, let six to ten folks in before you, and sit toward the far end of the row. This maneuver will give you a good view of the stage and a relatively quick exit.

6. Walk back under the arch and turn right to ride *The Great Movie Ride*. Ask a Disney attendant at the entrance or inside how long the wait is. If it is more than 15 minutes, skip to step 6 and return to this ride in the hour before closing.

7. Turn left from the exit, then left again down Mickey Avenue. Get

in line for *Who Wants to Be a Millionaire — Play It!* Or get a FAST-PASS if the wait is too long.

8. Turn left at the exit, walk straight across the park with Echo Lake on your left to enter and ride *Star Tours*. If the line is too long, use the FASTPASS option if it's available to you. If you are holding a FASTPASS for *Millionaire* and aren't yet eligible for another (see *Chapter One*, "Good Things to Know About"), return after lunch when you are eligible again and either ride *Star Tours* or get a FASTPASS for it.

   Caution: This is a rough flight simulator ride, maybe too rough for seniors and children under 7 or 8 years of age. If you have reluctant kids, ask the Disney attendant inside about switching off. If you're prone to motion sickness, take a remedy before entering the park.

   Height alert: Kids must be 40" or taller to ride.

9. Keep your priority seating reservations for lunch. If you don't have priority seating, try the Backlot Express for burgers and sandwiches, the Toy Story Pizza Planet for pizza, or the ABC Commissary for salads and stir-fry.

10. After lunch, enjoy *Jim Henson's MuppetVision 3D*. Use FASTPASS if eligible if the wait is too long.

11. Now it's time to consider some alternatives. If the park is open past 7:00 p.m., I recommend taking a break about now. If the afternoon parade is about to start, find a shady spot near (or on) the steps in front of the ABC-TV Theater (or in the area with statues called The Academy of Arts and Television Hall of Fame) and enjoy the parade. Then consider leaving the park for a couple of hours' rest in your hotel. If the parade is scheduled later in the afternoon, consider leaving the park now for a nap or swim at your hotel and return 20 minutes before parade time.

   Alternative: If you don't want to nap or swim, consider boating to the Epcot Resort area: Walk out of the Studios; turn left to the boat dock; embark, and then disembark at the BoardWalk. Wander around the shops and go to one of the hotel lobbies to rest awhile on the comfortable couches. Return to the Studios 20 minutes before parade time.

   Note: Remember to have your hands stamped at the exit for re-entry and keep any parking and stroller receipts.

   Tip: If the park is too crowded for your comfort and your ticket allows, switch to a non Early Entry Disney park after your break and start with the afternoon or evening section of the appropriate touring plan.

12. If you stay in the park, head for *Disney-MGM Studios Backlot Tour*. Walk to Mickey Avenue and turn left. You'll find the entrance at the end of Mickey Avenue on your right.

13. Exit and walk back to Mickey Avenue toward *Voyage of The Little Mermaid*. On your left past the *Backlot Tour* entrance is the entrance to the *Backstage Pass* walking tour. Get in line and take it.

14. Get some refreshment at the Studio Catering Co. (back past the *Backlot Tour* entrance). Tell your kids you will return to the nearby *"Honey, I Shrunk the Kids"* playground later in the afternoon.

15. If you have young children, catch a performance of *Playhouse Disney - Live on Stage!* (or its replacement); check the Times Guide for show times.

> **Watch out! If the sprinkler is on in Vern's front yard, folks seated in the right side of the tram may get wet.**

16. See the afternoon parade (if you haven't already) from a shady area near *Sounds Dangerous*.

17. When the parade has passed, get in line to see *Sounds Dangerous*.

18. Now you have some more options. If you haven't already done the *Backlot Tour*, head up New York Street. Turn right past *"Honey, I Shrunk the Kids"* playground to get in line at the tour entrance on Mickey Avenue. If you've already been on the *Backlot Tour*, go left and then under the arch to get in line to take *The Magic of Disney Animation* tour. Or if the timing is right, go to the *Beauty and the Beast*, *The Hunchback of Notre Dame* or *Indiana Jones* (check your Times Guide for show times). Try to arrive 20 minutes or more before show time to get decent seats.

    Tip: If you aren't sure which option to choose, check the Tip Board at the intersection of Hollywood and Sunset Boulevards for approximate attraction waiting times to help you make up your mind. If fireworks are scheduled, work them into your evening plans.

19. Next, let your kids play in the *"Honey, I Shrunk the Kids" Movie Set Adventure* playground for 20 or 30 minutes.

20. At the appropriate time, honor any priority seating reservations you made for dinner. Again, if you don't have reservations, try the Backlot Express for burgers and sandwiches or Catalina Eddie's for pizza and salads.

21. Visit the "Walt Disney: One Man's Dream" exhibit.

22. Head for the *Fantasmic!* amphitheater 30 to 45 minutes before show time (consult your Times Guide). Grab some refreshments to enjoy while you wait. If you have a blow-up seat cushion in your tote, get it out now. The benches are hard.

    Note: You can save a space for someone, but only up until about 15 minutes before show time.

23. Enjoy the show and be prepared to be patient on the way out. It takes a long long time for this huge crowd to exit.

    Tip: Try for seats on the right side of the amphitheater to speed your exit, if ever so slightly.

Day Two Plan for Early Entry Days

(WDW property guests only)

Note: Because guests generally take advantage of the Early Entry privilege only once at each park — or want to do the same popular rides again if they do two Early Entry days in the Studios — the Early Entry tour plan today is the same as yesterday's, with the exception of step 6. I include them under both days so that you don't have to flip back and forth in your book.

1. Pick up a Guidemap and Times Guide at the turnstiles or just inside at a vendor. Check to see if a "Star of the Day" (an entertainment celebrity) is scheduled to appear. If so and you're interested, make time for this special event in your touring plan. Ditto if a parade is on and you want to see it (or see it again). Then find out what attractions are open for Early Entry. Plan to skip any attractions that don't appeal to you.

2. Rent strollers, if needed, at Oscar's Super Service inside the entrance turnstiles on the right.

3. If you like fast roller coasters, make *Rock 'n' Roller Coaster Starring Aerosmith* your first ride. Walk to the end of Hollywood Boulevard. If a rope is up, line up at the rope with the other guests. When the rope drops, you may be asked not to jog or run, but to follow several Disney attendants to your first attraction. Turn right on Sunset Boulevard and follow the attendants down the right sidewalk. (If the rope is already down, head for the coaster at the fastest pace that's comfortable for you.) Before you get in line, stop and get a FASTPASS for *Tower of Terror*. Now line up and ride the coaster.

Height restriction: Kids must be 48" or taller to ride. Switching off is available (see *Chapter One,* "Good Things to Know About"). Don't force unwilling children or seniors to ride the coaster.

4. Turn left at the exit and ride *Tower of Terror* at your FAST-PASS time.

    When you're safely seated in the Tower of Terror elevator, place a penny in your open palm before the drop. Try to catch the floating penny when your elevator "hits" bottom.

    Height/fright alert: Riders must be 40" or taller, but the elevator drop can frighten even adults. Don't force unwilling members of your party onto this ride. You'll all be unhappy. Again, switching off is available.

5. Walk back down Sunset Boulevard. Turn right to Mickey Avenue. Get in line for *Who Wants to Be a Millionaire — Play It!* or any other attraction open for Early Entry.

6. Turn left at the exit and walk straight across the park, with Echo Lake on your left, to ride *Star Tours.*
    Note: This is a rough flight simulator ride, too rough for many seniors and children under 7 or 8 years of age. If you have reluctant kids, ask the Disney attendant inside about switching off. Use FASTPASS if the line is too long to suit you. If you're prone to motion sickness, take a remedy before entering the park.
    Height alert: Kids must be 40" or taller to ride.

7. Exit and calm down with some refreshments; a good source is the Starring Rolls Bakery on Sunset Boulevard just past the Guest Information Tip Board.

8. After your refreshments, go to step 3 of the following plan. Skip any attractions you've already experienced.

Day Two Plan for Non Early Entry Days

1. Pick up a Guidemap and Times Guide. If you like rough coasters, walk fast to the end of Hollywood Boulevard, turn right on Sunset Boulevard. Stop to pick up a FASTPASS for *Tower of Terror,* then get in line and ride *Rock 'n' Roller Coaster Starring Aerosmith.*
    Height restriction: Kids must be 48" or taller to ride.

2. Head for the tall, menacing building to your left and ride *The Twilight Zone Tower of Terror* at your FASTPASS time. If you're up for it, jump back in line and ride *The Tower of Terror* again!

Height/fright alert: Kids must be 40" or taller to ride. Use switching off if needed.

3. Walk back down Sunset Boulevard, turn right on Hollywood Boulevard and ride *The Great Movie Ride*, especially if you didn't have a chance to ride it on Day One.

4. Exit left, go under the arch, and get in line for *The Magic of Disney Animation* tour if you didn't take it on Day One. If the tour isn't open yet, return at its scheduled opening and take it then (consult your Times Guide or the Tip Board at the intersection of Hollywood and Sunset Boulevards for times).

5. Exit and turn right down Mickey Avenue. Get in line for the *Backstage Pass* walking tour if you haven't experienced it yet.

6. Honor your 11:30 a.m. lunch priority seating reservations (for recommendations, see above). If you don't have reservations, try the Backlot Express for burgers and sandwiches, the Toy Story Pizza Planet for pizza, or the ABC Commissary for salad and stir-fry.

7. If you haven't already done so, enjoy *Jim Henson's MuppetVision 3D*. Use FASTPASS if the wait is too long.

8. Plan to see *Beauty and the Beast*, *The Hunchback of Notre Dame*, and/or *Indiana Jones*. Check your Times Guide for show times and put any or all of the shows into your afternoon touring plan. *Tip:* Arrive 30 minutes or more before show time to get decent seats.

9. If your children want to see it, catch a performance of *Playhouse Disney - Live on Stage!*. Check your Times Guide for show times.

10. If your kids want more autographs, check your Times Guide for today's character greeting locations.
    Tip: The Animation Courtyard and Mickey Avenue are popular areas to find characters.

11. Shop in a few of the interesting stores, such as Sid Cahuenga's One-of-a-Kind (movie memorabilia) and the Animation Gallery (Disney movie cels) at the exit of the Animation Tour.

12. Check Hollywood Boulevard for the Streetmosphere performers: starlet wannabes, gossip columnists, and a host of other entertainment-related characters who interact with each other and passersby in short, impromptu scenes. They often appear on the half-hour.

13. Visit any rides, shows or parades that you want to enjoy again if the waits aren't too long. Get FASTPASSes when appropriate. If fireworks are scheduled, work them into your evening plans. Visit the "Walt Disney: One Man's Dream" exhibit (or its replacement attraction) if you haven't yet seen it.

CHAPTER FIVE:

Disney's Animal Kingdom

Walt Disney World Resort's newest theme park is a grand zoological kingdom (over 200 species of animals) with a mix of Disney shows and attractions similar in scale to those at the other major Disney theme parks. Disney's Animal Kingdom pays tribute to all animals while warning humans to do more to help save our fellow creatures and the plants on which all of us depend. The majority of animals here are out in the open. You see them on "hills" and savannas from the vantage point of safari vehicles and in gardens and small parks as you stroll the kingdom's many walking trails. You have to search far and wide to find any cages or bars.

Note: To protect the animals, no balloons, straws, or cup lids (except for hot drinks) are allowed in the park. Your balloons can be stored at the park entrance.

The Oasis

You enter and exit Disney's Animal Kingdom through the Oasis, a lush garden filled with exotic plants and animals that's located just inside the entrance turnstiles. Here you encounter plants and animals while walking along winding trails. You will either see the animals as you walk or read the explanatory tablets and then try to spot the animals in the sloping gardens, in the trees, or by the winding streams. The identification tablets are colorful, easy to read, and downright poetic.

discovery island
1 The Tree of Life
2 It's Tough to be a Bug!

camp minnie-mickey
3 Pocahontas and Her Forest Friends
4 Festival of the Lion King
5 Character Greeting Trails

africa
6 Kilimanjaro Safaris
7 Pangani Forest Exploration Trail
8 Train to Rafiki's Planet Watch

rafiki's planet watch
9 Conservation Station
10 Affection Section
11 Habitat Habit!

asia
12 Flights of Wonder
13 Maharajah Jungle Trek
14 Kali River Rapids

dinoland u.s.a.
15 Tarzan™ Rocks! at Theater in the Wild
16 The Boneyard
17 TriceraTop Spin
18 Primeval Whirl
19 Cretaceous Trail
20 Dinosaur
21 Dino-Sue T Rex

Some animals are easy to spot: The two-toed sloth usually reclines in a tree and stays in the same position for long periods of time. Others are more difficult to locate in their designated areas. After all, they have their own schedules, and even though they're technically "Disney animals," they aren't particularly interested in how your vacation day is going at their kingdom.

Tip: To expeditiously enter or exit the main park, head straight for one of the walkway trails on either side of the Oasis as you enter through the turnstiles. The walkway on the left side may be a bit shorter and straighter.

Discovery Island

Discovery Island lies in the middle of Disney's Animal Kingdom, connected to its other lands by bridges. Like the Magic Kingdom hub at the end of Main Street, Discovery Island is the central area from which you enter all the other lands in the park. It offers attractions, shops, restaurants, and walking trails. Soaring over the island is the 14-story tall *Tree of Life*, the central symbol and centerpiece of the park. It is analogous to Cinderella Castle in the Magic Kingdom, Spaceship Earth at Epcot, and Mickey Mouse's Sorcerer's Hat at Disney-MGM Studios.

The Tree of Life

This amazing structure has over 325 animals sculpted into its roots, trunk, and branches. Walking trails, designed to resemble natural forest trails, snake around the tree and under its roots. These trails offer multiple vantage points for close-up viewing of the tree's beautiful, intricate artistry. *The Tree of Life* is unique and so original it's difficult to stop marvelling at it. Disney's Animal Kingdom parade follows a route around it. Walking paths through gardens, with plants and animals to view, lead you gently away from it and on to the Kingdom's other attractions.

It's Tough to be a Bug!

Rating:	* * * *
Type:	3-D movie in a sit-down theater
Time:	8 minutes
Steve says:	Insects were never so enjoyable!

This 3-D experience takes place indoors in a theater under the roots of *The Tree of Life*. *It's Tough to be a Bug!* is an eight-minute 3-D film using advanced computer animation techniques. Packed with surprises, the show is nonstop fun. You meet many different bugs up close and personal, including a stink bug who releases a cloud for the benefit of your nose. The special effects are reminiscent of and on a par with Epcot's *Honey, I Shrunk the Audience*.

To find the sign marking the entrance to the show, bear to your right after you walk across the bridge from the Oasis toward *The Tree of Life*. (The entrance site changes from time to time, so consult your Guidemap if you have any difficulty locating it.)

Insider tips: From the holding area, the doors to your extreme left admit you to the back rows of the theater, while the middle two sets of doors admit you to the middle rows. Aim for one or the other, because the middle and back of the theater offer the best vantage points for the show. The long rows are divided into seats by small ridges. The back and bottom of each seat offer the sitter surprises during the show. Just sit comfortably and enjoy the special effects!

And don't worry; the stink bug's not that stinky.

Camp Minnie-Mickey

Camp Minnie-Mickey is a forested area containing character greeting areas and two stage shows. While some characters can be found signing autograph books along the main trails, most characters are located in the rear of the camp at the end of four short trails that snake off to the right of the main thoroughfare (see below). The stage shows are fun-filled live performances.

Pocahontas and Her Forest Friends

Rating: * * *
Type: Outdoor live stage show with animals
Time: About 15 minutes
Steve says: Especially entertaining for kids

This shaded but uncovered stage show features Pocahontas, along with Grandmother Willow and their animal friends. They all remind us of the obligation of humankind to protect the earth's flora and fauna. Live animals, including a skunk and a snake, make appearances and children can sit in their own special area near the stage.

Note: The Festival of The Lion King show is next door, so make sure you're in the correct queue.

Festival of The Lion King

Rating: * * * * *
Type: Live musical show in a covered theater
Time: 25 - 27 minutes
Steve says: Superb, one of the best shows at WDW

This theater-in-the-round show is a high-energy musical and dance performance interspersed with audience participation and breathtaking acrobatics. The dancers wear animal costumes, and the fashions, floats, vocals, and choreography are sensational. You'll have a rousing good time.

Tip: The bleachers inside the covered Lion King Theater have separate queues. If you have children or short adults in your party, sit higher in the bleachers for a better view.

Character Greeting Trails

Rating: * * *
Type: Outdoor area for meeting characters
Time: If only a few folks are ahead of you, 5 - 10 minutes per trail; the time lengthens as the lines do
Steve says: Can be time-consuming

Four trails (named Arbor, Mickey, Forest, and Jungle) with four separate queues lead to different characters. Minnie is usually at the end of the Arbor Trail, while Mickey greets you at his own trail. The Forest Trail leads to several Winnie the Pooh characters, while the Jungle Trail serves up several characters from *The Lion King* and *Jungle Book*.

Note: Trail names and characters may change from time to time.

Africa

The gateway to Africa is Harambe, a re-creation of an East African village. Harambe, like any decent gateway, offers shops, fast food counters, and a cocktail lounge. You must pass through Harambe (which means "coming together" in Swahili) to reach Africa's attractions.

Kilimanjaro Safaris

Rating: * * * * *
Type: Outdoor guided safari ride
Time: 20 - 22 minutes
Steve says: The animals are nearby, behind camouflaged barriers. There are no cages.

At the end of Harambe's central street is the entrance to the safari ride. The large open-air safari vehicles carry you on a bumpy ride over dirt trails through forests, around hills, and over flat savanna. One short bridge feels especially creaky and unstable (Disney designed it that way for your benefit). Inside your vehicle are pictures of the animals you're likely to spot. Zebras, gazelles, elephants, lions, ostriches, giraffes, and rhinos are visible in open grottos, on hilltops, and by streams on either side of your vehicle. Along the way, your driver entertains you with a humorous and informative spiel. You will help him (or her) chase and trap some evil elephant poachers before the ride ends.

Note: Lines for this one build quickly once the park opens.

Pangani Forest Exploration Trail

Rating: ★ ★ ★ ★
Type: Walk-through animal exhibit
Time: About 25 minutes
Steve says: Well-designed zoological nature trail

Next to the exit from *Kilimanjaro Safaris* is the entrance to *Pangani Forest Exploration Trail*. This beautiful walking trail winds by a troop of lowland gorillas, a hippopotamus pool with an underwater viewing area, colorful African birds, agile meerkats, and an interesting glassed display on the naked mole rat.

Rafiki's Planet Watch

This outpost between Africa and Asia will acquaint you with research on the habits and health of animals in the wild. You reach it by a train, leaving from Africa.

Note: For those who may have missed the movie, *The Lion King,* Rafiki is a wise baboon with a very distinctive voice.

Train to Rafiki's Planet Watch

Rating: ★ ★
Type: Outdoor guided train ride
Time: 5 - 6 minutes one way
Steve says: A means of transportation to Rafiki's Planet Watch

The entrance to this train ride is to the right, at the end of Harambe's central street and across from the entrance to *Kilimanjaro Safaris.* The train itself conjures up images of a real African train, with luggage, boxes, and bicycles roped precariously to the roof of the train cars. All passengers face to one side of the train in tiered seating. During the ride to (past Africa) and from (past Asia) Rafiki's Planet Watch, the conductor gives a short educational spiel on how the Kingdom cares for these creatures. You'll get to see the back of the animal keepers' metal housing for the Kingdom's larger African and Asian creatures, such as rhinos and elephants.

Note: You may spot a few animals inside their houses.

Conservation Station

> *Rating:*   * * *
>
> *Type:*   Indoor animal science exhibits
>
> *Time:*   15 - 20 minutes minimum, longer if your kids stop in the petting zoo
>
> *Steve says:*   Like an interactive science museum

You'll find a series of walk-through educational exhibits in this building. An animated cartoon Rafiki talks about various endangered animals. A children's show presented by mechanized puppets focuses on conservation and saving our planet. You can experience the sounds of an endangered rain forest (queue up for sound booths in which you don headphones) and watch researchers and veterinarians working with and treating live animals, often ones with injuries. Video cameras project close-up shots of the animals and their caretakers onto overhead monitors, so even the shortest can see what's going on. Other imaginative exhibits include computer interactive sessions on conservation.

Outside the building you'll find **Affection Section**, a large petting zoo, and **Habitat Habit**, an outdoor animal viewing area.

Note: The hike from the train station to Conservation Station takes a few minutes (about the same length as the time it takes to walk through the Oasis).

Asia

There are two routes to Asia, a path from Harambe that parallels the river and a bridge from Discovery Island. You enter this land through the village of Anandapur (which means "place of all delights"). The animals you'll see when you get here are all indigenous to the Asian continent, with roots in such countries as India, Indonesia, and Thailand.

Flights of Wonder

Rating: * * * *
Type: Outdoor amphitheater bird show
Time: 25 - 30 minutes
Steve says: Sensitive, high-quality avian show

This open-air stage show stars many amazing birds, including a falcon, a hawk, a singing parrot, and other trained avians that perform unusual tricks. These delightful stunts are not mere tricks, they're enhancements of the birds' natural behaviors.

Maharajah Jungle Trek

Rating: * * * *
Type: Walk-through animal exhibit
Time: About 25 minutes
Steve says: Well-designed zoological nature trail

This nature walk on the left side of Asia brings you close to such animals as Komodo dragons, tigers, antelopes, giant fruit bats, and many more. The jungle settings are lush, especially the palace ruins.

Kali River Rapids

Rating: * * * *
Type: Raft ride
Time: 5 minutes
Steve says: Not too wild, but definitely wet

A large, circular, free-floating raft takes 12 adventurers twisting and turning down a jungle river past waterfalls, white water rapids, archeological ruins, and a rain forest ravaged by loggers. Your raft drifts perilously close to burning logs and falling lumber. Be prepared to get wet! Consider putting your shoes, socks, and camera into a plastic bag or the waterproof container at the center of the raft. In fact, you might want to do both.

Height restriction: Kids must be 38" or taller to ride.

DinoLand U.S.A.

A thematically rich land, DinoLand U.S.A. is filled with all manner of dinosaurs and fossils. The animals of this land may be long dead, but DinoLand U.S.A. is really lively! A 50-foot long brachiosaurus forms the entrance gateway. Fossil and excavation exhibits are scattered throughout the area. "Field notes" by paleontology graduate students (with critiques from their professors in red ink) explain the exhibits. And if you feel the need to eat or shop, DinoLand U.S.A. has a shop and several fast food stops. Many folks here eat turkey legs in homage to the carnivores of this land, or maybe just because they're hungry.

Theater in the Wild

Rating: * * * *
Type: Live musical show in a covered theater
Time: About 30 minutes
Steve says: Vibrant, lively show

Located on the far left side of DinoLand U.S.A., this theater seats 1,500 people and presents animal-themed shows such as *Tarzan Rocks!* This show features a live rock-and-roll band along with jungle gymnasts and rollerbladers. Tarzan, Jane, Terk, and their monkey friends reprise segments of the Tarzan story in an energetic and fast-paced show spiced with swinging song and dance.

The Boneyard

Rating: * *
Type: Imaginative outdoor playground
Time: As long as you want, minimum 10 - 15 minutes
Steve says: Great place for energetic kids to let off steam

A wild and crazy playground, *The Boneyard* swarms with running, crawling, and yelling kids (and smiling adults). You'll find it on the left, just inside the entrance to DinoLand U.S.A. Reminiscent of the *Honey, I Shrunk the Kids* playground at Disney-MGM Studios, *The Boneyard* is modeled after a fossil dig site. Budding scientists can dig to uncover dinosaur skeletons embedded in fossil sand pits. (The Disney staff thoughtfully re-conceals them every night.) Unlike real dig sites, *The Boneyard* also has rope ladders and tunnels to climb up and through and plastic tubes to slide down from the rock walls.

TriceraTop Spin

Rating: * *
Type: Flying, steerable dinosaurs
Time: About 2 minutes
Steve says: Circle ride with prehistoric twist

These four-person dinosaur vehicles (like *Dumbo* with horns!) revolve around a hub, but levers let riders control some of the motion. The two rear riders can make the vehicle go higher and lower, while the two front riders can tilt the beast's nose up and down.

Note: Nearby is **Fossil Fun Games**, a small carnival-style midway area with dinosaur-themed games. Playing them will set you back $2 to $4 per game.

Primeval Whirl

> *Rating:* ★ ★ ★
> *Type:* Roller coaster with spinning ride vehicles
> *Time:* About 2 minutes
> *Steve says:* The spins add unpredictability to your ride

This relatively mild coaster ride has drops and curves on the way down. The round, four-person ride vehicles spin freely at times.

Height restriction: Kids must be 48" or taller to ride.

Dinosaur

> *Rating:* ★ ★ ★ ★ ★
> *Type:* Motion-simulator indoor track ride
> *Time:* 3.5 minutes
> *Steve says:* Realistic, high-energy simulator thrill ride in the dark

This jolting joy ride takes you back in time about 65 million years. You and the rest of your crew board a time vehicle (a motion simulator vehicle that also moves along a track). Your objective is to find a living (vegetarian) dinosaur and bring it back to the present before its species becomes extinct. During the mission, you encounter nonstop near-death experiences, confront angry or hungry carnivores, and barely escape the asteroid that collided with earth and (allegedly) blotted out the dinosaurs. This attraction is a magnificent high-tech achievement by Disney's Imagineers.

Tip: As your vehicle nears the exit area, watch the monitor above you for a "real time" view of the dinosaur you just brought back.

Caution: If motion simulators make you queasy, you may want to skip this one, or prepare for it by taking an over-the-counter motion-sickness remedy an hour or so before you board.

Height restriction: Kids must be 40" or taller to ride.

Cretaceous Trail

> *Rating:* ★ ★ ★
> *Type:* Nature trail
> *Time:* 10 minutes, or as long as you want

Steve says: Relaxing diversion

In the middle of DinoLand U.S.A., the winding *Cretaceous Trail* takes you through a lush forest populated with plant and animal species that have survived since dinosaur times. "Field notes" from eager paleontology graduate students introduce you to numerous changing exhibits, such as soft-shell turtles and small Chinese alligators.

Note: Along the way, you'll find some shade and some places to sit.

Dino-Sue T-Rex

Rating: **
Type: Outdoor exhibit
Time: 2 minutes
Steve says: Worth a visit and family photo

Billed as the largest and most complete tyrannosaurus rex ever found, Sue is 40 feet long and once weighed 6 to 8 tons. Don't get too close; she looks hungry!

Attractions With Minimal Waits (Usually)

- The Oasis. Explore this area anytime.
- *The Tree of Life Garden* and *Discovery Island Trails*. Explore these anytime.
- *The Boneyard.* Especially fun for children; anytime, but it is exposed to the sun.
- *Cretaceous Trail.* Explore this area anytime.

Attractions That May Frighten Children

Remember that "switching off' is available at some of these attractions (see *Chapter One*, "Good Things to Know About" and below).

- *It's Tough to be a Bug!* Loud, intense 3-D effects may frighten children.
- *Kali River Rapids.* The turning raft and rough white water may frighten small children. Switching off is available.
- *Dinosaur.* Intense encounters in the dark with realistic dinosaurs can frighten anyone, especially kids. Switching off is available.

Least Crowded Restrooms

- The restrooms next to Chester and Hester's Dinosaur Treasures

in DinoLand U.S.A.
- The restrooms along the trail to the right, before the bridge to DinoLand U.S.A.
- The restrooms at the rear of Tusker House Restaurant in Africa.

Resting Places

- The shaded chairs in the large sitting area on the waterfront by the Flame Tree Barbecue restaurant.
- Scattered isolated benches along the winding trails (some shaded) around *The Tree of Life*.

Hidden Mickeys

Here are just a few of the hidden Mickeys you may want to look for in Disney's Animal Kingdom:

- *Tree of Life*. As you enter Discovery Island from the Oasis, walk to your right and stare at the tree. Partway up the trunk on the right side is a cluster of green algae shaped like Mickey's frontal silhouette.
- *Kilimanjaro Safaris*. More than halfway through the journey, you pass a flamingo pond to your left. An island in the middle of the pond is shaped like Mickey's frontal silhouette.
- Find Mickey's head atop a flagpole that's located just before the second bridge leading into Camp Minnie-Mickey.
- *Pocahontas and Her Forest Friends*. On a path to the right of the stage are three rocks forming the frontal outline of Mickey's head.

Touring Disney's Animal Kingdom

The fastest way to get to Disney's Animal Kingdom is to drive your car to the main parking lot. On-property guests can take a Disney transport bus instead (check your Transportation Guide) but it is slower and less convenient. Off-property guests will probably not be satisfied with the bus transportation available, because it tends to run irregularly. Ask at your hotel Guest Services how long it will take you to get to the entrance.

Note: Unlike WDW's three other major theme parks, Disney's Animal Kingdom has never had Early Entry days for Disney resort guests; thus there is no Early Entry touring plan.

How early should you arrive?

Plan to be at the entrance turnstiles about 45 minutes before the official opening time. Add 10 minutes if you have to buy your admission tickets. Pick up a Guidemap and Times Guide at the turnstiles or just inside at a shop or stand. If you arrive later in the day, plan to use FASTPASS or the singles line option (if available) at popular crowded attractions.

Tip: If the morning lines are long at all entrance turnstiles, line up in an outside queue. Sometimes, an attendant will open up a nearby turnstile at the last minute, and you may be positioned to move with other excited guests to the new and shorter queue.

One-Day Touring Plan for All

(*Note:* I consider a wait of more than 15 to 20 minutes "too long.")

1. If needed, rent strollers inside the entrance turnstiles on the right at Garden Gate Gifts.
2. Go to *Kilimanjaro Safaris* by walking through The Oasis. Turn left in Discovery Island and follow the path to the rear of Africa. Walk at a comfortable pace; there's no need to jog. Enjoy the ride.
   Note: Kilimanjaro Safaris may not yet be open when you get in line. However, this popular attraction should be your first stop

since the queue can become very long soon after opening. Alternatively, get a FASTPASS and return later to ride.

3. After *Kilimanjaro Safaris*, cross Africa and turn left along the river toward Asia. Then cross the bridge to Discovery Island and walk to DinoLand U.S.A. Ride *Dinosaur* (if you like it, ride it twice!) then take a picture with *Dino-Sue*, a large T-Rex skeleton near the *Dinosaur* ride.

Don't forget to check for a "real time" view of the dinosaur you just brought back with you.

   Height/fright alert: *Dinosaur* may be too intense and rough for seniors and children under 8 years of age. Kids must be 40" or taller to ride. Switching off is available.

4. See *It's Tough to be a Bug!* in *The Tree of Life*. During your winding walk near the theater, admire the spectacular sculpting on the bark of *The Tree of Life*.

5. Walk to Asia and ride the *Kali River Rapids*. If the waiting line is long (more than 20 minutes), get a FASTPASS for each person. After enjoying one or both of the following trails (see steps 7 and 8), return to *Kali River Rapids* at your designated FASTPASS ride time for a shorter wait.
   Height alert: Kids must be 38" or taller to ride.
   Caution: you may get wet or even drenched on the *Kali River Rapids* ride. Be prepared. Many folks don ponchos.

6. Get some refreshment in Asia.

7. Walk the *Maharajah Jungle Trek* in Asia.

8. Walk the *Pangani Forest Exploration Trail* in Africa.

9. Eat an early lunch. The Rainforest Cafe at the park entrance is a good place to eat and has an interesting ambiance. Tusker House Restaurant in Africa serves salads and sandwiches.

10. After lunch, work in the next *Tarzan Rocks!* show at Theater in the Wild in DinoLand U.S.A. (check your Times Guide for times). Arrive about 20 minutes before show time.

11. Ride *Primeval Whirl*. Get a FASTPASS to ride later if the waiting line is long.

12. Now ride *TriceraTop Spin*.

13. Play some midway games if they appeal to you.

14. Consider returning to your hotel for a nap and swim. Have your hands stamped at the exit for re-entry and keep any parking receipts. If you stay in the park, rest for a while in the covered seat-

ing area next to Flame Tree Barbecue restaurant to the right on the lagoon. While resting, study your Times Guide for the other theater show times. You may be able to fit in one of the parades; again check your Times Guide.

Note: If the park is too crowded for your comfort and your ticket allows, switch to a non Early Entry WDW park at this point and start with the afternoon or evening section of the appropriate touring plan.

15. Cross the bridge toward Asia and turn left to the Caravan Stage. Enjoy the *Flights of Wonder* show circa 3:00 p.m. (check your Times Guide for times). Arrive 15-20 minutes before show time.

16. If your kids want 'em, get autographs at one of the character greeting trails in Camp Minnie-Mickey.

17. Depending on the schedules for shows in Camp Minnie-Mickey, enjoy either the next *Pocahontas and Her Forest Friends* show at Grandmother Willow's Grove Theater or *Festival of The Lion King* at Lion King Theater. Go to whichever show is most convenient for your schedule; you'll have time to see the other later (step 19). Arrive about 25 minutes before show time.

18. Get more autographs, if your kids want them, at the character greeting trails in Camp Minnie-Mickey. Alternatively, explore the gardens and trails around *The Tree of Life*.

Shops anywhere in Disney's Animal Kingdom will send your bulky packages to "package pickup" near the front exit at no extra charge.

19. Catch the next *Festival of The Lion King* at Lion King Theater in Camp Minnie-Mickey (or *Pocahontas and Her Forest Friends* show at Grandmother Willow's Grove Theater). Try to get to the theater about 25 minutes before show time (consult your Times Guide for show times).

20. If you have more time in the park, you have several options:
    - Get a quick bite to eat at Pizzafari Restaurant in Discovery Island.
    - If you are visiting with kids, consider meeting more characters in Camp Minnie-Mickey at any of the four different character trails you haven't already visited.
    - Otherwise, take the *Train to Rafiki's Planet Watch* from the right rear side of Africa and explore the exhibits in the *Conservation Station* building, along with *Affection Section* and *Habitat Habit* outside it.

- Walk along the *Cretaceous Trail* and then let your kids play in *The Boneyard* playground in DinoLand U.S.A.

21. In your remaining time before closing, explore the gardens and trails around *The Tree of Life* and The Oasis. Keep your eyes open; the animals are often more active in the cooler evening hours.

CHAPTER SIX:

Downtown Disney & The Water Parks

Downtown Disney

Located on the shore of one of Walt Disney World's many lagoons, Downtown Disney has three distinct areas, Marketplace, West Side, and Pleasure Island. You'll find shopping, dining, and entertainment in all three, but distinctive pleasures in each one.

Pleasure Island

Surrounded by a moat in the middle of Downtown Disney, and linked to the other parts by bridges, Pleasure Island is one of Disney's nighttime entertainment areas. It charges a cover after 7:00 p.m., and guests under 18 who arrive after that time must be accompanied by a parent or legal guardian. A single evening admission ticket will cost you about $20 and is included with certain WDW passes (See "Admission Tickets," *Chapter One*).

Pleasure Island includes restaurants, shops, outdoor performance venues, and eight nightclubs: Comedy Warehouse, BET SoundStage Club, Adventurers Club, 8TRAX, Mannequins Dance Palace, Rock 'n' Roll Beach Club, Pleasure Island Jazz Company, and Motion (featuring Top 40 music and alternative rock music). The clubs open nightly at 7:00 to 8:00 p.m. and close at 2:00 a.m. All serve alcohol. While you must be 21 or older to imbibe, younger guests may visit all the clubs except Mannequins and BET SoundStage Club. Mannequins is off limits to those under 21 at all times, while BET SoundStage restricts access only on certain evenings, generally Thursday through Saturday. Outdoors, and open to all, the West End Stage offers loud and lively evening concerts.

On the night of your visit, park your car and pick up a Pleasure Island Guidemap at the entrance turnstiles for specific information about what's playing and when. If the parking lot in front of Pleasure Island is crowded, you can park near either the Marketplace or West Side.

I suggest you visit the **Comedy Warehouse** first. It features performances by an improvisational group, and the two early shows (usually 7:10 or 7:30 p.m. and 8:15 or 8:30 p.m.) are the easiest to get into. Next go the **Adventurers Club**, a wacky comedy club modeled on a 19th-century British sportsman's club. Ask the door attendant when the next show starts (sometimes a brochure available at the podium on the front steps will list the performance schedule). If you enter before or during a show, you will be asked to wait in the main club area, which features ongoing spontaneous entertainment by Disney cast members with British accents, who interact with the guests and do offbeat things. At show time, you will be ushered into the Library for an unusual comedy performance.

Tip: Sit on a bar stool and ask the bartender to make your (or your unsuspecting friend's) stool sink slowly toward the floor!

The other clubs at Pleasure Island have varying schedules; you can enter and exit them as you please. The late **West End Stage** show ends with fireworks near midnight.

Note: If you'd like to see Pleasure Island but aren't interested in nightclubbing, you can walk through it before 7:00 p.m. without paying a cover charge. The clubs will be closed, but you can look around and visit the shops.

Marketplace

The Marketplace is a colorful shopping and restaurant area full of visual delights and diversions such as interactive water fountains. The **LEGO Imagination Center** displays some incredible LEGO sculptures, including a sea serpent appropriately rising from the lagoon and a snoring man seated on a bench just outside the store. Here, too, you'll find **The World of Disney**, the largest Disney character shop on earth! Late in the year, Marketplace store windows exhibit Christmas scenes featuring Mickey Mouse and friends.

West Side

West Side offers dining, shopping, and a wide range of entertainment. Adventuresome video game fans will head directly to DisneyQuest. Music fans will gravitate to House of Blues, and dance and theater fans will seek out Cirque du Soleil.

DisneyQuest is an indoor interactive playground in a five-story building. Here you can ride a roller coaster of your own design in a flight simulator-like sphere at *CyberSpace Mountain,* navigate bumper cars that shoot big balls through cannons at your fellow drivers at *Buzz Lightyear's AstroBlaster,* experience innovative interactive and virtual reality games, and even play such classic video games as *PacMan.* One-day tickets cost about $29.00 for adults and about $23.00 for children 3 to 9 years of age.

Note: There are height restrictions for *CyberSpace Mountain* and *Buzz Lightyear's AstroBlaster.* You must be 51" or taller to ride either one.

Admission to DisneyQuest is included with Disney's Ultimate Park Hopper Pass and the Premium Annual Pass (see *Chapter One*). If you don't have one and you are staying on Disney property, buy tickets from your hotel Guest Services to save time waiting in line at the DisneyQuest ticket windows. Weekday mornings tend to be the least busy times to visit.

A New Orleans style eaterie with an attached music hall, **The House of Blues** features Creole food

The ticket windows in front of the House of Blues have free monthly entertainment schedules for the music hall.

plus live music in the music hall on most evenings (separate admission charge) and a Sunday gospel brunch. Tickets for the evening shows are available to all comers; the prices range from less than $10 to about $40 depending on the performer(s); call 407-934-2583 for information. If you want a table or bar stool for the evening show, arrive at the music hall an hour or so before show time. Sunday brunch seatings, which include food and music, are available for 10:30 a.m. and 1:00 p.m. Tickets cost about $30 for adults and $15 for children 3 to 9 years of age. Children under 3 are admitted free.

Next door to House of Blues is **Cirque du Soleil**, a unique, 90-minute circus, acrobatics, and modern dance show (call 407-939-7600 for information or tickets). It is often described by viewers as "the best show I've ever seen." Tickets cost about $67 for adults and $39 for children (9 and younger). I've never met anyone who was disappointed by it. Children 5 years of age and older enjoy it.

Tip: Make a bathroom stop before the show!

WDW Water Parks

Disney World offers not one but three distinctively themed water parks. Two, Blizzard Beach and Typhoon Lagoon, have much in common with the Orlando area's other water parks. The third, River Country (closed at press time), is closer to a fancy swimming pool. Whichever one you head for, it's easiest to wear your bathing suit under your street clothes, so you don't have to worry about a dressing room. Bring suntan lotion, a towel, a cap, money, and your Disney resort I.D. card if you have one. You can drive your car there or take a bus. Parking is free.

Admission to the water parks is included with certain WDW passes (see "Admission Tickets," *Chapter One*). Otherwise, a one-day adult ticket to either Blizzard Beach or Typhoon Lagoon costs about $30 and a child's ticket (for kids 3 to 9) about $24. Children under 3 are admitted free.

Plan to arrive at Blizzard Beach and Typhoon Lagoon 30 minutes before the official opening time (45 minutes if you have to buy a ticket) to be among the first in the park. That will give you a chance to stake out your area and enjoy the slides and other attractions without much wait during the first few morning hours. If you want to rent a locker, do so as soon as you enter the park.

Blizzard Beach

Blizzard Beach is Disney's wildest water park. The unusual theme is a failed ski resort, which was built (so they tell us) during a freaky, snowy winter in Florida. The park consists of a meandering creek on the outside, two children's areas, a gentle wave pool, and more than 16 water slides. The last include *Summit Plummet,* one of the fastest and tallest freefall speed slides on the planet.

Height restriction: You must be 48" or taller for *Summit Plummet.*

Typhoon Lagoon

Typhoon Lagoon is a "ruin," what was left of a tropical area after a typhoon blew through. The park has one of the world's largest wave pools (in which you can body surf), along with a meandering creek, a salt water snorkeling pool stocked with fish, a children's area, and 10 water slides. Your admission covers the use of snorkeling equipment.

Age restriction: You must be 10 years or older to snorkle.

River Country

Note: Like the other two water parks, River Country is open to all comers — when it is open. The park is closed as we go to press, with no announced date for reopening. So don't count on visiting it when you visit WDW. Should it be open by the time you come, expect to pay about $17 for adults and $14 for children 3 to 9.

On the chance that it may have reopened by the come you come, here is a description of what you'll find:

River Country is a sedate "swimming hole" playground straight out of a Mark Twain novel. Sporting swimming areas and three water slides, it appeals more to families with young children than to teens and young adults, so you can generally arrive after opening time and still stake out a good spot. Just be aware that it can get crowded on warm days, especially during the summer.

River Country is part of Fort Wilderness but has its own separate entrance. There are several options for getting here depending on where you are staying. If you're staying at Fort Wilderness, you can walk. Visitors staying elsewhere have several transportation options: You can take a boat from the Magic Kingdom or from the hotels on Bay Lake and Seven Seas Lagoon. You can ride a bus from the Ticket and Transportation Center. Or you can drive. If you drive, you have to park at the entrance to Fort Wilderness and then hop a bus either directly to River Country or to Pioneer Hall, which is just a short walk from the water park's entrance.

CHAPTER SEVEN:

Other Fun Things To Do At WDW

Magic Kingdom:

- Explore the Camera Shop next to Tony's Town Square Restaurant. Beyond the shop proper is a long hallway lined with interactive photo displays. In the very back they show vintage Mickey Mouse cartoons continuously.
- À la Lady and the Tramp, share a strand of spaghetti with someone you love at Tony's Town Square Restaurant (that's a photo op!)
- Get a haircut at the Harmony Barber Shop on the left side of Town Square on Main Street. For an appointment, call 407-824-4321 and ask to be transferred to the Harmony Barber Shop. The hours are 9:00 a.m. to 5:00 p.m. seven days a week, and prices are about $15 for adults and $12 for children under 12 years of age. You can often spot a young boy in the barber chair experiencing his first haircut.
- Catch a performance of the **Dapper Dans**, a barbershop quartet. They usually sing at the top of the hour from 9:00 a.m. until 5:00 p.m. with a break from 2:00 to 4:00 p.m. for the afternoon parade. You will find them at spots along Main Street, such as the Camera Shop, or even on the moving trolley. Ask at the Harmony Barber Shop for information about the Dapper Dans.
- Find the antique phone on the wall inside the Main Street Market House and listen in on a 4-minute re-creation of an 1890s' party line conversation between a mother and her daughter.

- Find the "talking trash can" in Tomorrowland. It speaks to you when you push the trash panel open. The Disney folks move this special trash can around but it is often located outdoors near Cosmic Ray's Starlight Cafe. Having trouble finding it? Ask a nearby Disney cast member (especially if he or she is emptying trash cans) where the talking can is located.
- At the Merchant of Venus shop in Tomorrowland, observe the robotic process for airbrushing T-shirts, or choose a design for your own T-shirt.
- Watch the **Flag Retreat**, complete with marching band, at 5:00 p.m. in Town Square on Main Street near the Railroad Station. Check your Times Guide to find out if it's scheduled for the day of your visit.
- Take a special tour: **"Disney's Family Magic"** is a 2-hour scavenger hunt through the Magic Kingdom aimed at families with children. The tour guide has families dancing, singing and searching for clues that will save the Magic Kingdom from evil spells. In the end, the kids not only save the MK but get to meet a surprise Disney character (cost about $25 per person, not including park admission).

  "Keys to the Kingdom" is a 4- to 5-hour, behind-the-scenes look at the Magic Kingdom (cost about $58 per person including lunch, but not including park admission).

  "Backstage Magic" offers a 7-hour guided tour to the inner workings of several of the major theme parks (cost about $200 per person including lunch and park admissions). The "Keys" and "Backstage Magic" tours are offered to guests 16 and older and include a visit to the tunnels under the Magic Kingdom, where you'll see (among other things) characters resting between appearances.

  The 2-hour **"Magic Behind Our Steam Trains"** tour shows off the steam locomotives of the WDW Railroads to guests 10 and over. The cost is $30 per person, not including park admission.

  Call 407-939-8687 for up-to-the-minute ticket prices, additional information, and reservations for any or all of these tours.
- **Cruise the Seven Seas Lagoon and Bay Lake** aboard a yacht or pontoon boat and watch the evening fireworks over the Magic Kingdom. For about $300 per hour, you and up to 11 other guests can cruise on the Grand 1 Yacht. For a $120 per hour, you invite up to 9 other guests to join you on a pontoon boat cruise. Food

and drink are extra and can be ordered through yacht catering. Call 407-824-2439 to reserve the **Grand 1 Yacht**, 407-939-7529 for a pontoon boat, and 407-934-3946 for yacht catering. Or, if you are staying on-property, contact Guest Services at the resort you are departing from for catering information. You can also rent the boats during the day.

Tip: These boats are popular, so reserve them 90 days in advance. If you will be visiting during high season, reserve your boat when you make your hotel reservations.

Epcot:

- Quench your thirst *free* at **Ice Station Cool** (a refreshment center that serves soft drinks popular in countries such as Japan, Mexico, and Italy). You'll find it at the end of Innoventions-West Side.
- Find the "talking trash can" at the Electric Umbrella restaurant. It speaks to you when you push the trash panel open. This special trash can is moved around by the Disney folks but is usually located inside the restaurant. Ask a nearby Disney cast member (especially if he or she is emptying trash cans) where the talking can is located.
- Check out the **Wonders of Laugh** show at the Wonders of Life Pavilion. Check your Times Guide for performances or check inside the pavilion.
- Buy a same-day ticket (at the Green Thumb Emporium) or reserve in advance for the 1-hour **"Behind The Seeds"** guided tour of the greenhouses at The Land Pavilion (cost is about $6 for adults and $4 for children ages 3 to 9; booking starts at 9:00 a.m.). Longer Epcot tours are offered to guests 16 and older. Among the offerings are the 3-hour **"Gardens of the World"** tour (Tuesdays and Thursdays, about $59 per person not including park admission) and the 3-hour **"Hidden Treasures of World Showcase"** architectural tour (Tuesdays and Thursdays, about $59 per person not including park admission). Or visit backstage in some of the Future World pavilions in the 4.5-hour **"Undiscovered Future World"** tour ($49 per person not including park admission). Call 407-939-8687 for information, ticket prices, and reservations for Epcot tours.
- At The Living Seas Pavilion, scuba dive (daily, about $140 per person including all necessary gear for a 2.5- hour session that in-

cludes a 30-minute "dive adventure"). Or learn about dolphins in depth (weekdays, about $140 per person for a 3.5-hour program). You must be 16 or older to participate, and park admission is neither included nor required. Call 407-939-8687 for information and reservations for either activity.

- Take a **free** guided tour of Norway or Morocco (check your Guide-map or at the pavilions for times).
- Visit the exhibits in China, Japan, and Morocco.
- Watch the evening *IllumiNations* from a boat under the bridge between France and the United Kingdom. Very relaxing and romantic! You can rent a pontoon boat or **The Breathless** (a sleek motor boat) by calling ahead to 407-939-7529. Cost is about $120 per pontoon boatload of up to 10 guests, and about $160 for up to 7 guests on The Breathless. Food and drink are not included but can be ordered (contact Guest Services at the resort from which you are departing, or call 407-934-3160). You do not have to be a Disney property guest to rent a boat or order food.
  Tip: **IllumiNations Cruises** are very popular. Start calling 2 to 3 minutes before 7:00 a.m. 90 days (even try 91 or 92 days!) in advance of the date you want. That's 7:00 a.m. Florida time!
  These boats can be rented during the day as well. The Breathless costs $25 for a 10-minute trip and $75 for 30 minutes for up to 7 guests.
- Enjoy any special seasonal festivals or events at Epcot.

Disney-MGM Studios:

- Take the 2.5- hour **"Inside Animation"** tour. Cost is about $59 per person, not including park admission, and you must be at least 16 years old. Call 407-939-8687 for information, ticket prices, and reservations.

Disney's Animal Kingdom:

- Enjoy the 3-hour **"Backstage Safari"** tour and meet some of the animal keepers! Cost is about $65 per person (not including park admission) and participants must be 16 or older. Or learn about this amazing park's creation in the 3-hour, inside the park **"Wild by Design"** tour for guests 14 and older. Cost is about $58 per person and, again, does not include park admission. Call 407-

939-8687 for information, ticket prices, and reservations.

At the Disney Hotels:

(*Note:* All the golf courses and some tennis courts are open to off-property guests.)

- Reserve Suite 1501 at the Beach Club Resort. This suite is the closest hotel room to any of the theme parks in WDW. 1501 is near the bridge to the rear entrance to Epcot. You can recline in the front room and see the Eiffel Tower in France from a side window.

- Enjoy your hotel pool. Some of them are elaborate attractions.

- Play **golf**. WDW has 6 golf courses. Greens fees for 18 holes vary with the course and season from about $90 to $165 per person. Twilight golf rates (after 3:00 p.m.) range from about $30 to $80. The 9-hole Oak Trail Course (a walking course) costs about $20 to $38 for adults and $10 to $20 for juniors 17 and under. Call 407-939-4653 to reserve tee times or golf lessons (about $50 to $60 per half hour for adults, $30 for juniors, and up to $159 for 9-hole playing lessons).

- Play **tennis**. WDW has 23 tennis courts. Some courts are free; others cost up to $15 per hour. Tennis lessons cost $15 to $40 per hour. Call 407-939-7529 for information.

- Go for a walk or jog near your hotel. Jogging trails are available at many hotels. Ask for information at your hotel Guest Services.

- Ride a **bike**. Bikes can be rented at Fort Wilderness, Wilderness Lodge, Old Key West, The Villas at the Disney Institute, Board-Walk, Port Orleans French Quarter, Port Orleans Riverside, Caribbean Beach, and Coronado Springs Resorts for about $5 an hour or $12 per day.

- Rent a **boat** at a marina if your hotel is on a lake or lagoon. Several types are available, including canopy boats, pontoon boats, pedal boats, sailboats, and the 2-person little white **Water Mouse speedboats**. Rental rates depend on the size of the boat and range from about $6 to $35 per half hour. You must be at least 12 years old and 5 feet tall to pilot a Water Mouse speedboat.

- Take a cruise on the Grand 1 Yacht from the Grand Floridian Resort. Cost is about $300 per hour for up to 12 guests. Reserve a late cruise to enjoy the evening fireworks over Cinderella Castle (407-824-2439). Food and drink are extra and can be ordered by calling yacht catering at 407-934-3946.

- Visit a **health club** (Animal Kingdom Lodge, BoardWalk, Contemporary, Coronado Springs, Dolphin, Grand Floridian, Old Key West, Swan, Villas at the Disney Institute, Wilderness Lodge, Yacht Club, Beach Club) or **spa** (Disney Institute, Grand Floridian, Wyndham Palace). The Old Key West fitness center is free to all WDW resort guests, and the Swan Resort's health club is free to its own hotel guests. At the others, you can elect to pay by the day or length of stay; or you can pay a single flat rate that admits up to 5 members of your family for the length of your stay. Health clubs charge from about $8 per day to a flat rate of $50 for a family length of stay. Spa services such as massages, facials, manicures, and pedicures cost extra (in the $50 to $110 range).
  Note: Some health and fitness centers are open only to their own hotel guests. Check with Guest Services.
- Stroll along the BoardWalk; check out the clubs and shops or **rent a surrey** to pedal along the promenade. Surreys rent for about $16 per half hour for a 2-seater; $18 per half hour for a 4-seater.
- In the evening, **dance** to older music or contemporary tunes at Atlantic Dance on the BoardWalk. Guests must be 18 or older, and the cover charge is usually $5 or more per person.
- **Sing along** with the piano players at Jellyrolls on the BoardWalk — a raucous good time! Hours are 7:00 p.m. to 2:00 a.m. Guests must be 21 or older. The cover charge is $5 or more per person.
- Relax with **afternoon tea** (2:00 to 6:00 p.m.) at the Garden View Lounge on the first floor of the Grand Floridian Resort. The cost is about $3 for tea only and $8 to $25 for various food packages. On Monday through Friday afternoons from 1:30 to 2:30 p.m., children ages 3 through 10 can enjoy tea, lunch, and cupcakes with Alice and her friends from Wonderland at 1900 Park Fare (cost is about $25 per child for the **Wonderland Tea Party**). These tea times are popular; reservations are recommended. Call 407-939-3463).
- Kids ages 4 to 10 can sign up for a 2-hour **Pirates Cruise** to find treasure along the lakes behind the Grand Floridian. The cost is about $25 per child. Call 407-939-3463 for reservations.
- Eat a dinner buffet while unraveling a **Mystery Show** on Saturdays at Baskervilles restaurant at the Grosvenor Resort (407-828-4444 for reservations). Cost is about $40 for adults and $11 for children ages 3 to 9. While in the restaurant, check out the detailed reproduction of Sherlock Holmes's office.

- Go to church on Sunday at the Luau Cove at the Polynesian Resort. Protestant services are at 9:00 a.m.; Catholic at 10:15 a.m.
- Check your hotel brochure for other activities you might enjoy.

Elsewhere in WDW:

Note: The following activities are open to all guests, whether they are staying on property or off.

- **Ride in the nose of the monorail** with the driver. When you line up for the monorail, ask the gate attendant if you can ride in the nose (usually a maximum of 4 riders). The attendant will check with the next monorail driver to find out if the nose seats are available.
- Explore the **activities at Fort Wilderness**. Rent a canoe (about $6 per half hour). Go fishing (on your own or book a 2-hour bass fishing excursion for about $150 to $200 for up to 5 people). Enjoy the petting farm with your children. Visit the horse barn, then meet the blacksmith who shoes the horses that pull the trolleys on Main Street in Magic Kingdom. Go on a hayride (about $8 for adults and $4 for children ages 3 to 9), carriage ride (prices vary) or a tame horseback trail ride (about $23 per person for 45 minutes; minimum 9 years of age; maximum weight 250 pounds). Have fun at the nightly (7:00 or 8:00 p.m.) outdoor campfire, which includes live musical entertainment, a marshmallow roast, meeting Chip and Dale, and a Disney movie. Call 407-939-7529 for information and reservations; 407-824-2832 for trail rides.
- Enjoy music by a country band, line dancing with Disney characters, and a barbecue picnic at **Mickey's Backyard Barbecue** at Fort Wilderness. It's offered on certain days in the late spring, summer, and early fall. Call 407-939-3463 for specifics. The cost is about $38 for adults and $25 for children up to age 9.
- Get rustic! Spend a night in a tent at Fort Wilderness (about $35 - $55 per night). The Disney folks will set up the tent before you arrive. Call 407-934-7639 for reservations. Then take a leisurely hike on the three-quarter-mile long **Wilderness Swamp Trail**, which starts behind the Settlement Trading Post.
- **Go fishing.** Arrange an adult or kid excursion at any hotel on a lake or lagoon. You can fish on your own or book a 2-hour **fishing excursion** for about $150 to $200 for up to 5 people. Call 407-939-7529 for information and reservations.

- **Play miniature golf** at Fantasia Gardens across from the Swan hotel or at Winter Summerland next to Blizzard Beach. Cost is about $10 for adults and $8 for kids ages 3 to 9. Be aware that Disney's Fairways, one of the courses at Fantasia Gardens, is one of the most difficult miniature golf courses on earth (no kidding!).

- Ride in or drive a fast stock car along the 1-mile oval WDW Speedway (near the Magic Kingdom) in the **Richard Petty Driving Experience.** The "Riding Experience" (ride-along) costs about $90; the 2-hour "Rookie Experience" costs about $370 for instruction and driving 8 fast laps; the "King's Experience" will run you about $750 for an 8-lap and a 10-lap session, and the "Experience of a Lifetime" costs around $1,270, for which you get to drive 30 laps over 3 sessions. Call 800-237-3889 for information or reservations.

- Play volleyball or basketball. Many hotels have courts.

- Go waterskiing, wakeboarding or tubing at the Contemporary Resort, or waterskiing at the Caribbean Beach Resort. Call 407-939-7529 for information and reservations. Cost is about $125 an hour for 1 to 5 guests.

- Learn to surf at Typhoon Lagoon. **Craig Carroll's Surfing School** offers lessons for ages 8 and over every Tuesday morning, 6:30 a.m. to 9:00 a.m. The $125 fee covers the lesson, use of equipment, and admission to the park for the lesson only (you have to pay regular park admission if you want to spend the rest of the day there). Call 407-939-7529 for information or to register.

- If you're really brave, **go parasailing** over Bay Lake from the Contemporary Resort marina. Call 407-939-7529; cost is about $75 for 1 person and $115 for 2 to ride tandem. Solo flyers must weigh 100 pounds or more.

- Test your football skills at the **NFL Experience** or watch the Harlem Globetrotters basketball or the Atlanta Braves baseball spring training at Disney's Wide World of Sports complex. Call 407-363-6600 or 407-939-4263 for information. Ticket cost, including access to the *NFL Experience* and any amateur events scheduled during your visit, runs about $9 for adults and $7 for kids ages 3 to 9. When Globetrotters or Atlanta Braves games are on, you can purchase a premium ticket, that includes general admission (if seats are available) to the pro game. When available, you can get these tickets on site or through TicketMaster (407-839-3900).

- Immerse yourself in virtual reality and other interactive fare at

DisneyQuest at Downtown Disney West Side. One-day tickets are about $29 for adults and about $23 for children 3 to 9 years of age. (Admission is included with Disney's Ultimate Park Hopper Pass and Premium Annual Pass.)

- Catch a **Sunday Gospel Brunch** buffet with live music entertainment at the House of Blues at Disney's West Side in Downtown Disney. For information or reservations, call the House of Blues Box Office (407-934-2583) or TicketMaster (407-839-3900). Brunch seatings are available for 10:30 a.m. and 1:00 p.m., and tickets cost about $30 for adults and $15 for children 3 to 9 years of age (children under 3 are admitted free).

- Also at Downtown Disney West Side, see the amazing, 90-minute acrobatic and dance show, **Cirque du Soleil**. Tickets cost about $67 for adults and $39 for children. Children 5 years of age and older enjoy it. Call 407-939-7600 or 407-939-6244 for information or tickets.

  Note: Make a bathroom stop before the show!

- Rent a boat (several types are available, including canopy boats and the smaller Water Mouse speedboats) at the Downtown Disney Marketplace marina. Rental rates depend on the size of the boat and average about $20 to $30 per half hour.

- Watch the **Electrical Water Pageant**, which floats through the waters of Bay Lake and Seven Seas Lagoon. A string of illuminated creatures moves gently to music as it passes by the Polynesian Resort at 9:00 p.m., the Grand Floridian at 9:15 p.m., the Wilderness Lodge at 9:35 p.m., the Fort Wilderness beach at 9:45 p.m., the Contemporary Resort at 10:05 p.m., and sometimes the Magic Kingdom at 10:20 p.m. Times are approximate; check with Guest Services at your hotel for current information.

  Note: The Pageant may be delayed a short while if the Magic Kingdom fireworks are scheduled for 9:00 p.m.

- Eat dinner at the California Grill. If the timing is right, walk outside afterwards and watch the **Fantasy in the Sky** fireworks over the Magic Kingdom. Then turn to your right from the rear outside walkway and watch the *Electrical Water Pageant* on Bay Lake.

- Consider visiting one of the WDW water parks in the evening. They're beautiful at night and usually less crowded.

- If you happen to get change in **Disney Dollars** (Goofy on the $5 bill, Simba or Minnie Mouse on the $10, and Mickey Mouse on the $20), you can keep them for souvenirs or exchange them for

U.S. currency at any of the WDW parks or hotels or at any Disney Store.

- Take a **VIP Tour** of WDW with your own WDW tour guide. The cost ranges from $75 to $95 per hour per group of 1 to 10 guests (minimum of 5 hours) and does not include park admissions. The guide tailors the tour to your group's wishes and will take you to any WDW attractions you want (so long as you are willing to pay the admission). VIP Tour groups do not get front-of-the-line privileges, which means they may have to wait in line (or use a FASTPASS when available) like anyone else. Call 407-560-4033 or 407-560-6233 for information and reservations.

Afterword

Orlando, Florida has become one of the premier vacation destinations in the world. WDW addicts abound; I know, I'm one. We keep coming back for our periodic infusion of Disney magic. Many folks who can only rarely accomplish the trek to Orlando have recurrent dreams about returning. Each day, theme park skeptics are converted into Disney aficionados, especially if they come prepared or with a seasoned tour guide.

What do people complain about after a WDW vacation? The cost, the crowds, the heat. But all of these irritants can be rendered inconsequential with advance planning and smart decision-making while you are in the parks.

Yes, you can drop big bucks at WDW and you can feel crowded and hot. However, the cost of theme park admission is recouped many times over in the course of a day, and you can minimize the cost of hotel, food, souvenirs, and incidentals if you plan well. As for the crowds and the heat, follow the touring plans in this book and you will minimize their irritation. Your visit to WDW can and should be as magical as any vacation you've ever taken.

See you there! (I'm the short smiling guy in the Disney floppy hat.)

Index

The following abbreviations appear in this Index:

AK - Disney's Animal Kingdom   E - Epcot
DD - Downtown Disney   MK - Magic Kingdom
DM - Disney-MGM Studios   WP - Water Parks

Other Books from The Intrepid Traveler

The Intrepid Traveler publishes money-saving, horizon expanding travel how-to and guidebooks dedicated to helping its readers make travel an integral part of their everyday life.

In addition, we offer hard-to-find specialty books from other publishers. For more information visit our web site, where you will find a complete catalog, travel articles from around the world, Internet travel resources, and more:

http://www.IntrepidTraveler.com

For this book's companion volumes, *Universal Orlando* and *The Other Orlando: What To Do When You've Done Disney & Universal*, plus updates to all three books, visit:

http://www.TheOtherOrlando.com

If you are interested in becoming a home-based travel agent, visit the Home-Based Travel Agent Resource Center at:

http://www.HomeTravelAgency.com